Follow F***ING ORDERS

Follow F***ING ORDERS

THE GANGLAND EXECUTION OF
A SWEDISH FOOTBALL STAR

Ann Törnkvist

First published by Pitch Publishing, 2020

Pitch Publishing
A2 Yeoman Gate
Yeoman Way
Worthing
Sussex
BN13 3QZ
www.pitchpublishing.co.uk
info@pitchpublishing.co.uk

ISBN 978 1 78531 648 7

Typesetting and origination by Pitch Publishing
Printed and bound by TJ International, Padstow, UK

Contents

PART FOUR: **THE WITNESSES**

PART SIX: **THE AFTERMATH**

PART SEVEN: **THE PRICE**

Dedication

To Fahd and Cajsa

And in loving memory of my
grandparents who taught me
to do my 'utmost'.

Acknowledgements

WITHOUT THE encouragement of Cajsa Collin and Fahd, this book would have never been written. And without the love of Johannes Rosendahl, Jacek Dabrowski and Annie Hellquist, I would have struggled even more than I did. Thank you, all of you, for being there for me.

Thanks to my family, especially my brother, who has always been my steadfast champion. To my father, who should have been an investigative reporter rather than a physicist slash poet. To my aunt and uncle who lent me their cottage so I could finish the book in peace. To my mum, for being cooler than me and for entertaining my police-protection officers with her war stories from Iraq where, she made sure to point out to them, her armoured car was, indeed, much bigger than theirs, and her bodyguards, one might add, were not 'just' cops, but ex-military.

To my friends who also happen to be authors and thus understand the madness: Joanna Jolly, Julia Wiræus, Alia Malek and Sofia Lundgren. Thanks to every one of my friends, and there are many of you, who read chapters along the way and shared your thoughts with me.

Richard Pike deserves special mention for his kind critique and wise words.

And, not least, my publishers and editors at Mondial and at Pitch Publishing.

Methodology

FOLLOW FUCKING ORDERS is based on interviews with witnesses, crime victims and their families, the gang leader and his friends, old classmates, teachers, with town hall politicians and public servants, the police, lawyers, the lead prosecutor, social secretaries and others who have followed the case. Several have asked not to be identified.

Source documents include the police case file, including testimonies from witnesses who have not been interviewed, the two District Court verdicts as well as the Appeals Court verdict, Dany Moussa's 1994 verdict, Bernard Khouri's criminal record and prison service documentation pertaining to his imprisonment, Khouri's letters to me and his letter to the appeals trial, and newspaper and magazine articles.

The football chapters were written with input from sports journalists.

A fact checker was employed.

All quotes are translated from Swedish apart from Milad's quotes as he spoke to me in English, *you know*.

Character gallery

The Network
Bernard Khouri, gang leader, known as Al Taweel, 'The Tall One' in Arabic.

His predecessor, Bülent 'The Godfather' Aslanoglu.

Abraham 'The Torpedo' Aho, Khouri's younger cousin and alleged assassin.

Sherbel Said, another of Khouri's cousins, paralysed in a drive-by shooting.

'Travolta', a young mafia errand boy and poet.

The Family
Yaacoub Moussa, eldest son in the Moussa family, manager of The Oasis, married father of four.

Dany, one of the middle sons, the black sheep of the family who set up X-Team in Södertälje.

Georges, who attacked a boy at school after his older brother Dany gave him a knife.

Eddie, the youngest, their mother's 'favourite child' and rising star in Assyriska FF.

Alexandra, one of their sisters.

Mohaned Ali, Dany's friend, X-Team member and a debt enforcer, father of three.

The Dead
Yaacoub, Eddie and Mohaned.

CHARACTER GALLERY

The Cicerone
Philip*, 'poker genius' and drug addict, with friends on both sides of the conflict, who witnessed the murders of the Moussa brothers.

The Extorted
Milad Bahnan, indebted small-business owner, married father of one.
His brother Bahnan, manager of The Parrot café.
Oritha Chabo, whose brother borrowed money from the wrong people.
Her eldest son Leon, who was born with a muscular disease.
Leon's personal assistant, who prefers not to be named.

The Kidnapped
Georges Abo, former owner of a car used in a drive-by shooting.

The Investigators
Gunnar Appelgren, superintendent and lead detective.
Björn Frithiof, lead prosecutor.
Alice Ekengren, beat police officer in Södertälje.

The Lawyers
Fredrik Ungerfält, Khouri's defence lawyer.
Jan Karlsson and Elsa Svalsten, The Torpedo's defence lawyers.
Claes Borgström, legal counsel for the Moussa family.

The Club
Conny Chamas, devoted Assyriska FF fan and long-time admirer of Eddie Moussa.
Aydin Aho, club director of Assyriska FF.
Andreas Haddad, team-mate and close friend of Eddie.

In the Stands
Issa*, small-fry gambler who witnessed the double murder.
Tony Khouri, Khouri's estranged uncle.

Özcan Kaldoyo, Assyria TV contributor and opinion writer.

Jakob Rohyo, furniture store owner, witness to Khouri assaulting a police officer.

Hosep*, witness to Eddie attacking one of Khouri's friends with a kebab skewer.

Olle Eriksson, editor of *Filen*, a magazine for prison inmates.

Ellinor Persson, Djurgården IF board member.

*To protect their identities, Philip, Issa and Hosep asked that their real names not be used.

PART ONE

THE BOSS

2013

Forgive me

'YOU CAN tell from the way Bernard Khouri looks at you that he is always angry. Not even Jesus can help him,' says Milad Bahnan.

No one could tell from his calm, average-kind-of-guy drawl that this middle-aged father of one holds the fate of a town in his hands; hands now busy lighting a cigarette – I can tell because I can hear the click of the lighter and the crackle of paper as the cigarette catches fire, and after exhaling Milad picks up the story. It's a long one.

Milad knows the dangers of owing money to men like Khouri. It is so dangerous that he has had to flee his beloved but crime-addled hometown Södertälje, just south of the Swedish capital Stockholm, in order to testify against Khouri, the alleged leader of 'The Network'.

The upcoming high-profile trial has been years in the making and the police are now wrapping up the most extensive investigation into organised crime in Swedish history. Witnesses such as Milad, who has defied the town's code of silence, are key to helping the prosecutors end Khouri's reign.

Milad, a small-business owner who borrowed money from the wrong people, has taken refuge in the police's witness protection programme. New name, new social security number, and the same for his wife and their daughter. And they're not alone; more and more victims have come forward, all being spirited away by the police to keep them safe.

The police talk about the tipping point, when enough people at last say 'enough is enough'. The lead detective likens the thaw in the case, with ever more people coming to the police for help, to a local Arab Spring, when protestors felt they had found safety in numbers. Never before have the Swedish police helped so many witnesses move and change their identities to feel safe enough to take the stand in court.

There's good reason for their fear. Milad has tasted The Network's wrath: a few years back he was assaulted with a captive bolt pistol, the kind used in abattoirs, and he still has trouble sleeping, but he's alive to guide me through the maze of threats, the never-ending demands to pay protection money, taking out loans to make the payments, getting new loans to cover the old ones, seeing 'fines' added to interest rates, handing over envelopes with cash once a month until he had no money left to put food on the table for his wife and kid – the shame he felt and why he kept quiet for so long. And he takes time to explain that the alleged gang leader has a theatrical bent and love of violence, expressed in grandiose fashion, that has made Khouri the most sought-after debt collector in town.

'The loan sharks who came before him were reasonable, you could talk to them, but have you ever looked Khouri in the eyes?' Milad asks me. I haven't, but I will soon as Khouri has granted my request for an interview.

'Khouri is on my list,' Milad says.

'What list?'

'I keep a list of everyone who has made my life hell. I'll celebrate when they end up in prison ... or when they die.'

At this point, there's still no certainty that the police and the prosecutor will see Khouri jailed for the crimes he stands accused of. There's a lack of forensic evidence tying Khouri directly to his alleged crimes, a weakness in the case that worries some of the victims' lawyers. Will the charges of usury, extortion, intimidation and assault stick? Fear can silence the best of us, and Khouri's not just a loan shark, he is being charged with ordering three murders.

The most infamous killing was the execution of a famous up-and-coming football player, Eddie Moussa, who was shot 17 times with a Kalashnikov, the semi-automatic Soviet rifle that has been gaining popularity in the criminal underworld.

Milad and his persecutors belong to the Assyrian and Aramean community in Södertälje – Orthodox Christians from the Middle East – and the local police note that the community's insularity is problematic; there's a culture of silence that makes pariahs out of 'snitches' who go to the police. Milad confirms the observation that Khouri and his men only threatened and harassed their kinsmen, because people in their community would rather turn to trusted mediators than to the authorities. By extension, that habit stoked impunity. Being told to behave by a community elder is not the same as being locked up: Khouri thought he'd never get caught.

As Milad and I continue our long phone call, I can hear tell-tale sounds in the background that he's out driving. 'Do you have a crucifix in the car, hanging from the rear-view mirror, like so many Arameans in Sweden have?' I ask. 'Of course,' Milad says, a smile embedded in the tone of his voice.

He pauses. He lights another cigarette, and it sounds like he's looking for a parking spot. I can hear the ticking of the indicators, the car slowing down. Then the engine dies. Faintly, car doors being closed? A parking lot … followed by the metallic whine as a train brakes upon arriving at a station?

These sounds could be reaching me from the north, maybe from the south. I don't know where his family live nowadays in this vast country, equal in size to California and almost to Spain. Milad did say that I was welcome to visit, to grab a coffee, or take a ride through the countryside. He sounds lonely and bored, like he wouldn't mind a change of routine, but I don't want to know where he is. It's safer that way, for him and his family, and for me. What you don't know won't kill you, as the Americans say.

Milad happens to sound just like an American. He lived in the US for a few years before moving to Södertälje and still prefers to speak English rather than Swedish, which he didn't really have to learn because he was surrounded by his compatriots – Milad was born in Syria and many of his former neighbours in Södertälje hail from Lebanon and Turkey.

Many speak Arabic but their mother tongue is Assyrian, the language of the Orthodox Christians. Many community members call Södertälje the new capital city of a people who can trace their lineage back to Mesopotamia – some refer jokingly to the town as 'Mesopotälje'.

Milad explains why he left the US for Sweden, speaking unhurriedly at the small-town pace common outside America's big cities. Adding a 'you know' to the end of every other sentence, he tells me that New Jersey was beautiful – the wetlands of the north yielding to forests and fields, the hills bordering Pennsylvania, the beaches by the ocean where the siren song of Atlantic City lures hunters of fortune. But, he says, it was just too vast and couldn't cater to his longing for his people – while speaking English he uses the Swedish word 'syrian' to name his people – not to be confused with being a citizen of Syria – often translated into Aramean, rather than the term 'assyrier'. Although there are those who think the divide, most common in Sweden, between Arameans and Assyrians has no historical justification: they're the same people[1].

Regardless, he felt lonely in New Jersey. 'There are Arameans in the United States as well, but they live so far apart from each other, you know. I was tired of driving. When I came to Södertälje, I felt so happy that so many of us lived in the same place.'

Södertälje, an old spa resort turned industrial hub, is the biggest town in Södermanland, one of the country's most picturesque counties with hundreds of Viking rune stones and thousands of the red cottages with white window frames so iconic for Sweden.

Here, Milad was given a new townscape to learn by heart. The small marina, the cobblestone central square overlooked by the District Court, which is housed in an angular modernist behemoth.

---

1 The terms are used interchangeably in the book depending in part on which term the interviewee has used.

The salt tang of Baltic Sea air arrives from the east, as do the container ships that squeeze through the canal past downtown's grand, turn-of-last-century houses towards Lake Mälaren. It's a town where the wealthy teach their children to sail on the lake's mud-green swell, while the less prosperous kids ride mopeds along asphalt paths that snake between the monotone hulks of public housing.

The mafia use Audis that shuttle them the half-hour north to the upper-class watering holes in Stockholm, spending evenings dedicated to booze and coke, to seeing and being seen, to power and prestige. To toasting their wealth.

Södertälje is not a big town compared with the cities Milad left behind in the United States, and also in Syria, but the community spirit made up for it, not least in the neighbourhoods of Ronna and Hovsjö, home to many Assyrians and Arameans. Nor is it a poor town. Shoals of commuters arrive in rush hour, the commuter trains passing the global headquarters of Scania, the world's fifth-biggest truck manufacturer, founded here in 1911. A walk under the bridge leads to the labs and offices of pharmaceutical giant Astra, which after a merger became AstraZeneca.

While still plagued by socio-economic divides, there are jobs in Södertälje and opportunities to be had for small-business owners, such as Milad, catering to the throng. Yet despite its multi-layered history, Södertälje has become synonymous with organised crime. But back then, when he first moved here, Milad still had years of happiness ahead of him: Sunday lunch with his parents, drinking coffee with friends, playing cards at his brother's café. Milad got married and became a father. When Milad drove his car up the gentle incline of Robert Anbergs Street, he would pass Khouri's old school, then on past The Oasis café, run by the famous footballer Eddie Moussa's brother. Satellite dishes picking up foreign cable stations sprouted like fibreglass mushrooms from Ronna's flat-faced buildings. As Milad continued, down the other side of the hill, toward the St Ephrem Syriac Orthodox Cathedral, each and every passing car had a crucifix hanging from the rear-view mirror. Milad was no longer alone.

But that was a long time ago now. He left Syria because he wanted to, leaving the US was a choice, but leaving Södertälje was the only option left to him because he feared for his life – a dark irony, as Södertälje has been, since the early 1970s, a safe harbour for so many who escaped the discrimination of ethnic minorities in the Middle East. But here, Milad found out that oppression can shed its skin.

'Your book shouldn't be about Khouri,' he says in a light-hearted manner that cannot conceal his sadness.

'What do you mean?'

'It should be about me.'

Milad is not wrong. In the media limelight, victims are crowded out by Khouri, who appears more than happy to take centre stage. It's the charismatic Khouri who has become a celebrity. It's Khouri whose friends have used his alleged diagnosis as a psychopath to boost his reputation and instil fear. It's Khouri who gives interviews about the upcoming trial, explaining to any reporter willing to listen why he's convinced that the charges won't stick – and we all do listen, because we are fascinated by this historic case.

While Milad's name can appear in print too, it's only because 'Milad' is no longer his name on paper – his new identity is meant to make him unfindable. When curious police officers ask me how I got hold of Milad, they get only vague answers from me. An older police officer, born and bred in Södertälje, reacts with less surprise than his less-experienced colleagues at Milad letting himself be found. 'The biggest danger to a person in witness protection is the person himself,' he tells me. 'Especially over time, once the trial is over. They think that people forget, that people forgive. They miss their family, their friends, they go back home to visit. They get sloppy.'

Milad knows this to be true. Some nights, when the loss and longing rob him of sleep, he sets off for Södertälje but always pulls the car over when he gets within 100 kilometres of his old town. He has established a safety perimeter, sitting close to tears on the motorway's hard shoulder.

Yet he doesn't even feel 100 per cent safe in his new hometown. 'You know how it works, gangs send each other pictures of people they want to take revenge on. There might be some gang around here, you know, that got sent my picture,' he says. 'And sometimes I think that I see Khouri's friends when I'm out driving.'

Those friends also get attention in the media, as do the people they now stand accused of having killed: the first mention always goes to the football player Eddie Moussa from the Södertälje club Assyriska FF, an underdog team that fought themselves into the top national league, the 'immigrant team' that both *The Guardian* and *Le Monde* have written about.

For years to come, Eddie's death will continue to be eulogised in headlines, because fame sells, and his celebrity ensures that the turf war in Södertälje sticks in the nation's collective memory.

So does the brutality of that summer's night. As Eddie fell lifeless to the floor, his body so peppered with bullets that the first responders would say they'd never seen anything like it, a second gunman walked up to Eddie's brother Yaacoub and shot him three times in the throat.

The double murder served up a smorgasbord of macabre details: Kalashnikov, check. Dead sports star, check. His brother executed at close range, check. Ricochets, check. Upended chairs as more than a dozen witnesses fled the scene in panic, check. A hit meticulous in both planning and execution, check. Mopeds at the ready to ferry the killers from the scene, check.

The suspects can deny the charges all they want, but after the police rounded up Khouri and his suspected accomplices and stuck them in jail cells to await the trial, one of his young foot soldiers cracked under pressure. The wardens found a note in the teenage boy's cell:

> *Forgive Me Eddie n Jacob*
> *I didn't know Please*
> *I'm sorry*
> *when I ask the Police*

was there a lot of blood
he said Yes
not even in a film have I seen so much blood
and never in my 30 years as a police officer

But there's no smoking gun – *not yet* – that ties Khouri himself
to the crime scene. So maybe Khouri's right, maybe he will walk?

The number seven

ORITHA CHABO, yet another extortion victim who's in witness protection, along with her three young children, says the police are focussing too much on Khouri. Don't get her wrong, she has no love for her former classmate from primary school, but Khouri's a fist-for-hire. 'There are others out there,' she says.

While Milad is sad and his boredom makes him willing to speak with me, Oritha's the kind of tiger mum who spits fury when she speaks of how Khouri's threats have taken a toll on her kids' lives. But both Milad and Oritha want to talk to me about what it has cost them, what it has cost their families.

Khouri, meanwhile, is not impressed with whom I'm talking to. In a letter from his cell, Khouri tells me it's easy to find 'losers' who want to talk shit about 'a Big Man' – those are Khouri's capital letters, not mine. He is scolding me, or trying to play me, to twist the narrative back to his version of events, to manipulate me, which I do not realise as I do not know him well enough – *not yet*.

If Khouri's words are meant to deter me, they have the opposite effect, instead reminding me that the 'losers' need to be given a platform, to explain the emotional storm triggered by intimidation, and to explain why they put their foot down – Oritha's family begged her not to – and why they think that Khouri, once a silent, somewhat shy kid, grew up to be a 'Big Man'.

Oritha has known Khouri since he arrived from Lebanon, she thinks it was, with his divorced mother in the mid-80s, when he was about six years old. His transition wasn't without its hiccups, she tells me, explaining that as he learned Swedish he couldn't get his tongue around the word 'sju' – the number seven. As she herself comes from an immigrant family, Oritha knows that the word often trips up newcomers learning the language, because 'sj' sounds less like a consonant and more like a sigh, a blend of the English 'sh' and 'h'.

'We used to tease him. We used to tell him to say 777 – "sju sjuttiosju" – which became "chu chuttichu",' Oritha continues. 'Then he'd chase after us and, sure, he was aggressive, but I never thought he would end up like this.'

Khouri was thus bestowed with the nickname 'Sabe' – Aramean for seven.

Like many of their other friends from school, Oritha soon found out what career Khouri had chosen when he grew up, that he'd taken over the reins of what would soon be known as 'The Network', and that he was less concerned, compared to the criminal generation just before his, with keeping a low profile:

'He did cause a ruckus when he came along, he made a lot of noise,' Oritha says.

She also grew up close to her cousin Eddie, who was making noise in the world of football as a rising star striker – her dad was Eddie's godfather and was close to his big brother Yaacoub. A few weeks before her cousins were killed, she had been forced to take notice of Khouri again for the first time in many years because he had some unfinished business with her brother, who'd borrowed 10,000 kronor[2] and failed to pay it back. The debt was then passed on to Khouri. The night that Khouri and half a dozen of his associates crowded into Oritha's parents' home, decorated with paintings of Jesus and the Virgin Mary on the walls, Khouri demanded they pay 300,000 kronor to settle the debt – 30 times the original sum. Khouri would, when later confronted by the police, say that he'd just wanted to help Oritha's family get rid of the debt, that he was a benevolent mediator. Oritha disagrees. Of course, her family wanted to pay back the money, but the amount was unreasonable.

---

2   In the late 2000s, the exchange rate hovered between 13 and 12 Swedish kronor to one British pound.

When Oritha and Khouri were kids in the Ronna neighbourhood, lending money to relatives and friends was just part of a culture of helping out. That's what their community had done back in their parents' home countries, they had helped each other out. Orthodox Christians trusted each other and family ties kept things cordial; inviting outsiders was to invite trouble. If someone struggled to come up with cash, mediators stepped in to quell conflict. They set up a long-term payment plan.

While the ebbs and flows of cash in the under-the-radar loans market were nothing new, and paying interest was a given, Khouri's demand was out of line, and Oritha's parents did something unusual for Arameans their age – they went to the police.

'I can understand that older people, our parents who are first-generation immigrants, have chosen not to report Khouri in the past,' Oritha says. 'And for the even older ones, our grandparents, their family and friends are all in Södertälje, they'd jeopardise their support structure. Many don't even speak Swedish, so who'd help them if they had to move and start over?'

Even though her family reported Khouri to the police, they decided to also pay him the money, but managed to get a 'discount' and negotiated 300,000 kronor down to 200,000 – albeit still a 20-fold hike.

Oritha's mum sold her gold jewellery, Oritha's sister dipped into her savings, and the debt was cleared.

Money is God

'MONEY IS God,' says Philip, offering up one of his many punchy one-liners. What he won't offer is his name. He's clear on that. His anonymity takes priority above all else, and he insists I call him Philip. And then there's a no-go topic: he won't talk about the double murder. He was there that night, he was one of the dozen witnesses who fled the scene when the shooting began, and he does not want to revisit The Oasis café.

I already know he and the other men there were all playing cards that night, it's what people do to relax at the cafés across town. But that kind of social small-fry gambling is not how Philip has earned his fame: he says he has thrown a die for half a million kronor, and the common acquaintance who set up our meeting calls Philip 'a poker genius'.

His personal philosophy on the matter is that if money is God, debt is Satan. He's kept the devil at bay for years and years, and he credits his talent at the gambling table. 'When I lose money, I make sure that I earn it back quickly,' says Philip, who needs the cash to finance his drug habit.

The one time he did lose a big bet, Philip picked up a blade to punish himself, but he won't let me share the details of his self-harm, because 'people reading your book could identify me'.

We have met up in an old café across the street from St Ragnhild's Church near the District Court. Older women make up most of the afternoon crowd, along with teenagers hanging out at the end of the school day. In this small town, everyone knows everyone, or at least someone who knows this person, who's related to that person … and thus Philip breaks his unflinching gaze at times to scan the surroundings, to make sure no one's watching us.

A group of boys come in and, as they look for a table, Philip grabs my iPhone, standing on its edge recording our interview, and places it screen down on the table. He says, 'They'll think I'm talking Säpo,' using the short form for 'säkerhetspolisen', the national intelligence service tasked with keeping the nation safe. Then he stares at one of the boys; that's all it takes for the teen's cocky ebullience to vanish with a nervous flicker of the eyelids.

Philip's gaze is part of his business model. He has hosted private gatherings for high-level gamblers behind locked doors, and that's the world, so foreign to me and populated by the underworld's finest, that he's agreed to explain. Night after night, Philip, my cicerone, has watched tight bundles of bills, inches thick, unrolled and cash change hands.

Philip had to maintain order at the joints. 'If someone trod on me, I had to show that I was ready to cut them,' Philip says. 'I had to show them how hard I was.'

He has seen his friends rack up debts, the weight of each loss amassing until it transforms into devastation. The loan sharks – many look like regular guys, a far cry from the suited gangsters of Hollywood lore – sit right next to them, and will at times play cards along with them, taunt them, tease them, open their wallets for them. A thousand kronor to tide you over, just one more set of cards … win it back, regain your pride.

The danger is in the interest rate. Philip has borne witness to a trifle of a sum multiplying in the heat of the moment, until all that's left is desperation. He knows the risks of cash, and of dodgy lines of credit, meant not just to catch but to ensnare – interest grows over time, after all. It's a money-spinner.

What Philip doesn't see is anything wrong with the system, neither the quick loans at the gambling table nor the cash offered to local businessmen. People borrow money, people place bets and lose it, or let bad business ideas drain them of capital. And then people have to clear their debts. What's the problem?

There is no problem, that's Philip's take on the matter, and nothing in his body language signals an invitation to debate.

The politicians in Södertälje Town Hall have pleaded with the police for years to close down the joints, as part of an effort to squeeze the cash economy dry, because that cash economy feeds violence. Help us because violence begets violence, the Town Hall nags, adding warnings by asking why wait for bloodshed before acting?

The understaffed police agree: 'In large part, the cash loans market forms the basis for organised crime in Sweden,' says Detective Superintendent Gunnar Appelgren, who, after years of Town Hall hand-wringing, was put in charge of catching Khouri. The police did so after a drive-by shooting, as Khouri left a nightclub with his friends, two of them ending up with serious gunshot wounds. The police also got a cash injection when the justice minister freed up and earmarked millions of kronor to combat organised crime; her political party had gone to the polls with tough law-and-order promises.

For Appelgren's colleagues on the ground, the beat cops – who for years had stood by, powerless, as The Network recruited young boys in the less-affluent neighbourhoods – the targeted investigation meant that their local knowledge at last added up to something bigger. They have logged every contact and sighting of The Network – who was hanging out with whom, when and where, in which car, who said what when they searched the trunk for drugs and guns – gathering intelligence for the analysts at police HQ up in Stockholm. There are patterns to be found for those paid to search for them.

At all levels of the police hierarchy, officers agree that cash has been the root cause of much of the troubles. One beat cop, who refers to money as 'nectar for the gangs', says that a wad of cash provokes facial expressions akin to sexual arousal among young gang recruits and also the grown-up 'career criminals'.

Philip doesn't give a damn about the cops' descriptions of his friends and associates who collect debts all over Södertälje, nor does he pass any judgement on the exchange rate between favours done and favours owed. It's a market economy, after all.

'What are you going to do if I owe you 100,000 kronor?' asks Philip.

'Call my lawyer? I don't know,' I say.

'No, but for real, what would you do?'

'Well, I'd … well I'd …' I stutter as my imagination fails me, because I have stepped over the boundaries of personal experience, and I'm stumbling.

'If I ignore you when you want your money back?' he persists.

'A debt collection company?'

'NO NO NO! I'm talking about cash!' Philip interrupts. 'I know what you would do! You would sell your debt to someone who won't hesitate to use violence to get your money back.'

Scarface

'HAVE YOU seen Khouri's eyes in that old picture from when he was younger?' Milad asks me.

He's talking about a photo floating about online, which looks like one of the line-up pictures the police use when asking witnesses to identify suspects. A photo of Khouri, possibly in his late teens or early 20s, with the ragged edge of his short hair capping his forehead.

'Look at his eyes,' Milad says. 'The men who came before him never gave you that look.' Milad mentions a man called Bülent Aslanoglu, widely known to be Khouri's predecessor who's sometimes referred to as 'The Godfather' by the media. Khouri isn't the town's first loan shark, he inherited a culture, but he represents a shift in that culture, according to Milad.

'Bülent wasn't like that, Bülent was a reasonable man,' he says. 'In the old days, when I, or someone else, needed a bit more time to repay our debts, we could talk to Bülent.'

Milad doesn't have a problem with Aslanoglu, who is a charismatic man. A former teacher said that the young Aslanoglu, upon entering the classroom, had a rock-star presence that drew everyone's attention, although as a boy he seemed to romanticise the gangster life.

We discuss an anecdote passed around town about Aslanoglu as a schoolboy. That he was caught red-handed scrawling the word 'Scarface' on the wall, and shrieked 'I wasn't here!' and the teacher said, 'What do you mean you *weren't* here? You *are* here, you're holding the pen in your hand!'

Milad laughs, which he does often with a dry kind of chuckle. But when it comes to Khouri, his laughter dries up. He sees no reason to laugh about him nor about Khouri's friends or any of the young boys in Södertälje who look up to the gang leader. They make up the tiers of what the police call a well-structured network. All members play their parts, and to get them to respond to the accusations levelled against them by Milad and so many others, I need to find a way to speak with them. I know that Khouri is the key. If he says okay, the door will unlock. I have to begin by speaking with him.

Before contacting Khouri, I look through the police's case file, known in Swedish as 'förundersökningsprotokollet' and most often referred to by its short form 'FUP', pronounced 'fupp'.

The witness testimonies in the FUP paint a picture of Khouri as the leader of a network with all the signifiers of organised crime. Put simply, they qualify to be called mafia, a controversial epithet but one that fits more neatly in a newspaper headline than the cumbersome 'organised crime syndicate' and also sells more papers with its Sicilian-sounding punch.

But the FUP is just one version of events, one truth among many, which I, at times, need to explain to friends who have blind trust in the police and the prosecutors; a faith characteristic of Sweden with its high level of confidence in the authorities.

'You know what happened, you've got the FUP,' a friend tells me, leading me to counter with yes I do, 'But that's the police and prosecutors' version of what happened, not The Network's version nor Khouri's.'

Receptionist

THE RECEPTIONIST is in a bad mood. 'Why can't people turn off their phones before they put them away?' she complains as a ring signal buzzes, incessant like a trapped wasp, from the wall of lockers opposite her desk.

The reception room is populated by defence lawyers set to visit clients who are being held in custody. The lawyers retrieve phones and keys from the pockets of their expensive suits, stowing them in the lockers, then almost all of them slick back their hair; they share an aesthetic code that signals wealth. Many of their clients are poor, or grew up poor before they started to earn cash from getting up to no good.

I follow protocol, stuffing everything I've brought with me into a locker as we register at the Kronoberg Detention Centre, known simply as 'Kronan', 'The Crown'. There are two senior detectives accompanying me to meet Khouri in a visiting room. I'd been told ahead of time that no recording equipment, not even a notebook nor a pen, would be allowed. 'But, why not?' I thought to myself. 'So that Khouri won't stab me in the eye?'

My imagination is running a bit too wild, because there's no point in attacking a journalist – 'In truth, it'd be kinda counterproductive,' I hear myself thinking, as it would just shore up his bad reputation before a trial that he hopes will lead to his acquittal. Stabbing me in the eye with a pen would, in fact, be illogical, but as I've never met a suspected killer before, my mind is thriller-tripping.

One of the detectives looks down at me from his considerable height and gives me one single piece of advice, which I do not fully understand – but will do much, much later, when it's too late. 'Be straight with Khouri,' he says.

Two wardens join us: a hefty woman, her belt digging into her midriff, and a slight and stooped older man who gives us not so much as a cursory glance, but I can tell he's eavesdropping. We set off into The Crown. It's undergoing renovation and heavy swing doors propel us through a temporary gangway that feels like a wall-panel sluice. An elevator, then another corridor. A janitor spots us and shoots me a curious look. I don't walk like a cop, I don't dress like a lawyer. 'Who are you?' his eyes ask me, before annoyance flashes across his face as he realises we need to squeeze past his cleaning trolley.

The wardens stop at a door, unlocking it to let the two police officers enter first. One of the cops is tall, the other fat – 'To overpower Khouri if something goes wrong?' I've already asked myself – and I feel like a lost child, even though I'm tall and powerfully built, slipping behind them into the visitors' room. I am, it turns out, much smaller than Khouri, who is waiting for us.

As one of his many nicknames is 'Al Taweel' – 'The Tall One' in Arabic – his height does not surprise me, but his bulk does; broad shoulders add weight to his top-heavy frame.

Khouri and I are the same age, in our early 30s, but he looks older. After being locked up for so long, deprived of sunlight for months on end as he has been denied requests to be set free in the run-up to his trial, his skin's not just pale – it's tinged green.

As the cops walk past him, to take a seat on a narrow bed in the corner, Khouri neither looks at them nor at me, busy as he is inspecting himself in the mirror above a small washbasin.

'You smell good today,' the tall police officer tells him.

'It's for Ann's benefit,' Khouri answers.

When I first contacted Khouri, he had already been arrested on suspicion of ordering three murders, including the grand-finale executions of Eddie and Yaacoub. What had aroused my interest was a question: 'Why does he have such power?'

The Crown

MY ROAD to The Crown started with a letter to Khouri's defence lawyer, Fredrik Ungerfält. He replied that his client did not want to meet me. My answer? That regardless I intended to interview every person who had ever met Khouri, 'including his daycare staff'.

Ungerfält countered with a rhetorical question: perhaps I would end up painting a rather skewed picture of Khouri if it relied solely on his pre-school teachers?

Instead, I wrote directly to Khouri c/o The Prison Service. I had no high hopes that Khouri would reply, and had mentioned what his lawyer said about no interviews, but then a small envelope arrived in the post.

'There are too many lost journalists for my lawyer to keep track of,' he replied from a maximum-security prison facility called 'Fenix' – nicknamed 'The Bunker'. I found out later, from another suspect, that all of them, not just Khouri, had been inundated with interview requests – 'Even from Japan!' he said.

Khouri's handwriting, I noticed, was old-fashioned, the capital letters written with curlicue flourish. About his life in 'The Bunker', he wrote, 'I'm completely isolated. It's me, the walls, and the push-ups.'

Our correspondence continued. He posed questions about the reach of any material I'd get from him. As I was working at a niche online newspaper at the time, he suggested selling a freelance reportage about 'the miscarriage of justice' – because, according to him, he'd been scapegoated, the justice minister had an agenda, the police investigation was a botch job made to look pretty, and the prosecutor was making an example of him.

After a short time of further correspondence, Khouri and I talked on the phone, with a police officer listening in to make sure he wasn't using me to pass on messages to his men on the outside.

'Our first meeting can be off the record if you want,' I told Khouri.

'Off the record does not exist,' he said, seemingly delighted by his street-smart know-how.

After a few more letters, best described as a semi-flirtatious power play during which I was careful not to promise anything, Khouri invited me to see him – by then he'd been transferred to The Crown in central Stockholm, which is connected by underground passageways to 'säkerhetssalen' – 'the security courtroom' – a windowless room; only the worst of the worst bad guys are put on trial in this airless box. Family, friends and reporters wanting to watch proceedings have to go through airport-style security with a metal detector and a pat-down by either security guards or police before climbing the stairs down to the basement courtroom.

Above ground, The Crown overlooks a small courtyard; from some cell windows suspects can catch a glimpse of the inner-city streets surrounding the complex.

Eager not to be late for my meeting with Khouri, I had made my way downtown far too early, ending up browsing the shops, snatching some free beauty product samples and applying blusher and eye shadow at a cosmetics store. Although I rarely wear make-up, I'd been battling a cough and fever for the few days before so I thought I'd take the opportunity to make myself look less ill.

As there was still time left until the meeting, I grabbed a coffee with a cop who used to work in Södertälje, and was met with bemusement when I told him who I was about to meet.

'Ah, you have been granted an audience with His Majesty?' the cop joked, followed by seriousness. 'I've never interrogated Khouri,' he added. 'Could you send me a text message when you're done and just describe him in three words?'

As for me, I had been looking forward to meeting Khouri. His letters testified to a certain kind of humour. Among other comments, he wrote that my abysmal and paltry Arabic, which I had sewed into a joke, was worse than his grandmother's Russian.

He called me 'Madame' in his first letter, but allowed himself to be corrected when I signed my reply with 'Mademoiselle'. 'You bite back as quick as the women in Paris,' was his riposte.

Khouri apologised to me for his bad Swedish. It wasn't bad. Sometimes, in his letters, he mixed up the genders of nouns, but who doesn't when writing too fast, when the hand holding the pen can't keep up with the manic mind.

'The cops have always hated me'

I HAD been summoned and now he's standing right here, I could reach out to touch him. I've had nightmares about this man, yet he looks so normal. There's about four feet between us, my face turned towards him as I search for acknowledgment of my existence. At last he breaks the impasse by reaching out to shake my hand. His is dry and warm and so huge it swallows mine.

Khouri's wearing black sneakers with tracksuit bottoms and a T-shirt, both also in black. The only dash of colour, a smudge in the run-down and forlornly beige visiting room, is in the prayer beads snaking around his fingers, with their pattern of linden green flowers.

It's time. We are about to take our seats. The cops sink down on a single bed in the corner – 'For conjugal visits?' I wonder – as I take my place at a small table, facing Khouri. Soon enough, the fat cop has fallen asleep, the tall one's paying attention but pretending not to – or perhaps, as these kinds of visits are mundane for them, the cop's busy wondering what to make his kids for dinner once he returns home from work.

Khouri asks what I want. He looks me in the eyes. I say I want to talk. 'I won't talk,' he says. It's not the tone, which is polite despite its force, but the rapidness of his reply that jolts me. Leaning forward with his elbows on the table, Khouri does not shy away from my gaze. As his head's a bit big for his body and his eyes quite large, it's like a human teddy bear staring at me. I'm confused. Why invite me if he's not going to talk?

We do end up talking. Khouri is well-mannered, jokes at times, but we are skimming across the surface of the unspoken – the murders – until we do get to something more serious than his fiancée's wedding dress: the drive-by shooting, a few months before the double murder, that almost cost his friends their lives.

Khouri tells me that after leaving a nightclub together, he had stepped out of his cousin Sherbel Said's car to go get a hamburger, that when he heard the shooting a few streets away he knew his friends were in danger. That he sprinted, taking the wrong route at first, doubling back, at last reaching the shot-up red Volvo. His cousin's body was half-hanging out of the door.

The cops, who had arrived at the scene before him, tried to stop him from driving his cousin to the hospital, because, Khouri says with a look of disgust, they assumed he was already dead.

Khouri ignored them, as he had done for most of his life – 'The cops have always hated me' – and he drove his cousin to hospital where the doctors saved his life. But nothing could fix the damage from one of the bullets that had burrowed into his spine, paralysing him from the waist down.

Back in the centre of town, just blocks from the police station, forensics were called in to pick up every casing and photograph every bullet hole in the car where Khouri would have been sitting – and was likely to have been the prime target – if not for that late-night snack.

I don't bother asking Khouri who he thinks was holding the gun that night, because he wouldn't tell me anyway.

Time's up. The wardens let me out and I obediently plod after them down the corridor, descend in the lift, and let the swing-doors spit me back out into reception. Mentally, I drag my feet out of frustration: I have so many questions that time didn't allow me to ask.

Outside on the street, with the barbed wire on top of The Crown's gates behind me, I fish out my phone and type those three words I promised the Södertälje cop, and I describe Khouri:

'Funny, macho, scary.'

PART TWO

THE TOWN

2005 to 2009

Nemaline myopathy

NO EXPLANATION of what happened in Södertälje in the summer of 2010 is possible without rewinding; back to before meeting Philip, before finding Milad despite him being in hiding. And before tragedy changed Oritha's life so drastically that she finally felt 'free to talk' to me. Rewind to revisit everything that happened before I interviewed Khouri after he was incarcerated in The Crown for his alleged involvement in extortion and murder.

Oritha's fight began in 2005. Soon after giving birth, the young mother realised that something was not right with her firstborn. At first, the doctors searched in vain for explanations of Leon's breathing difficulties. As they laid a puzzle with the symptoms, a diagnosis emerged: Leon was suffering from a muscle disease, but which one?

'There's an untold number of muscles diseases in the world,' Oritha told me about first hearing of nemaline myopathy. It is a congenital disease that can weaken the muscles in the chest, making it difficult to breathe. The disease is so rare that the doctors told her Leon could be the only child with the disease in all of Scandinavia.

Looking back at the first few days and weeks of Leon's life, Oritha told me that she felt helpless, even when Leon was examined by specialists at the Astrid Lindgren Children's Hospital in Stockholm. 'It felt like we weren't getting any help from the public health service, but it's not true, they did so much for my son,' she said.

After being allowed to take her son home from the hospital, the everyday task of keeping him alive fell on Oritha, but with the help of the Swedish welfare state, which kicked into action, paying for personal assistants to care for Leon at home. The caregivers helped him turn over frequently so that excess mucus did not get stuck in his lungs, they made sure that the breathing tube that went into his throat was fitted correctly, they fed him with a tube, they showered him. Physiotherapists made sure that Leon's muscles didn't atrophy.

As Oritha learnt about the nitty-gritty of everyday care, she also learnt about the admin involved when applying for personal assistance, and she put that knowledge to use, setting up her own personal-assistance company with about ten employees. Then she also took a job as customer manager at another company in the same field.

While proud of her career, she came to realise that that kind of success attracted the wrong kind of attention. 'The Network knew that I had money,' she told me.

Months became years as Oritha kept the household afloat. Leon survived his first year, then his second … From time to time, one of his personal assistants sent me emails about working for the family. 'God chose Oritha as Leon's mother,' she told me, 'because God knew that she would take good care of him.'

And while the assistant was technically the one who cared for Leon, she had never seen it that way – according to her, the little boy, even though he could only breathe with the help of a respirator, was the one taking care of everyone around him, by teaching them to live in the moment.

'He can barely do a third of what other kids do – the machines are his constant companions – but despite that, life for him is about love and joy,' the assistant told me.

And when Oritha later made her decision to fight back against the mafia, it was her fight to care for Leon and his fight to stay alive that had inspired her to do so.

The national team

FOUR YEARS later, Leon had made it to his fourth birthday, but his health stopped him from taking part in the activities that all other little boys love; many of them had already started to kick footballs around. As they grow older, some boys dream of playing professionally, and in Södertälje the star of Assyriska FF shone with unrivalled splendour.

The dream of the football field – the admiration from the stand, the lucrative sponsorship agreements, the prestige – is difficult to achieve no matter where you spend your childhood. Most people will find other jobs once they grow up. Most will live ordinary lives, also only reading about the mafia in the newspapers, but in neighbourhoods that the police have categorised as 'especially vulnerable areas' the boys run a higher risk than their well-to-do peers of being drawn into crime. Living next door to young men who have already taken their place in the criminal underworld, who may even be related to the young boys, create, what social workers have referred to as 'the risk of infection'. The danger, however, usually only becomes acute in early teenagers, not among the young boys whose only dreams are of football.

Once upon a time, Conny Chamas was one of those boys, learning to love the beautiful game at a young age. At his first practice, he and the other boys had scratched their names in the field's gravel. Some years later, Chamas's uncle picked him up at home in a Stockholm suburb for a special outing, heading south on the E4 motorway. 'Conny, we're going down to Södertälje to see Assyriska play,' his uncle told him.

Conny Chamas was only seven and too young to understand what Assyriska FF meant to so many Assyrians, not only in Sweden but also across the global diaspora. He had not yet learned to love the white strip and club crest with the Assyrian flag and its blue and red rays.

'This is our national team, Conny,' the uncle told the child, who, with his pensive, green-eyed gaze, watched as the motorway snaked past forests and fields. Then at last they reached Södertälje, the industrial town sprawling in a shallow valley.

Parking near the Bårsta football field, tucked in between the town centre and the neighbourhood Ronna, they walked towards the clubhouse, Chamas eyeing his surroundings. Beyond the field he saw high-rise buildings on a wooded ridge. As they approached the clubhouse, Chamas noticed that the ground was covered in the husks of sunflower seeds, which the football fans would always eat as a snack.

Shortly afterwards, something else caught his attention: the game. It enchanted him. The men on the pitch were to become his heroes. And Chamas joined the ranks of countless boys who followed the team's ups and downs with devotion. He learned to hold two players in higher regard than the others: Kennedy Bakircioglü and Eddie Moussa, who Chamas had admired since first seeing him play – Chamas thought Eddie was fantastic.

The underdog club's highlight was 2005 – the same year Oritha's son Leon was born – when Assyriska FF fought their way into Allsvenskan, Sweden's premier league. Their triumph was short-lived, however, as they lost their spot at the close of the season, and saw no return for many years thereafter.

As the 2000s drew to a close, Chamas, by then a teenager, had not abandoned his hopes for the team and still kept an eye on his favourite players. He, like many others, couldn't help but notice that Eddie Moussa's skills on the pitch were evolving. Chamas and the other fans kept close tabs on his progress, hoping that Eddie would make his mark, not just at home but in the world, adding Assyriska FF's star to the galaxy of global football.

Surely, Chamas thought to himself, a bigger club would buy Eddie soon. 'Eddie had fantastic opportunities to go a long way, he was without a doubt the club's best player,' he told me. 'Eddie was explosive and technical, keeping the ball glued to his foot, playing in his own special style. He had a European style of play, and by that I mean he played an intelligent game where he assessed every situation.'

Chamas then added what everyone says about Eddie. 'And he was fast.'

Would 2009, four years after their Allsvenskan season, become another great year in the annals of Assyriska FF? The team were again approaching the highest league, and their on-again-off-again track record added a certain frisson of unpredictability for opposing teams, even such Allsvenskan giants as Djurgården IF. 'This is a compliment: with Assyriska FF you never know what you get,' said Djurgården's board member Ellinor Persson, before her team faced Assyriska FF in a crucial double meet to battle it out for a spot in the top league.

As others have done before her, Persson acknowledged the Södertälje club's courage and perseverance, always admiring them for their warm and welcoming fan culture, including whole families who'd make a day of it in the stands.

The story of Assyriska cannot be told without speaking about family and the community's history – the burning desire to rebuild a nation that geopolitics had torn apart. A desire that had translated to fervour in the stands. Grown men bursting into tears as the team loses. The same men standing up to dance when the team scores, moving joyfully in a line led by a piper playing the oboe-like zurna.

At a noisy derby I went to against the Aramean club Syrianska FC, a boy, who couldn't have been more than 12, sitting in front of me, screamed, 'Damn Aramean!' at the referee for handing Syrianska a free kick. His older sisters giggled, seemingly part amused, part embarrassed. Their father caught my eye and shook his head in a 'boys will be boys' kind of way. Across the field were Syrianska FC's supporters, who'd a few years later become notorious for growing ever more noisy. But no matter in which stand the fans had taken a seat, they were united in all being survivors.

They are the children and grandchildren of the Christians who survived the odds when the Ottomans slaughtered their families during the purge of ethnic minorities that Turkey still won't call a genocide. It had long been a sore point in Södertälje that the Swedish government had yet to label it a genocide either.

Over the years it had become such a sore point that the Social Democrat mayor of Södertälje had, on several occasions, explained to her local electorate that she did not agree with her party's stance at government level.

Anyone with any connection to Södertälje knows that Assyrian and Aramean families were decimated, that the survivors had to count their dead on more than one hand, often two or more. A shocking number of residents in Södertälje have told me that only their grandma had escaped, too many spoke of a cousin who had lost all his brothers and sisters, too many with an aunt who had been abducted, never to be seen again.

In the late 2000s, nearly a century had passed, but, unlike physical wounds, memories of oppression do not heal. The survivors had carried their memories with them to Sweden and their children built their homes here in Södertälje, thus, the players on the pitch had come to represent survival, not just football, each time when they stepped out on the grass and looked up at the stands. Facing the old and the young, the seated and the dancing.

The long reach of war

IN THE years when Eddie Moussa could be found playing football for Assyriska, there were also rumours in town that he was earning money on the side as a loan shark.

Philip, the gambling addict, didn't know Eddie well, so he showed no interest in talking about the matter when we spoke, but we talked about money on a more general level. 'This town's flooded with cash,' Philip told me.

That the cash economy was thriving did not go unnoticed by others in town, and it was a cause for concern in some quarters. Downtown, the local government politicians complained that the police wouldn't listen to their warnings about the emergency of a below-radar economy where cash is king.

The local police, however, knew this all too well. The cash in question didn't stem only from loan sharking, but from other black-as-night sources. In raid after raid, the police seized drugs and weapons, but could not pinpoint who was masterminding the illegal trade.

Nor had the situation escaped the Swedish Tax Agency – once the authorities had begun to cooperate in the Södertälje clamp down – where a senior agent explained the most basic of set ups to me: a cash register where the cashier simply 'forgets' to register a few too many payments – the cash put to the side becomes untraceable and thus untaxable, unless the Tax Agency had sent out its employees to lunch, where they, in between each bite, took note of the number of customers and then, after their coffee, seized the register to compare the numbers.

There was, however, a bigger problem that had only grown – the housing crisis.

Already squeezed for space, Södertälje's lack of flats became acute in the 2000s when Christians fleeing from Iraq arrived in the town. Following the US invasion in 2003, the ensuing chaos in Iraq had reverberated more in Södertälje than in any other city in the world, providing sanctuary once again to Christians running for their lives. And their number caught Södertälje officials by surprise.

'Of course we'd been watching the evening news like everyone else, but, when we saw American combat vehicles roll into Baghdad, we didn't think it would set off such chaos that Christian Iraqis would flee to Södertälje,' said one senior civil servant, who wanted to be quoted anonymously.

'In Town Hall, we hadn't see this coming and weren't prepared,' he added.

So many refugees made their way to Södertälje, where about one third of its 90,000 people are first- or second-generation immigrants. By the time the town had welcomed more Iraqis than all of the United States had, the situation prompted a visit from curious US senators. It was an irony not lost on many Swedes that Sweden had taken on the task of providing refuge, despite not having been part of the US-led coalition that invaded Iraq in the first place.

But where to put people? The pressure on the housing market made Södertälje vulnerable; high demand created a thriving market for those with a shrewd mind for business. In 2006, as the Iraqi asylum seekers began to head for Sweden, Södertälje's Social Democrat Member of Parliament Yilmaz Kerimo wrote an open letter to the Integration Minister Nyamko Sabuni of the Liberal Party saying it was time for other towns to show solidarity and help take care of asylum seekers:

'My town Södertälje has worked with introduction and integration for more than 30 years,' Kerimo wrote. 'Despite all our efforts, we're seeing signs of overcrowding, unemployment, social-benefits dependence, inadequate language skills, poverty, children faring badly.'

A law known by its acronym EBO had since 1994 allowed asylum seekers to choose where to live in Sweden; newcomers had thus often opted for towns where they had relatives, or at least picked neighbourhoods where the high number of immigrants meant they could get by speaking their native language. Critics of the EBO Law have said it leads to segregation and also puts an undue financial burden on just a few of the country's local governments; municipal taxes pay not just for schools but for several key welfare services, including social benefits and care of the elderly. And it's also the local government that takes care of social housing. Desperation and fragile dreams of safety lead to rising rents – even though sub-letting is allowed, it must be approved by the housing association, and rents are capped to avoid usuary. But few bother to send in sub-let applications because why should they when there's money to be made?

In a block of flats close to Assyriska FF's old football field, Bårsta IP, a co-op board member told me that he had reminded a neighbour to apply for permission to sub-let his flat. In response, the neighbour had threatened to kill him if he flagged him officially.

Sub-lets, known in Sweden as 'second-hand contracts', are sub-let yet again, and then again. Second hand, third hand … social workers had told me they had made house calls and encountered families who had 'fifth-hand contracts'. These families had very little legal protection, and there was no improvement on the horizon; new housing would take time to build. With few, if any, choices, families took what housing they could find. The lucky ones were sleeping on relatives' sofas. The unlucky ones were in the hands of what can only be described as lease-holders moonlighting as slum landlords, and overcrowding became a fact.

The Town Hall had long tried to estimate the extent of the problem: 'If you look through the windows in some Södertälje neighbourhoods during the day, you can see stacks of mattresses,' the senior civil servant said. 'Who knows how many people sleep there at night?'

There were plenty in this small town who were cashing in on 'fauda', the Arabic word for chaos.

Qualifier one

IN LATE autumn of 2009, as the days went by, the sun set ever earlier. October served up sweets to children who adopted the American trick-or-treat tradition from Hollywood movies, while many of their parents held true to the Swedish tradition of placing candles on the graves of relatives on 'Alla helgons afton' – 'All Hallows' Eve'. At dusk, the fading light transformed the graveyards into shadowy fields of flickering light. When October yielded to November, people found the resolve to brave what many Swedes consider to be the most difficult month of the year. On days that are not overcast, the sun sinks below the horizon at around 4pm. There was no snow yet to offset the gloom and no frost to add early-morning sparkle.

In the world of football, there were other woes to ponder. With their glory year of 2005 behind them, Assyriska had spent several seasons in the second-tier league Superettan, but if they put up a proper fight, the club could get back into Allsvenskan.

After a 3-3 draw against Jönköping, Eddie scoring two goals, they qualified for the play-offs, but to get back into Allsvenskan they would have to bring down Djurgården, the prestigious Stockholm club that had taken home the national championship three times since the millennium, and 11 times in total so far in the club's history. Yet despite their historic victories, Djurgården had recently struggled to stay true to their legacy, which meant Assyriska had a fighting chance.

4 November 2009 drew near. The Stockholm club travelled the short journey south to Södertälje's new arena on the edge of

town, nicknamed Jallavallen. 'Jalla', pronounced yalla, meaning 'Let's go' in Arabic, while 'vallen' means embankment in Swedish. 'Jallavallen' thus fuses two of Södertälje's main languages and cultures.

Both *The Guardian* and *Le Monde* had visited Södertälje to report on Assyriska's football prowess, and about the community that had given birth to the club.

With 3,500 seats and space for another 3,000 fans to stand, the arena had hit a record attendance back in May 2009 during a derby against Syrianska FC. There had been, however, quite a few fans, like Chamas, who'd grumbled about the arena, 'too cold in the stands', he explained. Furthermore, he felt nostalgic for the old sports filed with its rickety clubhouse where he, as a young boy, had seen his first Assyriska match.

With temperatures hovering around 5°C for the previous few days, November had been nippy but not nasty so far. The Swedish weather service, staying true to its penchant for poetic summaries, ended up describing November as a month with 'many nuances of grey'.

The players were ready. In striker Andreas Haddad's eyes, Eddie was the undisputed star of Assyriska FF. Yet it was only in the last few years that his friend had managed to meld his raw talent into something more controlled and much more powerful. 'Eddie used to complicate every situation just like young players do,' Haddad said. 'He wanted to do difficult things instead of just going for a simple forward pass, but all young players do that before they realise that taking what is easy and making it even easier, that's the hard part about football. Eddie always had the speed, but not the technique.'

As Eddie and his team-mates walked out on to the pitch, the tension was palpable. If he scored, Eddie would treat his supporters to his signature victory move: a swift backwards trot that gave the fans the best possible view of the number 18 on his back.

The fans had to wait 38 minutes until a curling, wing-back cross from Assyriska's Kristoffer Näfver reached Dennis Östlundh, whose header left the enormous Djurgården goalkeeper Pa Dembo Touray defenceless.

Having put Assyriska back on course towards Allsvenskan, Östlundh beamed with pride.

A local sports journalist later told me that Östlundh exemplified Assyriska's fresh recruitment drive, they had been adding trusty workhorses, steady but never quite star material, who could join the club without losing any prestige. Assyriska offered them an acceptable step sideways to a club with future prospects, the journalist said. And thanks to the short commute to Södertälje, Stockholm-based players would not have to relocate with their families.

As the players reassembled after the first goal, the game picked up pace straight away. Djurgården steered the ball from kick-off straight to the Assyriska goal, threatening to equalise. But the fervour didn't translate into a goal; Mikael Dahlberg's attempt missed the left post by a mere foot. As the teams walked off the pitch at half-time, Assyriska were leading 1-0. Once they returned, it was soon clear that the second half would have more action in store.

Within just a few minutes, Eddie got hold of the ball and sprinted clear of Patrik Haginge, who couldn't keep up with the player so famous for his speed. And once Eddie turned to pass, he had laid the groundwork for the second goal. When he passed the ball to captain Göran Marklund, another former inner-city player from AIK Fotboll, they scored a second goal. At 2-0, Assyriska had the top league in their sights once again.

Towards the end of the match, Eddie had a problem: a recent leg injury started to act up. Even though Assyriska had already burned through their substitutions, he had to step off the pitch, but despite being one player down, Eddie's team-mates managed to keep Djurgården goalless until the final whistle.

The match lodged itself in Haddad's memory forever. 'When we played our [first] qualifying match against Djurgården, Eddie was Assyriska's best player,' he said. 'He'd been retrained into a forward and he was the absolute best. A lot of top teams were keeping an eye on him, he'd been outstanding all year.'

The problem was that a different kind of team were also keeping a watchful eye on Eddie at the time, a team that didn't like him crowding their turf one bit – Khouri and his team-mates, ready to defend their lucrative loan-sharking business.

Once the police started to look long and hard at the events unfolding that autumn, they kept their narrative simple: Eddie, along with his brothers, and The Network were on opposing teams, and there wasn't a referee to keep the peace.

Thou shalt not kill

THE CREATION of football clubs had become one of the success stories of Södertälje's Orthodox Christian community: building their churches was seen as another success, as they stood testimony to a culture that had resisted all attempts at extinction in the Middle East. 'Södertälje is a biblical city,' a former criminal said to me one afternoon – he had agreed to be interviewed about his journey back to his faith, how he went to prison and then found God in solitary confinement.

A biblical city – it struck me as a fitting description. The town's patron saint, the 11th-century pilgrim St Ragnhild, had not only been chosen to give her name to the church by the central square, across from the District Court, but also been chosen to adorn the town crest.

As well as the Lutheran church bearing her name and the Orthodox churches, I discovered many other iterations of Christianity. I visited a Pentecostal church near the train station that were handing out bags of food to those in need. The volunteers told me there were more and more people turning to them for help. A short stroll across the bridge, I spotted the town's Catholic church nestling above the banks of the canal.

In the Hovsjö neighbourhood, the Chaldean community, also from the Middle East, had commissioned architects to build them a church. It was to be clad in black-stained wood – the budget didn't go further, the community association chairman told me – and thus the blueprint melded the structure of a grander church with the minimalism that the Nordic building material provide.

Just like the football arena's nickname Jallavallen, it was to become an example of fusing traditions.

Among the youth, Jesus tattoos had become common, as were necklaces with crosses worn by both men and women. In the same neighbourhood as the Björn Borg Promenade, named after the legendary tennis player and Södertälje's most famous son, a new evangelical church was set to join Hillsong, the ever-expanding global congregation.

As a reporter in Södertälje, I couldn't avoid religion even if I'd tried. On a bitter afternoon, I was out walking close to the St Ephrem Cathedral, just a few bus stops from the arena, when I stopped to speak to a woman pushing a pram. I was doing a story on street lighting and accessibility during the dark winter months, because uncleared pavements were seen as a public health hazard, but she still managed to steer the conversation off topic. 'Ann,' she said earnestly. 'Do you believe in God?'

I told her I'd chosen to be agnostic, which appeared to leave her flummoxed, not knowing how to respond, so I said with a teasing tone, 'Ah, I can see a twinkle of hope in your eyes, you think that as an agnostic I'm not beyond all hope!'

The woman gave me a confused smile, like she didn't know what to do with me, before shoving a pamphlet about her congregation into my hand.

Nor was I spared such conversations at the office, situated in a co-working space with commercial companies. An Aramean woman who worked next door, and with whom I often had lunch, spotted a small plastic cross hanging on my office wall (a gift from a corner-shop owner) and asked me with genuine, happy surprise, 'Ann, are you Christian?'

'Well,' I said, 'I'm only Christian when it suits me.' Her response was uproarious laughter.

This generous, curious, joyful woman had become one of my favourite people in Södertälje. We talked about everything: jobs, relationships, and how infuriating it was to be served cold fries at McDonald's. As a first-generation immigrant, from the mid-

2000s wave of refugees, she also offered a fresh perspective on the already established Assyrian and Aramean communities in town. In fluent, albeit imperfect, Swedish, she told me the first wave of Orthodox immigrants were much more conservative than newcomers like her.

Södertälje, I realised, was not only a biblical city, but more generally a religious one. The small Islamic Association had tucked its mosque into a modest commercial space behind a supermarket. On a nearby road, Jehovah's Witnesses had established their Kingdom Hall. Most often, I'd spot the witnesses at the combined railway and bus station in rush hour, distributing their pamphlets in a cornucopia of different languages.

Working full-time in Södertälje was enough to make me ponder about most Swedes' agnosticism – whether the loss of religion entails other losses, spiritual and emotional – but as I ploughed through thousands upon thousands of police case file notes on Khouri and The Network, I was reminded that faith never has and never will be a vaccine against wrongdoings.

The Ten Commandments could not be found in the interrogation transcripts: chief among them in its glaring absence – thou shalt not kill.

A hunger for power

LOCAL ENTREPRENEUR Jakob Rohyo had picked out a spot next to St Ephrem to establish his furniture store, an aesthetic hub, in sharp contrast to strict Ikea minimalism, inviting customers into a wonderland of Eastern glamour. Rohyo had chosen to offer endless choices, from sofas in leather to armchairs in velvet; the colour palette stretching from turquoise to creamy vanilla.

Rohyo always made time for his customers, chatting and catching up on the latest. One of those customers had been Khouri, who'd usually brought his long-term girlfriend, whose poise and intelligence had earned her a great deal of respect from Rohyo. 'She looks like Kim Kardashian but she's tall,' he told me, sizing me up. 'Like you, Ann, she's at least 5ft 9in.'

He told me that on one of the couple's visits to the store, they had looked for sofas. To show me, Rohyo pulled out a large catalogue of furniture from a shelf by his desk and flicked to the page with a photo of a sturdy creation in leather that the couple had shown an interest in. A Roman pattern ran along the sofa's dark-wood base. The design was called Cesar. 'She has good taste, his girlfriend,' Rohyo said.

While he had grown to respect Khouri's girlfriend, he'd wondered if she knew about the accusations against her boyfriend. Had she not heard the rumours? And why hadn't she questioned why so many people feared her partner?

During my meeting with Rohyo, a friend of his, who didn't want to be named, started to rattle off an extensive list of business owners who had been forced to pay protection money to The

Network. He gave me names and places but forbade me to look them up because he didn't want to run the risk of the information leading back to him. He, like so many others in town, was honest about his fears.

Instead, he expanded on why so few victims went to the police. 'It isn't just a question of being scared of The Network, it's a fear of the authorities that stems from the Middle East. Having lived with public servants and politicians who were at times as corrupt as any mafia, people learned that attracting attention was dangerous. Therefore, conflicts were resolved within the community,' Rohyo's friend explained.

While he personally regretted that the first generation of Assyrian and Aramean immigrants had not been able to shed this habit of never asking the authorities for help, he showed great sympathy for them, saying that many hadn't been able to step out from 'the long shadow of oppression'.

The well-spoken man continued: 'Many are still afraid. It's that simple. And it will probably take several generations until everyone has thrown that fear out.'

'It's easy to exploit that fear and to reinforce it with intimidation and violence. There's a rumour,' he said, shaking his head in disapproval, 'that has spread far and wide, that Khouri has started to tell his victims, "I own Södertälje".'

As the old man gave me a 'Dear God, what's wrong with people?' look, Rohyo placed the furniture catalogue back on its shelf. Sitting back down by his desk, Rohyo told me that Khouri had disappointed him – he used to be quite fond of the young man. He was also scared, not that Khouri would hurt him, but that Khouri's enemies would follow him to the store, when Khouri's guard was down and his friends weren't with him, and take revenge here in the store, which could lead to Rohyo's customers and friends being hurt.

Neither they nor Rohyo and his family came to Sweden to yet again be exposed to risk. They had left danger behind, they thought, as they headed north. A set of family portraits hung on

Rohyo's office wall, a picture gallery that encompassed several generations. There were studio-lit monochrome portraits of older women wearing black headscarves, their cheeks sunken by decades of hard work raising families. Next to these portraits hung school photos, popping with colour, of Rohyo's handsome sons, who'd only ever known Sweden as their home.

These were not just portraits of loved ones, together they sewed the patchwork of one family's history. While equally unique in its many details as any other family's, it was ubiquitous as a testament to the universal drive to make life easier for one's children. This wall was a portrait of hope, faith and charity, and told a story of exodus – a topic that Khouri used to be fond of. 'Especially when he was younger,' Rohyo said, 'Khouri was smart and curious when we talked about politics and history. The history of our people.' That's why Rohyo had clung on to hope for so long that Khouri would mend his ways. 'Once I told him, "If you choose to go down this road you are no longer welcome in the store",' said Rohyo.

Not only did Khouri not stray from his criminal path, he had kept on returning to the store, like a magpie unable to resist gold and all that gleams. And it was right here in the shop, among the gilded mirrors and the glass dining tables, that Rohyo began to see the contours of an ambition turned to madness in a boy raised by a single mother. 'Khouri's family were poor,' he said. 'They had no status. I think that's why he became hungry for power.'

The loss of hope

ROHYO WELL remembered the day when he had, at last, been forced to give up hope that Khouri would change course. A few years before meeting with me, he had watched as a police car pulled into the store's parking lot, approaching Khouri's car.

One of the cops explained to me later that Khouri had recently been sentenced to prison but hadn't bothered to show up and 'check himself in', so to speak: 'I told him, "Come on, it will be better if you just come along with us the right away",' the officer recalled. He had just engaged in conversation with Khouri when his colleague walked to the front of Khouri's car to discourage Khouri's friend at the wheel from driving off. But the driver had hit the accelerator hard. The officer first stepped out of the way then lunged towards Khouri's open window. The first cop, who'd been speaking with Khouri, pulled his gun, taking one shot to stop them from getting away. But as he watched Khouri wind up the window, trapping his colleague's arm and then dragging him 'at least 200 metres' as the car picked up speed, the officer lowered his gun out of fear he'd shoot his colleague by mistake.

At last, Khouri rolled down the window, freeing the officer's arm. The policeman hit the asphalt hard, but escaped without any broken bones. 'He was wearing a protective vest,' his colleague recalled, 'but that vest was torn so badly that you could see the metal plates inside.'

'Khouri has never paid us any regard, he has never shown us any respect nor any respect for the law, no respect for the system,' he added. 'Khouri is cold and indifferent.'

The witnesses at the furniture store would never forget that day. That was the day a shocked Rohyo had at last understood that his hopes that Khouri would change course had been in vain.

Hold the line

THAT AFTERNOON several years ago outside the furniture store, Khouri had added aggravated assault to his criminal record. Once he'd served his sentence, he came back to Rohyo's store and ordered more furniture. Where Khouri was getting his money from – Rohyo's store is high-end, the furniture not cheap – was a question best left unasked.

Down at the Town Hall, Khouri and his loan-sharking ilk were not the only item on the agenda. The politicians and public servants were still nagging the police to do something about crime, but they were also busy grappling with the effects of high-level immigration.

In the preceding few years, Södertälje's schools had been struggling to keep high teaching standards – not just because of the increasing number of students, but due to the fact that the new students didn't speak Swedish.

The Town Hall were scared of 'white flight', the American term for middle-class and often white families packing up and moving away. A long list of parent signatures accompanied a letter published in the local paper asking Södertälje Town Hall to invest heavily in the schools so that they wouldn't feel forced to transfer their kids to better schools in nearby towns. Some families had already decided to quit not just the school, but the town forever.

'I never thought I'd be that person,' a middle-class woman told me about her decision to leave Södertälje, where she grew up. 'But it's difficult to keep your political conviction that everyone needs to chip in when your kids' education is at stake.'

The Town Hall – scared that 'white flight' would drain the budget because the well-to-do pay more in municipal taxes – decided to appoint more teachers, aiming for a two-teacher-per-class system that ended up being studied by education researchers at Stockholm University. And the Town Hall decided to hold firm its anti-alarmist 'We'll deal with it' line. They faced journalists, including foreign correspondents, who viewed Södertälje as a symbolic microcosm of all of Sweden's immigration challenges, which in many ways was true, but the Town Hall kept their cool.

Because organised crime clustered in a few poorer neighbourhoods and, as Milad described it, The Network didn't bother 'Swedes', the violence hadn't affected everyone in Södertälje. Yet Social Democrat politician Boel Godner, who was next in line to lead the municipal council, described an undercurrent of concern across town. When she gave me an interview, she brought up all the local newspaper headlines about crime, the burnt-out cars across town, and going to the pub and being forced, more or less, to check your coat in even when it felt unnecessary. Coat checks were always a great and easy way to bring in cash, a cop later pointed out to me, and the gangs were very fond of cash.

And whether one was directly affected by the crime or not, the rumours reached everyone: loan sharking, protection money, threats, reprisals … an extortion victim, who ended up in the witness protection programme, described how The Network's hierarchy worked in an interview with the police: 'The first group are teenagers, from 15 to 17 years old. When they perform tasks like burning cars, they are paid between 4,000 to 10,000 kronor. You haven't been able to sell your car, so you hire the teenagers to torch it at night,' said the man, explaining that that way the owner at least got insurance money.

The somewhat older, tier-two criminals were in charge of bothering business owners who refused to pay protection money, which could be as much 30,000 kronor a month, according to the witness.

'Long live Södertälje'

THERE ARE always at least two sides to a story. What was the street angle if one asked the boys roped into crime? I turned to a local rapper for answers, but he said he wouldn't give me an interview if I didn't pay him, which for press ethical reasons I couldn't do. So instead I watched his music videos online. One video started with an orchestral version of national anthem playing over drone footage of expensive lakeside properties, but when the clip cut to Södertälje's stark public housing, the music ended and he started to sing about racism.

The video was well made, with drone footage interspersed with street scenes and close-ups of young boys' faces as they loitered on a pavement. In a scene in the back of a car, a man in a Lucha Libre mask held an automatic rifle – I couldn't tell if it was real or fake. The videographer had filmed cop cars as well as boys on mopeds. The video ended with the rapper singing, 'Long live Södertälje'.

Most of the footage, I noted, was from the Hovsjö neighbourhood, where the beat cop Alice Ekengren had been stationed since arriving in Södertälje. I mentioned the rapper to her.

'My god, I remember when some of the boys in the neighbourhood took part in one of his music videos. They were so happy!' Ekengren told me.

Hovsjö at the time was no picnic for the cops. Geographically, her beat was limited: the bus station by the central square with shops and a restaurant, a kiosk and a primary care centre including the physiotherapy clinic that used to treat Eddie and his teammates for injuries.

Hovsjö had been built between a lake, an industrial sprawl and not much else. Allotments had been added on its outskirts and much of the dense forest had been left untouched, stretching in unbroken wilderness for mile upon mile upon mile, populated in folklore by goblins, trolls and elves.

But under the yellow haze of streetlights at night, parents didn't worry about their children going into the woods, they worried about them ending up in bad company, and feared the traps that made their kids vulnerable to being recruited into a 'gangsta life' to stave off boredom. Lured by a chance to make a living despite bad grades in school, and by an invitation to brotherhood that'd protect them from bullying.

It was a neighbourhood where young boys were surrounded by older boys who dabbled or were already well established in crime – sometimes their own brothers or cousins. Some social workers had used the term 'the risk of infection' to explain to me how the dangerous inter-connectivity worked.

During her first years in Södertälje, Ekengren felt that the autumn and winter weather could be merciless – cold and raw – but she still spotted boys out during the chillier months loitering on the square, where the 'local talents' – cop code for those who dabble in crime – used to hang out. Ekengren told me she understood that a teenager wanted to spend time with his friends, but outside on cold nights? Why weren't they tucked up on the sofa watching television, keeping warm?

These boys were a handful; they did stupid shit, and they did racist shit. Which came as no surprise to the beat cops, given how the boys' parents expressed themselves about other ethnic minorities. Nor had the racism come as much of a surprise to me. In the little local kiosk by the square, selling cheap wood crosses decorated with small plastic portraits of Jesus, the shopkeeper had looked me straight in the eye, several times, and explained – in broken Swedish despite decades in Sweden – that those Muslims, they had only come here to breed like rabbits and to live off benefits. The kiosk owner, still not breaking eye contact, once stroked his chin to illustrate a long beard, as worn by devout Muslim men including community leaders, and then added, with a slightly more reconciliatory tone, that it was the 'mullahs' fault'. That's why Muslims were bad, their leaders were no good. Then he kissed the cross around his neck to tie up his argument. His lips glued to Jesus's face; case closed.

Children as young as eight had looked Ekengren straight in the eye and told her that Muslims were 'disgusting'. While most of Hovsjö's new arrivals in the late 2000s were Christians from Iraq, a few Somali families had moved in too, but most, Ekengren noted, had left as soon as they could. Ekengren remembered one incident in particular, when several boys attacked a young Somali girl outside the supermarket. 'They were just kicking a football around and decided she was as good a target as any,' Ekengren explained. 'So they attacked, tried to pull off her headscarf and pushed her to the ground. One boy spat in her mouth.'

As 2009 started to draw to its close, Ekengren would spend less time chatting to the boys, and more time doing her part in what would become the biggest organised-crime investigation in Swedish history. And what would become a nightmare for Eddie Moussa's family and friends. And for his fans, who'd just received happy news.

On 19 December 2009, Assyriska FF's supporters' club, Zelge Fans, announced that Eddie had extended his contract with 'the mother club':

Despite his young age, Eddie Moussa is somewhat of a veteran in Assyriska FF. Eddie, who was nurtured by the club, is on his eighth season in the A-team since his debut in 2001. This year, Eddie Moussa has seriously developed as a striker. In the past season, Eddie produced seven goals and six assists. And the readers should have in mind that he only made his debut as a forward in nine of the matches.

Godless

AT WORK one day – a day like any other, Milad later pointed out – there was a knock on the door to his wholesale business. Milad let an acquaintance into his office and offered him something to drink. Milad, a quite short man who had not become overweight but was robust and who admitted the days he played a lot of football were long gone, noticed that his visitor – 'a vain man' according to Milad – had managed to keep fit, unlike many other men of their age who had not been able to hold off a beer belly.

Milad thought he knew the reason for the man calling on him at his place of work – probably to order chocolate, one of the many goods that Milad imported in large quantities in order to offer discounts to the shops and cafés in town.

'You are doing well,' the visitor said. 'We see how hard you work.'

While Milad treated the man with kindness, he had never liked him much, finding him arrogant. Milad's friends held the same view and over at The Parrot café they had tried to teach Tyson, an actual parrot sitting in a cage by the window, to squawk 'faggot' in Aramean whenever the man entered the establishment.

Despite his reservations, Milad was flattered that the man praised him for having a successful business. The man's next line came as a shock to Milad. 'You have to pay us 30,000 kronor a month.'

At first, Milad didn't understand what he meant – and who 'us' were. And then he realised who 'us' were, confirmed by the man mentioning one of Khouri's many nicknames, 'Al Taweel', which in Arabic means 'the tall one'. He was being told to pay protection money; the lack of shame on his extortioner's face really struck Milad. And behind this man's demands stood an army led by Khouri, he realised.

'They never say Khouri's name because they don't have to say more than 'Al Taweel'', Milad would later tell me. 'All my people, all Arameans, know who Al Taweel is.'

Nevertheless, Milad tried to bargain. 'But what are you thinking, that I even earn 30,000 kronor a month?' The visitor wouldn't budge at first, but Milad persevered and got the 'fee' down to 27,000 kronor. The man, at long last, left.

'That man has no God,' Milad recalled thinking. 'He only believes in money.'

As the door shut behind his visitor, Milad started to take stock and do the maths. He was expecting a big shipment of toys from Dubai, and he would have to find buyers at once. He then decided to moonlight as a driving instructor to earn more money. There were always parents who'd rather pay for an instructor than subject themselves to sitting in a car with their own teenager at the wheel.

With a feeling of deep regret, Milad realised he'd have to ask for cash in hand. If he paid taxes, he'd not scrape together enough money to pay The Network. Milad didn't want to dodge taxes, but asked himself, 'What choice do I have?' He knew better than to pick a fight with Al Taweel.

The police, once they started hearing about Khouri's nickname, struggled to transliterate it from the Arabic. Going through the transcribed witness statements, I spotted both 'Altavil' and 'Altaville', which sounded like the name of a small American town – 'With Khouri himself mayor,' I thought to myself.

Al Taweel … AKA Bernard Khouri, AKA Berno, and he had been given more nicknames such as Jarecho, Aramean for 'the tall one', and Sabé, Aramean for 'seven'.

The old Swedish proverb 'kärt barn har många namn' roughly translates as 'a beloved child has many names'. Ironic, as Khouri couldn't be further from beloved in his victims' eyes.

Milad, so desperate to get The Network off his back, turned to an old acquaintance, a local goldsmith, who gave him a loan of 200,000 kronor so he could pay off Khouri's associates. That loan would come to haunt Milad. And his fear of Khouri would come to rob him of sleep for years.

And as I continued digging into The Network's business model, I'd grow to deeply empathise with Milad. There may be a fine line between being careful and good old-fashioned paranoia, but Khouri even ended up getting to me. Soon after starting my research into The Network, I saw two young men sitting in a car outside my house. At the time, I lived on a quiet suburban street, and there was no reason for them to linger, so I wondered if Khouri had sent them.

And after I spoke with Milad for the first time, and as I kept on reading statement after statement made to the police by terrified witnesses, my sleep suffered. Some nights, I had nightmares as a tall shadowy figure loomed over me.

Clues

WHO WAS this man who had destroyed so many people's peace of mind? Khouri's criminal record offered some clues. The document provided to me by the District Court spanned six pages and included several convictions of assault as well as vehicle theft, robbery, carrying a knife ... the list was long.

In 2002, the year Khouri turned 22, he was convicted of resisting arrest and aggravated assault; the date, I noted, matched up with Khouri dragging that police officer 200 metres across the car park outside the furniture store.

Because crimes committed under the age of 18 are always confidential, and thus not included in the document I was holding in my hand, I couldn't tell if Khouri had gotten into trouble with the law before his first adult conviction: a drug-related crime in 1999, the same year he turned 19. I had heard, however, that social services had tried to help Khouri back when he was still a minor, but my source, whom I'd tagged as reliable, refused to give me details. Another source had told me that 'something happened' to Khouri as a child. He wouldn't tell me more. Neither of these sources were keeping quiet out of fear, but as they were both working as public servants, the law prevented them divulging details.

In my search for information I instead turned to the people who knew Khouri as a child. When I got hold of the grade transcript for his entire ninth-grade class, I phoned all of his old classmates; about two-thirds of them were willing to talk, but none of them wanted me to use their real names.

Most of them remembered him as shy and withdrawn in the beginning when he'd just moved to Sweden. Once they'd all left school, and lost track of each other, one of his former classmates tried to figure out the identity of 'the gang leader' referred to in all the newspapers. When a friend told her, she had been shocked, replying, 'But that's not possible! Has he done all these horrible things? He must have completely lost his way.'

Another classmate did remember Khouri misbehaving even as a child. Before breaking for the holiday, Khouri and the other children – 'We were nine or ten, I think,' the classmate said – assembled to sing summer songs and thank their teachers. As is customary, the teachers had put all the children's assignments and projects into little bags for them to take home. When Khouri had received his bag, he emptied its contents on the ground. 'Our teacher was absolutely furious!' the classmate pointed out.

Upon growing a little older, Khouri had started to unpick bicycle locks while the other kids were still busy with kiddy pranks such as stealing apples out of people's gardens. And Khouri started to demand more attention. 'I thought he was cocky,' yet another classmate told me as I made my way down the list of names in front of me. 'He tried to act tough,' he added, 'but I always knew he wasn't tough. I could see he wasn't doing well, that he was sad. You could see it in his eyes.'

Several people talked about Khouri's sadness. 'He didn't have a father. They said his dad was dead, but I never bought it,' one said. 'If he'd had someone to take care of him, I think he'd be working at Scania or Astra today. He wouldn't be a gangster.'

Qualifier two

THE YEAR 2009 was turning into an odd one, and not just in football. Swine flu had reached Sweden and Djurgården board member Ellinor Persson had gotten the vaccine; inoculation centres had opened across the country, people were tense, and Persson, at one point, thought that the atmosphere 'felt almost like war'.

The second qualifier was coming up. Last time, down at Jallavallen, Djurgården coach Andree Jeglertz had left star striker Mattias Jonson out of the action because he'd been having problems with his calf. Then Assyriska started stealing goals off them. 'After that second goal, I felt hope abandon me,' Persson recalled.

Ahead of the impending second match, she was hoping that Jonson could pull them from the quagmire. They needed a 3-0 win. Building a team is like laying a puzzle; she called it a 'lottery', and pointed out that just one injury could throw the dynamics of a carefully planned and trained first XI out of balance – 'These damn constant injuries,' she said.

Three days to go. She felt fine. The next day, fine too. Then, on the morning of the second qualifier, a few days after taking the swine-flu vaccine, she woke with a high fever, her face flushed and her throat dry, every inch of her body sore. There was no way she'd make it to the Stadion arena later that day. She turned on the TV instead.

Right from the start, she noted that Djurgården were playing much better than the first qualifier, which she called 'a catastrophe'. With hope restored, she fell asleep.

Over at Stadion, it was Assyriska's turn to face catastrophe. In a run on goal, Eddie faced off with Djurgården's giant goalie, who grabbed the ball right in front of him, forcing Eddie to leap over him. As he landed, Eddie started to limp, grabbing the back of his thigh. The television commentators didn't miss a beat, calling game over on Eddie's turf time before he even had time to turn around to face the bench. He looked resigned, rather than angry, when he signalled to his coach to sub him off.

From then on, Djurgården pinned back Assyriska. Marklund's beautiful pass to Kosovan player Xhevdet Llumnica was one of the few chances Assyriska had during the opening 45 minutes. It came to nothing, and at the end of the first half both teams had to walk off the pitch goalless.

Persson, still asleep in front of the TV at home, was oblivious to the drama. After the referee called half-time, her children woke her.

'What's the score?' she asked them.

'0-0,' she was told.

'You're kidding!'

Neither she nor the TV commentators were sure Djurgården could pull off a win: 'Djurgården are doing everything right, except scoring,' reporter Suzanne Sjögren commented during half-time. 'Is it reasonable to think we'll see the same kind of grind in the second half?'

'I don't think so,' journalist Olof Lundh responded. 'If they don't score, desperation will take over. They need to score a goal quite early on. [Djurgården's] Mattias Jonson's very active, he's winning all his duels.'

Fifteen minutes later, as the second half kicked off, Persson tried to keep awake despite aching joints and fever. She couldn't abandon her team. In the 52nd minute, an opportunity appeared when the referee awarded Djurgården a free kick, which after a deflection found Jan Tauer clear through on goal. Tauer raised a finger – just one more goal needed to level the tie – and reignited the Djurgården fans' fervour. Their chants turned into an invocation for the next goal.

Eight minutes later, Tauer's team-mate Christer Youssef answered them by netting Djurgården's second goal of the evening. They had levelled. Then the game slowed down. As the clock edged towards the 90th minute, there hadn't been any more goals from either side, then the referee's whistle sounded.

As extra time began, Persson sank into a kind of squat, a sort of prayer position. She stayed there for the first five minutes. Nothing. Then another five, still nothing. With four minutes left and with a penalty shoot-out looming, Jonson answered her prayers: the third goal in the 116th minute. This was it, they'd done it. They were going to stay in Allsvenskan.

Persson flew to her feet. She hadn't been able to speak all day, yet all of a sudden she was screaming. She interrupted her screaming only to start laughing. Tears of joy streaked down her cheeks.

Christmas

WITH ASSYRISKA beaten, the fans faced a gloomier-than-ever November. But life went on. Waking up before dawn, travelling to work, attending meetings, answering emails ... end-of-year reports, coffee, more coffee, then home, helping the children with their homework, figuring out what to get them for Christmas.

It had become rare, with ever milder winters, for dreams of a white Christmas to pay off so far south in Sweden, but this one was a winter like no other. In early December 2009, after the children had celebrated the St Lucia festival of lights, donning white robes and using cheap tinsel as crowns to sing traditional songs for their adoring parents, the temperature sank below freezing and stayed there. Swedes use the term 'vargavinter' – 'wolf winter' – when the world turns into an icebox.

A couple of days before Christmas Eve, Detective Superintendent Gunnar Appelgren was on leave yet still busy, not with pondering the weather nor crime, but logistics: putting together the traditional Christmas smorgasbord for the family was no mean feat. On work days, Appelgren, a muscular man pushing 50, would drive to work from the family home in the countryside to Stockholm, the seat of both county and national police HQ, passing Södertälje on the way. He'd often glance down at the town's truck yards, and the grinning griffin of Scania's logo looming up at the motorists. It was rare for Appelgren to turn off to Södertälje. While his job covered all of Stockholm County, including Södertälje in its southernmost reach, the town had no special significance. While there were weapons and drugs in circulation in the town, weapons and drugs also plagued Stockholm's suburbs. Södertälje didn't stick out – *not yet*.

A few months from now, Södertälje would became Appelgren's one and only focus, and he'd come to realise that he'd have to navigate a unique town where all roads led to Khouri.

That evening, however, all roads led to Christmas preparations. Appelgren wondered what time it was and glanced at his mobile – it was late. His work phone had been connected to a special messaging system. When reports came in of serious crimes, an alert would ping his phone. Beep beep: Murder. Beep beep: Shooting. Beep beep: Explosive device. Beep beep: Anything connected to organised crime. Beep beep: Anything relating to Nova, the special task force tracking the most dangerous criminals. In criminal circles, being on Nova's rader had become a badge of honour; an attitude that Appelgren, just like a lot of other cops, found somewhat cringeworthy.

On paper, when it came to law and order, Appelgren should have been to the left on the political scale, given that his Social Democrat mother raised him in a working-class suburb, Bredäng. But during his more-than-two-decades-long career, Appelgren had moved towards a less liberal attitude on some issues. I'd once run into Appelgren at a conference on organised crime, shortly after an American lecturer's talk on repeat offenders, when he pointed out that longer sentences would keep the criminals, 'who are just gonna commit crime again', off the street.

'I don't know how many times I've bumped into someone on the street and said hello before realising that I recognise them because I helped put them in jail a few years ago,' Appelgren had told me at the time.

In our interviews over the years – he'd become so senior he frequently appeared in the press – the detective always spoke with a relaxed, old-school candour, not shying away from slang. He'd say 'the slammer' instead of 'prison'. As I asked him questions about Södertälje, we had conversations rather than Q and As. He was not offering soundbites, not weighing his every word in fear of being too outspoken or misquoted. There was never an anxious press liaison officer hanging over his shoulder.

He liked to talk and he liked to put problems into perspective. My audio recordings filled up with innumerable 'on the one hand but on the other hand' quotes from Appelgren.

He seemed keen to make a good impression, and to be a good colleague and a good boss; at one of our meetings, he had just completed a course on workplace communication. 'I'm sorry I'm sitting this way,' he told me mid-interview as he caught himself man-spreading in his chair, leaning back with his hands clasped behind his head. 'At that leadership course, we were taught that sitting like this is a classic posture to show dominance,' he explained, unclasping his hands and sitting up straight.

He had been working hard during 2009 and was looking forward to Christmas. No need to be the boss or get things done, apart from the Christmas lunch. He was asleep when his work phone went off … beep beep … of course the criminals hadn't taken time off for the holiday. He scanned the message on his phone: a man had been shot in Södertälje.

An ordinary shooting didn't fall into his remit, he was too senior for that. The local police would take care of it. He went back to sleep, unaware that this shooting was not ordinary; it was the kind of tremor that risked triggering an avalanche.

PART THREE

THE VIOLENCE

December 2009 to
August 2010

Oasis

THE 'VARGAVINTER' SNOW HAD kept falling during the events that had led up to the shooting, and that message pinging Appelgren's phone. A man carrying a gun had made his way to 'Oasen' – 'The Oasis' – community club. He'd pulled his hood up and entered the club, identified his target and shot the young man several times before running off. His victim, Mohaned Ali, sunk to the floor.

Emergency services logged the first call at 2.41am. It took 14 minutes for the first patrol car to arrive. As they waited for help, Eddie Moussa's older brother Yaacoub took care of the gravely injured Mohaned Ali at what had turned into a crime scene. Mohaned was conscious but in pain. 'Does it look bad?' he asked Yaacoub.

Inwardly, Yaacoub must have been cursing his younger brother – not Eddie, but Dany, the wayward one, who'd set up a Södertälje chapter of the X-Team, apprentice club to the motorcycle gang Bandidos. Yaacoub had told Dany and Dany's close friend Mohaned, now lying injured on the floor in front of him, not to wear their X-Team vests at the community club. Yaacoub didn't want trouble. Having balls is one thing, Dany's need to show them off all the time, that was just bad for business, because it attracted the wrong kind of attention, as well as being in poor taste. Despite being brothers, Yaacoub and Dany had a troubled history. And Eddie had not been making matters better.

And then this. A shooting in his club. The Oasis was supposed to be just that, an oasis, a place for people to feel safe and relax and to catch up with the gossip. Yaacoub was a married man with four children, he had responsibilities. This kind of violence didn't fit in well with that kind of life, and he had told his wife many times that he was worried about an escalation of conflict in Södertälje.

At last, the ambulance arrived and the staff drove Mohaned north to a hospital in Stockholm.

A police dog handler arrived too, and, standing outside The Oasis, she looked up at the woods right behind the building. Pedestrian paths cut through the trees. The officers already at the scene, who had local knowledge, pointed out the gunman's most likely escape routes, so she and the dog got to work.

She let him search along the paths and 15 to 20 metres to either side; a gunman couldn't throw a gun further than that if he tried to get rid of the weapon as he fled. But there was too much snow. If the gun had been flung into a drift, the snow lay so deep that the hole would have caved in on itself after impact, effectively sealing the gun in a snow pocket and making it harder for the dog to pick up the scent. And this dog hadn't been through specialised training to seek out weapons. Yet the handler didn't give up. She steered the dog to a playground. They didn't find anything there either. In her official report, the handler wrote:

'If you intend to search the area again one should use a metal detector as the likelihood of a dog being able to find a weapon under the snow is very small. But if one wants to try again with a dog, it should be a dog trained in finding weapons.'

The police would never find the gun. But there were other ways to find forensic evidence. As the police looked into suspects, they asked forensics to look for gunpowder traces on the clothes of a man called Abraham Aho – one of Khouri's younger cousins who became known as 'The Torpedo' in the ensuing media coverage.

Yaacoub Moussa was no stranger to violence. He had broken up plenty of fights when he was younger and worked as a bouncer, but this attack was extraordinary – so brash and so audacious. It was infuriating. Perhaps he should have known that trouble was on its way. Thanks to Dany and Mohaned and their stupid X-Team vests. And then this.

The Oasis didn't feel like an appropriate name any more, but at least Mohaned was alive. As they headed north, the ambulance crew made sure to alert the accident and emergency room at Karolinska Hospital up in Stockholm of their estimated time of arrival. Mohaned, who'd been floating in and out of consciousness during the journey, was awake as they arrived. The doctors surveyed the damage: multiple gunshot wounds to the chest. Mohaned was intubated and taken to surgery where the doctors confirmed that the 25-year-old had sustained injuries to the liver and the pancreas, and to the left kidney, which had to be removed. They drained two litres of fluid from his abdomen. When the surgical team opened up Mohaned's chest, they put a clip on his aorta.

It was no use. At ten past nine in the morning, Mohaned died. He left a wife and three kids. After receiving news of his death, his wife told the police that she had known that something was about to happen to him. The last time he left the family home, she had had a hunch that he was leaving forever. Mohaned also left his friends, not least Dany, and the rest of them who wore the red and black of the X-Team.

The wife

AFTER LEAVING The Oasis, Yaacoub returned home. His wife Sara was used to him coming home late, but this evening was different. She had rarely seen him so upset. 'The Oasis was like Yaacoub's home, his second home. That's where people knew they could find him, if he wasn't at home or at the football,' she would later tell the police.

Legally, the couple were no longer married. Yaacoub had been worried that the tax agency would go through his assets – his wife never specified why – and as the house was in her name, it meant they wouldn't lose it. So on paper, they divorced, but still considered themselves married in the eyes of God. She paid the bills, he paid the rest, usually in cash.

They had celebrated two weddings. A civil ceremony soon after meeting back when Yaacoub worked as a bouncer. The second wedding was in church. Photos were put up on social media showing Yaacoub in a pinstriped, three-piece suit with a white rose boutonnière. She had worn a figure-hugging dress with dainty flowers embroidered across her bust, with a large bouquet of white roses in her hand.

'My husband gained a great deal of respect, not by getting into conflicts and threatening people, because he worked as a bouncer for many years and became known as someone who was honest and fair,' she told the police.

The Oasis had been where people went after work, sometimes late at night, to relax, gossip, to unwind. Some town residents used to call The Oasis and similar venues 'kindergarten for adult men',

85

others likened it to a British pub, where everyone and anyone could spend time together.

Even when Yaacoub was at home, his phone never stopped ringing; people asking where he was and when he was planning to show up at The Oasis again. 'A lot of people turned to him when they had problems,' his wife said. 'My husband, he stood up for what he thought was right. It didn't matter if his brother [was involved]. If his brother was in the wrong, he said, "No, you're wrong!"'

Nor was Yaacoub the kind of man to take kindly to pressure. 'That's how he earned so much respect,' she said. 'Because there was no one who could bribe or scare him.'

But after the shooting at The Oasis, she saw how scared he was. The family didn't need any more tensions. Ever since her husband's father had died two years before, her mother-in-law, who'd never liked her, refused to visit them at home. Her mother-in-law instead visited Yaacoub at The Oasis, often bringing him a home-cooked meal. The matriarch had always used food to show her love: when her boys were at school, she'd bring their teachers cucumbers from her allotment.

As well as tension with her mother-in-law, Yaacoub's wife had to deal with her brother-in-law, Dany, who had long struggled with addiction. Making sure Dany didn't get into trouble had been her husband's 'full-time job' for years. And then this.

He isn't Zlatan

DANY … over the years, Yaacoub's wife had heard so many stories about him. One time Yaacoub had stepped in to pull Dany out of a fight and Dany's only thanks for being saved had been to pull out a gun and threaten his own brother. But Yaacoub had promised their mother he'd keep him alive and that had become an 'eternity project'.

'Dany never showed Yaacoub any real respect, even though Yaacoub guaranteed his safety,' she'd later tell the police. 'It doesn't matter if his brothers are good or bad people, they're still his brothers.'

The youngest of the brothers, Eddie, the football star, may have become the darling of her football-crazed neighbours, but he could be rude.

When her mother had come to babysit the children, she'd heard engine sounds coming from the garage. Having gone to look, she'd found Eddie in there and asked what he was up to. He had told her to mind her own business and that she had no right to ask questions in his brother's house. 'He told my mum to call the police if he was disturbing her,' the wife said.

That anecdote, which I'd encountered in a copy of her statements to the the police, did not shock me, because I'd heard others refer to Eddie as arrogant. He may have been loved on the pitch, but off it he had a bit of a reputation. Often, when I chatted to people about Eddie, I was met with a counter-question: how can a person who plays in the second-tier league afford an expensive car?

'How did he afford it?' Milad asked me. 'He is not Zlatan Ibrahimović!'

Wannabes

AFTER THE first murder, the poker wunderkind Philip – although it was a long time ago he was truly young, in truth he had started to look a bit world-weary – noticed a shift in mood. Something was changing in Södertälje. At the gambling joints, the attitude had become rougher, in particular among the young men whom Philip called 'wannabe gangsters'.

'Nowadays it's all "Fuck your mother!",' he complained to me.

Admittedly, those kinds of gatherings – with big players and big sums in 'other places' (Philip's purposefully vague answer) than the small gambling joints dotted across town – weren't all cuddly before the murder of Mohaned, but there had been rules of respect.

When Philip used to step in as host, he'd always had to hint at violence to keep the peace; to show, not state, the price of transgression. 'I've been so strong,' Philip told me. 'When someone's tried to trample me, I have shown that I cannot be trampled. Sometimes I had to show that, no no, you can't play your games in here.'

While he and all of Stockholm's heavyweights go way back, and while they may have been a kind of family, as host Philip had to maintain control. 'If you wronged me at the club, then I had to cut you,' he summarised.

The hint of violence had been enough, the insults kept to a minimum. That was the gambling culture that Philip had been introduced to so many years earlier.

But after the murder, Philip's girlfriend thought it was time for him to quit. She was afraid. Not just for his health – the booze that had made him fat, the cocaine that made him tense and unpredictable – but because Philip had become more and more aggressive. Would he too fall foul of the surge in violence?

Should he quit while he still could? While he was on top? Before things went bad … something big was going on, Philip knew that. Someone would avenge the murder of Mohaned. But where and when? Philip was feeling the tug and pull as people weighed in on whose fault it was, as people started to pick sides in the brewing turf war.

Philip was refusing to pick a side. He was friends with Bernard Khouri and with Yaacoub Moussa, and he wanted it to stay that way.

Bread

MILAD'S LIFE was in free-fall. It wasn't just that he could no longer afford a big car to go pick up his daughter from school – which she'd loved – but that he could no longer afford to buy bread. And he still hadn't told his wife about the monthly protection money payments of 27,000 kronor.

The situation had become untenable. So Milad phoned the intermediary and said he couldn't work magic, he hadn't got the money to pay. The man's reply? That Milad had a few days to conjure up the cash. A few days was not enough. Even though he could, in theory, report the man to the police for extortion, Milad didn't go to the cops.

People's reluctance to get the police involved didn't mean the police were clueless about what was going on. And, as one of them pointed out when I later discussed Milad's case with him, the loan sharks and extortioners in Södertälje had produced a few examples of impeccably poor judgement over the years. 'You can't lend someone 100,000 kronor on a Monday than ask for it back, plus interest, on the Friday. It doesn't add up,' he told me. 'I've grown so tired of hearing these stories about The Network over and over.'

Sometimes, when people told The Network they couldn't pay, they really were truly unable to pay, my source pointed out. About Milad, he said that 'to ask a guy for so much money that he goes bankrupt and then can't pay any money *at all*, it's idiotic!'

In lieu of cash, Milad risked having to pay in pain. He didn't notice the man sneaking up around the back of his van. The blow came out of nowhere. Milad stumbled, then saw another man approach from the front of the car, a man who was holding a type of weapon that Milad had never seen before. His attacker thrust the object against Milad's thigh. The pain was like being stabbed and being electrocuted at the same time.

Usually, Milad would have had no problem sprinting to get away, because he played so much football when he was younger, but the searing pain turned his muscles into lead. Yet somehow he managed to break free, muscle memory from a time long ago on the pitch brought to life by adrenaline. Flight or fight? Flee, flee, flee.

Milad managed to get indoors and lock himself in. He had the number of a local cop on his phone and contacted him, and the officer saw to it that emergency services sent an ambulance.

That strange weapon – what was it? Although there was no way to know for sure, after he was examined an x-ray revealed some telling details. A 36.2mm bone fragment had been prised loose from Milad's femur. There was no bullet or shrapnel, nor any other object, left in his leg. And there was no exit wound. Whatever the attacker had shoved against Milad's thigh – the wound did not indicate that it was a knife – had been retracted. Milad came to believe that it must have been a captive bolt pistol, the kind used to slaughter animals and brought to infamy as a murder weapon by the film *No Country For Old Men*. That would explain the damage: a projectile long enough to chip the bone, but not reaching deep enough to push through the other side of his leg. And thus no exit wound. 'I had big pain for almost one month,' he recalled when we spoke. 'It felt like they dropped 500 kilos on my leg, it was the first time I'd felt [anything like it].'

As he returned home limping, he could no longer conceal the situation from his wife. 'She cried, sure she cried. My daughter too she cry. She feel sorry for me, she feel mad about how much money I pay,' Milad said. 'Because if I don't pay they shoot me. For so many years The Network controlled everything in Södertälje.'

The police started to investigate the attack, trying to find witnesses. They spoke with a shop owner who gave them useful information. A few days before the attack, he had spoken to a man who had alluded to the fact that something was about to happen, telling him that Milad would 'at least' spend the rest of his life in a wheelchair. It was the same man who had visited Milad's office at the start of all the misery and demanded that Milad pay protection money. The information was strong enough for the prosecutor to press charges, and the man in question was found guilty and sentenced to six months in prison for ordering the assault.

What should have been vindication instead instilled a new kind of fear in Milad – that he'd just made things worse. 'Khouri will never forgive me,' he thought to himself.

Pingu

WHEN MILAD first heard about Mohaned being shot at The Oasis, he had realised that The Network had gone from threatening to kill people to actually killing them. As gangland murders so often went unsolved, because criminals were brainwashed so thoroughly into never 'snitching', Milad didn't think the police stood a chance of catching the killer.

But this time the police struck gold thanks to a witness at the scene who told them that even though the attacker had his hood up to conceal his face, he had recognised the man's body language. There was a teenager in the neighbourhood, Abraham Aho, who was also a young cousin of Khouri, who walked in a special way, a bit like the character *Pingu* in the popular animated kids' TV programme about a family of penguins.

Two days after Mohaned died, the police arrested Aho, who then gained his media nickname: The Torpedo. In essence, he was suspected of working as an assassin for Khouri. The police found CCTV footage from a local petrol station that showed the two men arguing – about what was impossible to tell without audio, but the police thought it looked like Khouri was giving Aho orders.

The prosecutors were working on the hypothesis that because Khouri was the boss, The Torpedo did as he was told. The Torpedo's defence attorneys did not buy into that line of argument.

Jan Karlsson, a lawyer since the 80s, answered my questions during an interviw with a near-growl, somewhat befitting, I thought, his long experience. A tall and slender man, he was discretely well-dressed, and had a confident yet unassuming air. His associate, Elsa Svalsten, younger but also tall, was equally elegantly dressed, with flawless make-up.

According to the prosecution, the motive for shooting Mohaned appeared to be straightforward. Mohaned had been working with two of the Moussa brothers – Eddie the loan shark and Dany the debt enforcer. Their attempt to get their hands on a slice of the Södertälje loan-shark pie had sparked a fight over market shares with Khouri and his associates.

But where was the evidence, The Torpedo's lawyer asked? 'It's not enough to walk like Pingu – if it was even the case that my client walks like Pingu, which he doesn't,' Karlsson said. 'The prosecution has to prove that our client is the perpetrator, and our standpoint is that they can't prove it.'

The police had drawn a timeline of The Torpedo's movements on the night of Mohaned's murder, step by step from order to alleged execution – based on CCTV, police surveillance in the neighbourhood and witness statements.

I'd discussed that timeline in detail with a colleague, who'd been helping me with research and accompanied me to meet The Torpedo's defence lawyers. It was true, they told us, that their client and Khouri had had an argument. It was true, they said, that their client then returned home. But no, he had not, like the police were claiming, then gone out again and made his way to The Oasis and killed Mohaned, no, he had gone to bed.

'That's the *only* difference,' they told us.

'It's a pretty *big* difference,' my colleague interjected.

Cinnamon

WHEN I, at a later date, mentioned The Torpedo's name to Khouri, he looked annoyed yet amused; it was well-known in Södertälje that he saw him more like a brother than a cousin, with all the attendant irritation that any sibling relationship can cause.

'He's not allowed to drive my cars,' Khouri said, 'because he fucks them up.'

'Why?' I asked. 'Because he's high all the time?'

'No no no, he's not like that,' Khouri protested, searching for words.

I already knew, from the beat cops, that The Torpedo was pedantic and wanted things to be just so. And that unlike his friends, including Khouri, he didn't do drugs – 'He'd never allow himself to lose control,' was one officer's succinct comment. When the police began to wiretap their phones, they recorded other members of The Network joking that they'd 'snorted all our profits'.

Despite all the work I'd done in Södertälje, I had never quite understood the extent of drug use in the town. During a meeting with ex-addicts, a young man told me, 'Södertälje is Sweden's Amsterdam,' but another man added, 'All of Sweden is Amsterdam.' One of them described his own drug use to me. That he had alternated between uppers and downers: hash to be able to fall sleep, cocaine to muster enough courage to leave home, always wondering who was pissed off with him, and then smoking hash again to get down from the cocaine buzz. One time, he'd taken so much cocaine that it was obvious to just about everyone because he'd been on his tiptoes, his hands dancing about, stiff fingers spread wide. 'Are you practising for a piano concert?' a cop had asked him jokingly, as she'd noticed his twitching fingers.

Khouri's drug use had caused some laughter, too: like the time some cops on a stake-out had watched him stalk into a shop and buy spices for several thousand kronor, which he then proceeded to snort.

'I don't think that could have been healthy?' I told the cop who shared the anecdote with me. 'Yeah, no,' he responded. 'Cinnamon is toxic.'

Leisure centre

WITH THE Torpedo taken into custody shortly after the Christmas murder of Mohaned, reporters at the local newspaper, *Länstidningen*, went through the archive and noted that they had written about the suspect before. A couple of years earlier, The Torpedo had been charged with assaulting a man in front of about 30 onlookers.

'No one identified him during the trial, which led to the District Court acquitting him,' the old news article said.

Thirty onlookers, zero witnesses. Under the online article, the comments section was brimming with anger. One reader had written, 'You worthless excuses for human beings! What kind of people are you? I hope something horrible happens to you and then no one stands up to testify for you in court.'

Another reader had engaged the caps lock. 'SWEDEN IS THE CRIMINALS' PARADISE!'

A person with the username 'Angry Aramean' stood for one of the longest posts:

'I have the following to say about Sweden's laws: Obsolete, tame, not adapted to today's society and with unreasonably short sentences. Criminals are not stupid. They calculate possible returns versus risk. And if they are caught? Well, either they're let go or they end up in something called "prison". I refuse to use the term "prison" because, the way I see it, it's more like a leisure centre with steak for dinner and access to cable TV and magazines.'

The comment concluded with 'Frightening!'

In Södertälje and other areas with high crime rates in Stockholm County, I had heard similar criticism of Sweden's prison sentences many times, which had long stuck out as short by any international comparison. The sentiment didn't spring from anything as simple as a desire for vengeance, I saw them as an expression of the desire to feel safe in your own neighbourhood where criminals were too often allowed to roam free.

If criminals were caught, they'd be out of prison again soon. Even sooner if they were young. When The Torpedo allegedly murdered Mohaned, he hadn't reached the age of 21 – and anyone younger than 21 would, upon conviction, get what's called the youth 'sentence rebate' ('ungdomsrabatten'), a one-third reduction in length of the sentence.

When I, at a later date, spoke to Yaacoub and Eddie's sister Alexandra about the youth rebate, she was furious, saying, 'How old do you have to be to be held accountable?'

Windscreen

WHY DID Khouri expect The Torpedo to follow his 'fucking orders'?

That's what he yelled at him on the phone one evening, a quote that a police wiretap picked up and which made it into the case file. 'When I give you orders,' Khouri had shouted that evening, 'you follow fucking orders.' But what had happened that night? I put that question to Khouri, who took it from the top:

After taking his fiancée out for dinner in Stockholm, they returned to his flat, where a nice evening in an instant turned into the kind of chaos that only The Torpedo could leave in his wake. In the bathroom – 'My favourite bathroom,' Khouri pointed out, 'with underfloor heating and a jacuzzi' – there was water everywhere. His near-obsessive cousin was so particular about not touching the toilet seat that he had lined it with reams of toilet paper before sitting down, and then that mass of bog roll 'and everything else' had blocked the toilet.

'My fiancée and I tried everything,' Khouri said. 'Prodding it, using a toilet sucker.'

Furious, Khouri phoned The Torpedo, who, to make matters worse, was out driving one of Khouri's cars. Or rather, had been out driving it before he'd managed to lock the keys in the car. 'He asked me whether he should break one of the windows to get in and I said yes, break one of the side windows,' Khouri recalled.

He drove his fiancée home first – 'She can't stay over, we're not married' – then met up with The Torpedo, and was met again by chaos because his cousin had smashed the windscreen to get into the car. 'There's glass everywhere, the alarm's wailing, the car lights are flashing like a god damn Christmas tree,' said Khouri, who said he had then called his cousin yet again, shouting at him to 'follow fucking orders'. Khouri claimed the orders in question were about breaking one of the smaller side windows, nothing else.

The police and prosecutor were considering using that very quote in the indictment – if they got as far as pressing charges against Khouri – as they believed that his tone of voice was evidence of his unwavering assumption that he ruled the roost; that quote along with many other pieces of evidence could be used to prove Khouri's undisputed leadership of The Network.

As for Khouri, he thought the context of that particular evening shouldn't be forgotten. 'Who wouldn't have been furious?' he asked me.

Omertà

WHILE THAT one quote on its own may have sounded banal, the fact that so many people were simply expected to follow fucking orders and shut up said something about the unwritten laws of the criminal underworld. And were a witness to break those laws, they'd pay a heavy price.

Breaking through that wall of silence was a problem for the investigators. Getting people to talk was an uphill struggle. Up at HQ in Stockholm, lead detective Gunnar Appelgren was informed that a potential witness, who'd been at The Oasis the night Mohaned was fatally shot, had been assaulted in order to silence him.

'There are parts of Södertälje that stink of skunk,' Appelgren told me.

Appelgren, known simply among his colleagues as 'Appel', had long since grown used to witnesses either saying nothing from the very beginning or changing their stories from one statement to the next. Some would claim that the police didn't understand their broken Swedish or that the interpreter had done a bad job of translating their witness statement. Others, who spoke perfect Swedish, just ended up claiming that the police had gotten it wrong.

And given all of Appelgren's experience with recalcitrant witnesses, he had been delighted that the man who'd identified 'Pingu' that night was considering talking to the police on record. But 'he was scared', Appelgren said, adding that his colleagues down in Södertälje had tried to convince the man several times to give an official statement and then testify in court. The witness had said something to the tune of 'okay maybe, but I need to talk it through with some friends first'. Which he had done, but news of his question had been passed on straight away as one of his friends had phoned The Torpedo's father, who'd shown up within an hour and a half and attacked the potential witness, Appelgren told me.

The witness was offered police protection, which he declined. Appelgren empathised. 'He's got a family,' said Appelgren. 'And we have the same problem with protecting witnesses as we have when we protect women fleeing domestic violence. Who has to move? Who has to leave their life behind? The victim.'

That's why Appelgren, despite his frustration, had long ago understood why so few people testified against organised crime. It was just easier to keep quiet.

In Sweden, the term 'culture of silence' was becoming a hot topic for politicians trying to get to grips with the mafia and the gangs. When I wrote an article about The Network for English-language newspaper *The National*, based in the UAE, the editor inserted, by way of explanation, the term 'omertà' – the Sicilian mob's code of silence.

While I had thought the editor was being a bit dramatic, I later came to accept the description. I changed my mind in part due to the investigative journalism programme '*Uppdrag granskning*' – 'Investigative Mission' – which aired interviews with two brothers involved in crime. One of them was trying to get his life in order, the other, who spoke of his links to The Network, was about to face a long prison sentence. The latter had tattoos, including the word 'omertà', inked across his face. He said that anyone he 'might have' killed had deserved it.

There are other ways to instil fear. In the case file on The Network, I noticed that one of the debt enforcers – an older man with a slight figure who Milad had implicated in his extortion – was referred to as a former member of the 'mukhabarat', the Arabic word for intelligence service.

That word can create fear in anyone from the Middle East, and in particular in Syria where more than a dozen different agencies are charged with gathering intelligence. They are infamous for their brutality.

In her book *The Home That Was Our Country*, the Syrian-American journalist Alia Malek retold a macabre joke about the mukhabarat:

The best way to explain this is with a joke I first heard back in Syria in the 1990s. It goes like this: the world's intelligence services gather at an elite training site. Present are the CIA, the KGB, Israel's Mossad, and the Syrian mukhabarat. They are brought to the edge of the forest and told they must each go in, track a certain fox, and bring him back.

Both the CIA and the KGB get it done in an hour. The Mossad completes the task even faster.

The last to go are the Syrian mukhabarat. They disappear for hours into the woods. When they return, they are holding a severely beaten-up rabbit. The other agents laugh at them or are perplexed. 'That's not a fox', they say.

The Syrians, in their leather jackets, are coolly smoking; one of them is holding the rabbit up by his neck. Their leader responds, 'He confessed. He admitted that he is a fox.'

After generations of being watched over and eavesdropped on, Syrians have internalized the mukhabarat; even in their absence they are present.

Given that kind of excessive violence, the police and many others in Södertälje told me, was it any wonder that immigrants from the Middle East tried to keep a low profile and not get the authorities involved? The investigators and the prosecution were well aware of the cultural baggage that had helped nurture The Network and was now hampering the investigation, but still the lead detective refused to give up.

'What we can do is encourage a new normal,' Appelgren said, explaining the concept of safety in numbers. 'If enough people stand up to them and have the courage to tell us what they know, then they won't be exceptions that prove the rule.'

Tortoise

DANY MOUSSA was just another Södertälje resident who thought the police should mind their own business. He had even told them so to their face, saying the police should let people sort their own problems out. His own problem, at that moment, was that The Network just shot his friend Mohaned to death.

When I tried to reach out to Dany for an interview, he didn't respond. I didn't expect him to because many criminals, though not all, think that the media should mind their own business.

But while Dany had a criminal record – I found his first conviction as an adult from 1994 in the District Court archive – when I pieced together the information he didn't seem very sinister, more like an addict with impulse control issues.

'He has always been crazy,' one of his middle-school classmates recalled. 'A day didn't go by without hearing that he'd done something. Stolen a moped or broken a window.'

The fact that Dany's family was religious had not been an antidote, remarked a former teacher, who wanted to remain anonymous. The teacher had watched with concern as the parents of his then pupils force-fed them religion. That that kind of black and white morality, he told me, the going to heaven versus ending up in hell rhetoric, hadn't worked. In fact, he thought it unhelpful. During our interview, Dany's old teacher picked up an imaginary Bible, saying 'Dany needed a bit less of this' as he imitated throwing the book on the table in front of me, and 'a bit more of this', he said, spreading his arms into a welcoming embrace. 'A bit more unconditional love,' he said

When he had reached his teens, Dany's behaviour made the family send him off to a monastery in their home country. The diaspora had used these monasteries, the most famous being Mor Gabriel in southern Turkey, as rehab. Monastic routine, the thinking went, could lead to some some calm, reintroduce structure, and inspire renewed faith. But in Dany's case it had inspired fear.

The teacher recalled that the young boy was so scared of being sent away that he'd gotten his hands on a gun to defend himself with. While Dany's mother declined to give me an interview, she had told another reporter that the monks hadn't taken care of Dany the way she had hoped.

Sending him to the monastery was not the first time his family made plans for Dany without consulting him. 'Already when he was a young boy, they decided who he was gonna marry,' a school friend told me. 'So he broke into our school and waited for the police to show up, because he thought that no one would want their daughter to marry a troublemaker.'

His old friend added that she'd heard the story from Dany himself, but as he was a bit of a joker, she wasn't sure it had actually happened. 'But that's what he told me, and that he was just ten years old.'

Betrothals of children were not unusual in Södertälje back then. Yet another teacher said that he regretted, looking back, that he had not addressed the issue with the children's parents. 'We were too lenient and permissive when it came to some cultural expressions, such as betrothals,' he said. 'I wouldn't call them child marriages, because the weddings would take place after [the students] finished school, but they were arranged long in advance,' he recalled. 'And sometimes the betrothals tied in with business deals.'

As a teenager, however, Dany had become more than adept at choosing his own objects of affection. At times his interest in girls verged on the obsessive. One girl, tired of Dany nagging her to go out with him, tried to get him to stop: 'Let's count how serious I am about saying "no",' she said. In front of a group of friends, one of whom told me the story many years later, the girl held up her thumb: 'No.' She held up her index finger: 'No.' She went from finger to finger, from one hand to the other, saying, 'No, no, no ...' Finally she bent over to point at every single one of her toes: 'No, no, no, no ...'

Back then, the cool kids used to meet up after school at the nearby basketball court to smoke Marlboro and Prince cigarettes; some of the boys bringing along a basketball to shoot hoops. One afternoon Dany turned up carrying a tortoise, meant as a gift for his latest crush. 'She didn't want it,' the girl's friend recalled. 'So he had to take it back.'

Yet, far from all stories I heard about the young Dany were light-hearted. In the early 1990s one of Dany's younger brothers, George, had a scuffle with a boy at school, which Dany got involved in.

When I spoke with the victim's twin brother he still had vivid memories of a friend sprinting from school to fetch him. 'She was out of breath and all I could get out of her was "stabbed" and my brother's name,' he remembered. 'I just thought, this can't be true, my brother's such a harmless guy. And the girl, she just kept saying, "You have to come now, you have to come now."'

As he rushed towards the school, he saw his twin brother being half-carried, half-dragged to safety. 'What happened?' he asked.

It turned out that his twin brother had been stabbed with a knife. George, the attacker, hadn't been carrying the knife at first, it was George's big brother Dany who'd handed it to him.

The knife, jammed into the base of the the young victim's neck, had only just missed his heart. After several days in hospital he was allowed to return home. Eventually, Dany and his brother George were charged with assault/attempted murder. 'I didn't go to the trial,' the victim's brother said. 'I just couldn't face it.'

Milad's list

SOME 16 years after the fight in the schoolyard, Dany was still getting into trouble with his attempts to encroach on The Network's loan sharking.

The Network had proved that there was money to be made, and extorting Milad was just a case in point. Just after the murder of Dany's friend Mohaned, Milad once again found himself in trouble. Apart from his previous protection-money tussle, he still owed a shop owner some money, a debt that had lingered ever since one of Milad's own ventures had gone belly-up a few years prior.

While he had down-paid the debt considerably, some 120,000 kronor in total, he still needed time to pay off the rest. But the shop owner was running low on patience. 'He said that if I didn't pay the rest straight away, he'd sell my debt on to Khouri,' Milad told me.

The shop owner also told Milad that just paying off the money was no longer enough, he was demanding an additional chunk of cash – a kind of late fee – which would, in effect, put the original loan's interest rate at 60 per cent … which Milad had no way of paying even in the long term.

Milad tried to negotiate, suggesting that they agree on a kind of late fee that was equivalent to about 15 per cent. The shop owner was not interested in negotiation.

That the shop owner had mentioned Khouri's name worried Milad. Once Milad drummed up courage to tell the police about the situation, the police went to speek with the shop owner, who offered them a mixture of denials and justifications. He hadn't done anything wrong, the shop owner told the police, he was a 'good Christian' and a 'peaceful man' and, besides, everyone knew that Milad was a 'swindler'. And, the shop owner emphasised, he'd never turn to Khouri to solve this kind of problem, he would go to the church and try to get mediation in order to get his money back.

Yet the police were well aware at this point that people often did turn directly to The Network, whose bread and butter was enforcing debts, but for a long time the cops had only a fuzzy idea of the sums of money that were involved. Milad helped them understand the extent of it, the large cash payments, and, more importantly, the kind of ad hoc interest rates slapped on debt in the heat of the moment.

Once that was sorted out, the police also asked Milad to help them with another confusing aspect: all the names and nicknames that were popping up during their investigations.

Older men in the Orthodox Christian parts of town were often referred to by their oldest son's name. So 'Abu Elie', for example, was simply 'the father of Elie', which required the police to sketch family trees in order to get a grip on the key actors.

And on top of many 'abus' there were all the nicknames to sort out.

'Do you recognise the term "Al Taweel?"' they asked Milad.

'Yes, it means "the tall one" in Arabic,' he replied.

'Is that what you call Khouri?'

'Yes, and they use it so you know who they're talking about without having to say his name out loud,' Milad explained.

The tall one … the synonym for a kind of violence that was meant to keep people in line. There had to be a price if you made bad deals. It wasn't dissimilar to getting a bad credit rating, except for the little detail that it's illegal to make threats and to get the money back using your fists, or worse.

Straight after Milad had had that initial conversation with the shop owner, Milad had feared that going to the police would make matters worse – he'd end up reporting him several months later – so Milad decided to sort it out himself. Otherwise the truce with The Network would be broken and he didn't want to pick a fight with Khouri because Khouri could make his life a living hell. The solution was crystal clear: go to one of the older mediators in town, someone who could calm Khouri down, and plead for a reasonable repayment plan.

Milad decided to turn to the older man who, rumour had it, used to work for the intelligence service back in Syria, and that man helped the warring parties agree to a monthly payment of 7,000 kronor. While it was a lot less than paying the debt plus interest off in full, the sum represented a third of an average monthly income before tax in Sweden. Few families could set aside that much. And Milad feared he'd never escape if more late fees and interest rates were added.

'They're gonna suck me dry,' Milad told me. 'They'll have me pay 240 million before this is over.'

After striking the deal, he pondered whether he should just stop working altogether, so the extortioners would back off – because if he went bankrupt, he wouldn't have any money to pay them anyway. But Milad couldn't bear the thought of living on social benefits. 'I don't want to live that way,' he said.

The debt took up all his mental and emotional energy. The more he spoke to his friends about the problem, the bigger his fear became because they told him so many of their own stories about The Network. One of them had been kidnapped and shoved into the boot of a car, just to 'remind him' about the money he owed.

After meeting with the mediator, Milad returned home. He found a pen and a scrap of paper and scrawled the word 'payments' at the top. He made the first payment just five days after the murder of Mohaned.

He would keep on filling the paper with dates month after month, not knowing that it would end up as a key piece of evidence when the police at last gathered enough evidence to bring The Network to court. But at the time, in those first cold months of 2010, that was still a long way away.

At the same time as he jotted down that payments on paper, Milad started a mental list of everyone who had betrayed him, everyone who had demanded money off him, and everyone who had turned his beloved Södertälje into a nightmare. While he often spoke to me about the importance of his faith, as we discussed right and wrong, he said he could no longer turn the other cheek. One day, he said, he hoped that every single person whose name was on this list would pay for their sins.

Get down

A COUPLE of months passed. Milad kept up his payments while the police continued their investigation into the December 2009 murder of Mohaned at The Oasis.

The weather showed no signs of spring approaching. Even getting out of bed each morning felt like a struggle due to the compact winter darkness that made it feel like the dead of night. Across driveways and parking lots, motorists created the tell-tale winter morning soundtrack of scratching and scraping as they tackled the frost on their windscreens.

In the evenings, people stayed indoors to watch television. Not Issa, however, who preferred to seek company at his regular joint, a community café where men met up to play cards. Issa had agreed to meet me to explain the more ordinary and low-key gambling culture. Because Philip, my guide so far, had been more interested in showing off about his role in the high-level 'I've thrown a die for a million kronor' world, I needed another perspective.

Issa told me about one evening that started off in a typical way, but ended up being one of the weirdest of his life.

One winter evening, Issa parked his car in the Geneta neighbourhood, home to the new football arena as well as St Ephrem Cathedral and the opulent furniture store, and headed inside. His friends greeted him, he was served a whiskey and sank down on to a sofa to watch the football match on the TV as the other men kept on playing cards around him.

Issa was a regular there. When he did join in a card game, he never bet big. The sum was never big enough to land him in danger. The cards were just props for a social activity, they didn't ever dictate his mood, not in the way it did for men like Philip, who needed to finance his drug habit, all while flitting around much closer than other gamblers in Khouri's periphery.

Issa hadn't ever met Philip, but, unbeknownst to them both, it wouldn't be long, when winter finally succumbed, before the two men would end up together in the wrong place at the wrong time, as the turf war in Södertälje entered its final chapter.

Issa had lived in Södertälje for many years. His grandmother had been the first to move here, leaving the town of Midyat in Turkey for Sweden, while he initially moved to central Europe, where he moved around for a while. Issa liked it well enough, but showed little interest in telling me more about those years, instead explaining succinctly that when his grandma asked him to come visit Södertälje he travelled north and ended up staying.

Like so many others, Issa had from the start considered Södertälje to be a safe haven for the many Christian minorities from the Middle East – Assyrians, Arameans, Chaldeans, Copts – but that winter, as he parked his car outside the café, he was no longer so sure. There was something in the air, something had broken. The community he'd joined was beset by distrust and the mood had changed. Just these last few years, the rumour mill had been on overdrive. And the rumours always concerned this new generation of young men whom no one seemed able to calm down.

Issa assumed the Swedish police were powerless, because if they had power, surely they'd have done something by now.

Inside the club, he was cradling his whiskey and focussing on the match on TV when the door was flung open and the shouting began. Men dressed head to toe in black barged in and screamed, 'Get down, down, down on the floor!'

It was the police. They looked oddly bulky, like Michelin Men, and Issa wondered if it was the equivalent of a special-response team, the kind of team usually in to keep the peace at high-risk events, such as demonstrations or even football games

– in particular derbies – when the police expected rival fan clubs to clash.

It was clear these police officers were dressed for a well-planned raid, but Issa was not afraid because, well, the Swedish police were weaklings, not like the police in his home country, so Issa ignored their orders to get down on the floor. Instead he just sank down on the sofa; he was lying down, after all, they'd said 'get down', so that should be enough.

From behind the sofa, he heard the police's footsteps and furniture being moved aside. Issa wondered what they were looking for, but still kept watching the match on TV. When an officer spotted him, Issa's nonchalance seemed to irritate him as he marched up to the TV to turn it off, but the policeman ended up hammering the DVD-player buttons by mistake, which mostly amused Issa.

Issa never found out what exactly they were looking for that evening, but afterwards he wondered if the raid had had something to do with that young man who had been murdered a few months before in The Oasis. Perhaps the 'weakling police' were ramping up their game.

The missing word

THE WOLF winter of 2010 was over at last. The days became longer. The many Södertälje residents who loved their allotments had waited patiently for spring. As the frozen ground thawed they could start planning for the planting season.

In March, the thermometer reading crept above zero degrees for the first time since the middle of December. By April, the weather was unsteady. When the sun did appear the light had a frail, washed-out quality but was strong enough to reveal the dirty shades of the early spring landscape: grey gravel and rotten leaves.

From the inside of his cell, however, none of this could be seen by The Torpedo. His days had offered him views of naked walls for almost four months – because of Swedish law the prosecutors could in theory keep him locked up almost indefinitely, as long as they convinced a judge that there was either a flight risk or that the suspect, if let loose, would hamper the investigation by, for example, intimidating witnesses. The only legal requirement was for the prosecutor to apply to a judge, every two weeks, who'd decide whether to keep him detained. Which they did.

The prosecution felt they had good reason to keep The Torpedo behind bars, but the lead prosecutor, Björn Frithiof, didn't think he and his colleagues could keep on convincing the judge to keep the young man detained much longer. The police investigation had stalled. And without compelling new evidence – the kind that made pressing charges in the near future look likely – it'd grow ever-more difficult to persuade the judge to extend his detention. Frithiof told me that he had never, in his many years as a prosecutor, run into such trouble securing testimonies from victims and witnesses as he had done in this case, which convinced him more than ever of the need to keep The Torpedo from returning home. Just seeing him in the street could scare off witnesses. 'We're not getting anywhere with our interviews with them,' Frithiof said.

Apart from testimonies, a missing piece of the puzzle was a forensics report on whether there was residue from firing a gun on The Torpedo's clothes, which the police had confiscated. 'The forensic technicians have taken some time getting the answer to us, which means the investigation has halted a bit because it really depends on that important piece,' Frithiof said.

When the prosecution at last received the official document from forensics, they appeared to have struck gold. There was indeed residue on his clothes, the report stated, which should be enough to convince a judge to keep The Torpedo locked up.

The session with the judge was over and done with quickly. One of the prosecutors simply read from the forensics report, the suspect was remanded yet again and stayed in custody. The Torpedo's friends, who'd travelled up to Stockholm in the hope they'd be giving him a lift home afterwards, were forced to leave without him.

'Then,' the prosecutor recalled, 'the kind of thing that shouldn't be allowed to happen, but happens because of human error, took place' … the forensics department called the investigators and confessed that there was a word missing in the report – the word in question was 'not'. They had *not* found any residue on the clothes, which meant that the prosecution had no hard evidence to justify keeping The Torpedo detained. They went back to the judge with the updated report and the suspect was released with immediate effect.

Once The Torpedo got hold of his friends on the phone they at first thought he was joking, then they double backed to pick him up and take him home to Södertälje.

Later that day, several of them decided to celebrate his release, and they headed to a club in Södertälje called The Strip.

Drive-by

ON 2 April 2010, Khouri partied with his friends at The Strip to celebrate The Torpedo being set free.

Khouri's friends had a habit of making sure they kept an eye on anyone trying to approach him; several of Khouri's childhood friends told me about incidents when they had spotted him out in town and gone up to him just to say hello, before being stopped by Khouri's friends and questioned about who they were and what they wanted.

There were many of Khouri's friends there that night, and the bouncers were keeping tabs not just on his entourage but also on Eddie's brother Dany, who, as it happened, was celebrating his birthday at the same venue.

The staff were on edge, but calm prevailed. Looking back at the events about to unfold, the club was an obvious tinder box. How far under the surface did the currents of anger flow? How strong was the desire for revenge in those men's hearts?

It had been months now since Dany's friend Mohaned had been shot and fatally wounded, but what use were months to count the effects of bereavement, of injustice? There was prestige on the line too, notions of brotherhood, questions of underworld commerce – childhoods intertwined meant nothing when this much money was at stake.

One drink turned into two, three … ten … no one was counting and no one was worried about the bill on a night like this.

When it was time to leave in the early-morning hours, Khouri decided he needed something to eat, leaving his friends in the car as he walked off to buy a hamburger; a last meal that in all probability saved his life.

Khouri's friends had not gone far in their old Volvo. They were a few streets from the club and around the corner from the police station when the shots rang out. Khouri's cousin was at the wheel. A bullet ripped deep into the cousin's spine, shredding the nerves. He lost control of the car. He lifted his hands to shield himself from the onslaught of bullets, as one of the two passengers in his car screamed 'Accelerate!' But having lost control of his foot he couldn't do anything.

The man in the passenger seat was struck by bullets in the abdomen, and he took several more bullets to his arms. Against the odds, the third man in the back seat escaped without a scratch.

As soon as Khouri heard the shooting, he knew his friends were in danger. He ran, picking up speed despite the considerable weight of his top-heavy body, but he ran up the wrong street, which forced him to find another route.

When he got there, a crowd had already gathered around the car. There was no sign of the gunmen's car. Also, the police had shown up: in the official log of that evening, one of the first responders wrote one single word to describe the scene: 'chaos'.

Then he added in the log 'a tall man arrives'. It was Khouri, the crowd parting before him as he ran up to his cousin, who was half-hanging out of the car door. As Khouri told me about that night, some time later, he recalled that the man in the passenger seat asked him, 'What happened?' And Khouri's only thought was, 'You tell me,' as he tried to get a response out of his lifeless cousin.

He shoved his body aside, readying to take the wheel, when a police officer tried to stop him, asking him to wait for the ambulance. Khouri ignored him. Another officer, who disagreed with his colleague, stepped in to say that Khouri was right, Södertälje hospital wasn't far, they shouldn't wait for the ambulance, they would get to accident and emergency faster if they drove themselves.

It didn't really matter what the cops said, Khouri would do what he always had done; not give a damn about what they asked him to do. When he told me about the incident, calmly going through the events step by step, a note of disdain crept into his voice.

He drove as fast as he could, the hospital was just across the canal, but his cousin beside him showed no signs of life as they approached accident and emergency. Yet the doctors managed to save Khouri's cousin, but he was left paralysed from the waist down.

Afterwards, looking at police photos of the old Volvo, it was clearly a miracle no one died that night; in one image, the forensic department had added arrows to show the angles of the bullets that had perforated the red chassis; the arrows, apart from being numerous, stuck out at odd angles, showing the chaotic result of shooting from a moving car at their target, which was also in motion.

The man who sat in the front seat, next to Khouri's gravely injured cousin, was so traumatised that he ended up seeing a psychologist for long-term treatment; the man in the back seat told the police that, while he escaped physically unharmed, he had become too scared to let his kids leave their home.

But it was Khouri's cousin who took the brunt of the attempted murder; one bullet in his spine, another in his jaw. He endured multiple operations in the following months – one left him with a 25cm scar – followed by several months in rehab where he had to learn how to use a wheelchair. His friends visited him there at the rehab clinic, where staff overheard the men whispering about revenge.

Copville

BEEP BEEP. When the high-alert message about the drive-by dropped into detective Gunnar Appelgren's phone, he made a note of the time. Just after 2am, when bars and clubs kicked out their hardiest, and drunkest, clients, and any slight could then be dealt with on the pavement. Young men fighting, that was nothing new. And he noted the date: 2 April 2010 was just three months after the murder of Mohaned. Of course, the police had feared a counter strike.

Appelgren was on leave for the long Easter weekend and, at his rank, officers didn't go to the crime scene, they instead managed investigations from their office, so he went back to bed.

The following week, however, as soon as Appelgren returned to the office, he was told that he was needed and that his role would be significant. It was time, his bosses said, to do something about Södertälje. The police chiefs were awake and alert, and as the justice minister had just earmarked millions of kronor to fight organised crime, the coffers were full – all that was left was to say thanks very much, and get going.

It was about more than the money though, the police couldn't ignore a drive-by a few streets from a police station, and no one should be able to walk free after trying to murder someone, there had to be legal consequences. 'It had become impossible, both from a police and a political standpoint, to not do something,' Appelgren told me.

His boss, Margareta Linderoth, a Guns 'n' Roses fans who had previously spent years working with counter-terrorism, gave Appelgren two days to draw up an action plan. It was a short deadline but everyone was aware that the risk of revenge actions after the drive-by was high, not least in this kind of context, because in the gangland revenge wasn't just about justice, it was about defending your honour, Appelgren explained.

As he sat down at his desk at county police headquarters on Kungsholmen Island in central Stockholm, he thought about all the warnings they'd received over the years, not just from their colleagues down in Södertälje, asking for help, but also from Södertälje Town Hall.

'We had had Södertälje on the agenda before,' Appelgren said. 'People down there had said that something had to be done, and they warned us that it could end up escalating.'

Appelgren was not sure where to lay the blame, if the warnings had not been stated strongly enough or, 'if we on Kungsholmen hadn't taken Södertälje seriously enough'. He did point out to me, however, that he wanted the county police to take part of the blame. 'The jargon up here on Kungsholmen had very much been "yeah yeah, but other places have problems too".' Then he did a classic Appelgren on-the-other-hand manoeuvre and flipped the coin: 'Possibly, it was Södertälje that didn't frame their problems in a way that was convincing enough.'

He did another volte-face and again pinned the potential blame on county police on Kungsholmen for not listening to the local police in Södertälje: 'Or maybe it was us who didn't see that the town is different from other parts of the county where we have the same gangland problems.'

Kungsholmen has long been a sort of capital city of law enforcement in Sweden: the imposing building houses not just county police but national police. It's right next door to The Crown detention centre, which in turn is connected by underground walkways to the maximum-security courtroom. For walking-distance access to their clients, many lawyers have chosen to establish their offices on this part of the island.

A colleague of mine once called this neighbourhood 'Copville', and I found it to be a fitting name. In jest, I'd also come to call it 'downtown', a reference to all those American cop shows where the police arrest suspects and snarl, 'We're taking you downtown.'

Here, at the heart of Copville, Appelgren would soon be heading an investigation unparalleled in size to anything Sweden had ever seen; only the unsolved 1986 murder of Prime Minister Olof Palme had taken up more police resources.

After the drive-by, it became impossible to ignore Södertälje. The town popped up ever more frequently in the newspaper headlines, and the news went from bloody to bloodier with every story. Across the country, Södertälje had become synonymous with the kind of violence that most Swedes associated with Latin American drug wars.

At the start of his career, Appelgren had worked in Södermanland County, just south of Södertälje, and as organised crime groups have ties across regional borders, he was not unfamiliar with some key actors in the town's seedier underbelly.

In the early 2000s, Appelgren had become a contact person for the police informant Max Åström, who later had to leave Sweden after testifying against known weapons dealers. Part of the information that Åström had given Appelgren concerned Yaacoub Moussa, who, Åström claimed, had stored weapons for the Hells Angels; a piece of intelligence that Appelgren had never shared publicly before being interviewed by me.

After the drive-by, the beat cops informed central command that Yaacoub's little brothers, Eddie and Dany, were at war with Khouri. All those pieces of intel – and with access to the police's own databases – meant Appelgren and his team had enough information to start planning their move.

When he presented his proposed roadmap to his bosses, they gave him more than 100 staff members for the long-term investigation – everything from expert analysts to officers who'd spent years on stake-outs keeping an eye on The Network and its rag-tag band of errand boys. Down in Södertälje, everyone already knew who led the dominant gang.

The team drew on police success stories in other countries, drawing a sketch of a pyramid to illustrate the structure of organised crime. The base of the pyramid represented the gangs on the street – the kids who burnt cars, the teenagers who intimidated business owners who didn't want to pay protection money, the young men who enforced debts for the slightly older men, such as Khouri, who oversaw cash-gathering assignments. Above them, in the middle section of the pyramid, there were big-scale loan sharks, money launderers, and in all likelihood drug kingpins importing narcotics from abroad. The top of the pyramid housed the marionette masters, but if the police ever identified them, they didn't let slip the names to me, and their investigation was focussed on the base of the pyramid: Khouri and followers.

A lot of the beat cops referred to Khouri simply by his everyday nickname 'Berno' but Appelgren kept to protocol, always, and always dryly, referred to him by his full name.

'Bernard Khouri is a little brat who terrorised an entire town,' he said. 'The question is what, or who, allowed him to do it.'

Rottweilers

A MONTH after the drive-by, the police had launched their special operation. Meanwhile, the Assyriska players faced their own challenge: Eddie, their star striker, was injured and had to get better – for the club's sake as much as his own.

Eddie's former team-mate, former Assyriska talent Andreas Haddad, who'd left Sweden to join a club in the Middle East, would be spending time back home in Södertälje. He had also been battling an injury and the two friends went to the same physiotherapy clinic, Hovsjö Rehab, in an outlying neighbourhood, not far from the arena.

Haddad, whose father is Assyrian, grew up in the north of Stockholm, where loyalty to the club AIK Solna runs deep. But as a teen he joined Assyriska, which he, in conversation with me, referred to as 'our national team', and that's how he met Eddie. 'Eddie had a bit of a temper, and I had a bit of a temper, so we clicked,' Haddad recalled.

The friendship at first grew slowly. 'We didn't spend that much time together at first because I was still living in Solna,' Haddad said. 'But when I moved here to Södertälje we spent a lot of time together before and after practice. We, like, clicked because we both had an attitude.'

'Eddie can be difficult, like that temper that a lot of us have, but he is wonderful. As a friend he is worth his weight in gold, he is always there for you no matter what, I really enjoy his company.'

The only thing Haddad disliked was his friend's insistence on bringing his Rottweilers, Edgar and Aurora, along with them.

Aurora in particular was always by Eddie's side; she rode in Eddie's car, accompanied them to the beach. Thankfully, Haddad laughed, she wasn't allowed to attend practice.

'Those dogs are crazily huge, but they're well trained,' Haddad said. 'They listen to everything Eddie says, I mean, they'll spin around, they'll jump, they'll freeze [at his command].'

Getting Assyriska to be as well trained that season, however, wasn't going as well. The team were still lingering in the second league, Superettan, and they'd lost the last derby against Syrianska FC 3-2. Then things had started to pick up. In June 2010, two months after the drive-by, Assyriska crushed Landskrona BoIS 4-1, then stalled as they drew against both Örgryte and Falkenbergs FF.

Haddad was worried about Eddie's injury, because Eddie was 'a really important part of the puzzle'. Eddie's sister Alexandra had followed Eddie's career from the start, explaining that, for Eddie, football was more than part of his life, it *was* his life. More than a profession, it was his identity. When he had still been just a boy, Alexandra used to hold his hand as they walked to practice. Apart from football and his family, Eddie's main focus was the dogs. And Eddie spent a fair deal of time grooming himself: 'He likes to look good,' she lovingly told me.

But football had become priority number one. She accompanied him to the Lebanese embassy to see whether he could apply for citizenship because he wanted to try out for the national team down there. Eddie told his sister he was also going to try out for Dynamo Kiev.

It was not just his family's pride that would be bolstered by a move abroad, it would help put Assyriska on the global football map if he became a star outside of Södertälje, where so many Assyrian boys join the club at an early age. The club chairman Aydin Aho explained that Eddie was an idol, even though Aho had been one of many doubters at the beginning: 'Some people thought that Eddie was too small, not much taller than 5ft 8in with a low centre of gravity and powerful legs,' he said.

Aho and the club's trainers had sent Eddie to another club a few years before, because they thought he wasn't developing as well as they'd hoped, but he ended up coming back. Upon his return, Aho thought he was not just a changed player but a changed person. Eddie started mentoring the younger players, and gone were the temper tantrums.

'When he was younger he could lose it sometimes and shout at referees and at his team-mates, that was one of the problems at the start of his career,' Aho said. 'When he came back he took that extra spark and aggression and moulded it into something positive instead. He could, in a way, control it.'

Eddie hadn't, upon his return, even been interested in negotiating his salary, telling Aho to just pay him what he thought was appropriate. 'It felt like the thing that mattered most to him was to come back, and when he put on the Assyriska strip you could really see how happy and proud it made him feel,' Aho said.

The fans adored Eddie and were 'extra happy', according to Aho, when he was the one to score a goal. 'After all, he's Assyrian, he was born and grew up here. And I think that all fans love a warrior who gives them 110 per cent, and who gives everything for the club shirt and the club crest.'

Fanatics

EDDIE'S COUSIN Oritha didn't have time to go to football games. In the early summer of 2010, she was still too busy taking care of Leon, who would turn six the following autumn, and making sure that he spent as much time as he could with the rest of the family. As June began, the long summer was stretching out ahead of them.

For Oritha and her four siblings, their parents' home was the family's hub. It was like any other family home, coats and jackets fighting for space in the hall, the heady aroma of scented candles seeping out from her little sister's room. In the living room, big bulky sofas in tan leather with a Mickey Mouse blanket, while her sister decorated her room with posters of Superman, which Oritha teased her about, but not too much as her little sister helped her so much with Leon.

But the joviality was about to come to an abrupt end; one sibling's mistake would haunt them all. Unbeknownst to Oritha, her brother had ended up in debt. At first, it was a medium-sized debt, but, having failed to pay back the 10,000 kronor, it had incurred interest.

Oritha was not at her parents' home the evening that a group of men knocked on the door; the men told her parents about the debt and that Khouri would like his money back asap.

Oritha's brother hadn't even borrowed the money from Khouri. Somehow Khouri had got wind of it and bought it from the lenders. And now, the men said, it was time to pay 300,000 kronor – a 30-fold increase on the original sum.

After the men left, Oritha's father was so distraught that he contacted one of his godsons, Eddie's older brother Yaacoub, to ask for help. Yaacoub told him to calm down, insisting that no, no, no the family didn't have to pay Khouri, adding that Khouri and his friends were 'idiots'.

Word that her father had gone to Yaacoub for help spread quickly, and it earned the family a second visit. And this time Khouri joined the group of men – a move that ended up being a monumental error on Khouri's part.

Two of Oritha's siblings were at home. As the men sat down with their parents in the living room, under the watchful eyes of the Virgin Mary, the siblings kept her abreast of what was going on through texts and phone calls. Her brother made sure the men couldn't see him as he called Oritha and told her to be quiet, then lowered his phone so the men wouldn't realise it was connected and went to stand in the doorway. He kept the line open, hoping that Oritha could snap up parts of the conversation. Their little sister, who had slunk into her scented-candle den, sent Oritha a text message telling her the men were smoking in the living room, and that the cigarette smoke had unfurled along the hall all the way into her bedroom.

Powerless to intervene, Oritha felt her blood start to boil. She thought about calling Yaacoub, calling the police, going over there herself, but then her husband, whom she described to me as 'a coward and a loser', grabbed the phone from her hands. 'He started shaking in fear even if you just mentioned The Network,' Oritha would tell me later.

After confiscating her phone, her husband locked her in the room. Furious, Oritha decided enough was enough, not just her husband's behaviour – she'd divorce him soon after – but the god damn Network's rampages. How dare they, she thought to herself.

At her parents' home, on the other side of town, Khouri was busy explaining that he had taken on her brother's debt as a favour, to get the lenders off his back, so he was just stepping in as a mediator to help them solve a problem. Oritha's shocked parents

127

memorised every word. Khouri told her father to not get Yaacoub involved this time, adding, 'I'm going to sweep him away'.

Oritha's mother – Oritha told me 'she is as strong as I am' – could not contain her rage. She argued with Khouri. For example, when Khouri said her son shouldn't have been hanging out with the people he borrowed money from because they were Kurdish Muslims, she wouldn't let his Islamophobic hypocrisy go by without remark: 'Your girlfriend is Muslim,' she said, provoking a protestation from Khouri that his girlfriend was going to convert to Christianity for his sake.

But the main issue was the outrageous hike-up from 10,000 kronor to 300,000. Against the odds, Oritha's mum managed to negotiate, but not by much, just down to 200,000.

It was an outrageous sum for a middle-class family to conjure out of thin air. Her mum sold her gold jewellery, her sister dipped into her savings, as did Oritha, and some relatives pitched in too.

When Oritha's father took the cash and met Khouri at a restaurant, Khouri poured him a drink and then, once the money had been handed over, kissed his forehead as a mark of respect. 'Creepy,' Oritha told me. 'To do that to a family and then pretend it's all normal. That kiss was creepy, and reading between the lines it meant he felt no shame.'

Shortly afterwards, her parents and one of her brothers went to the police, reported Khouri and the other men, and gave statements. Later on, when I read the statement her mother gave, it was difficult to keep up with the story; she was all over the place, going from indignant rage to scattered disjointed details of Khouri barging into her home, scrambling the time line, jumping back and forth.

As a crime reporter, I'd read a lot of witness statements and noted that that kind of garbled speech only showed up when the victim of a crime was deeply shocked, and in some cases even traumatised.

Oritha's father was calmer, but also deeply distressed, telling the police he could not believe Khouri's behaviour – the very kind of behaviour he'd wanted to escape upon moving to Sweden. 'I'm used to fanatics from my home country,' he said, 'but they were Islamist fanatics.'

Seen from a business perspective, Khouri's decision to join his men on the second visit was far from smart. In part because he was sowing the seed of anger that risked toppling him from his throne, but also because by showing his face he couldn't deny he was involved. He couldn't say 'it's not my fault people name-drop me in disputes about money' because he was there and an entire family were ready to testify against him.

'I memorised all the dates,' Oritha told me, 'so the police could cross-check the information.'

Which they did: accessing the suspects' text messages on the date in question, noting who called whom when to coordinate meeting up for a bit of extortion. And telephones pinging off mobile masts in the area can be used to discredit a suspect's claim they weren't in the vicinity. So Oritha's memorising the dates was valuable. She told me, with a fair dose of defiant pride, that 'it'll be my fault when they're caught'.

What had happened to her family was a good example of what the lead detective, Gunnar Appelgren, meant when he said Khouri was going too far. Appelgren used the Swedish expression 'fartblind', which means being blinded by your own speed, and said Khouri didn't seem to realise he couldn't push people forever.

Another police officer, a junior detective, wondered if Khouri's mental health was deteriorating. 'The way I saw it,' he later recalled, 'Khouri had become manic.'

A real man

ONE OF the personal assistants employed to take care of Leon remembered her reaction when she found out how Khouri had treated Oritha's family.

As I agreed not to mention her by name, she freely shared her opinions of The Network with me. 'They're so disgusting, who smokes indoors?' she said with a look of disdain, referring to Khouri's gang lighting cigarettes in Oritha's parents' living room.

The way in which they threatened the family, with Khouri's allusion to violence and saying he was going to 'sweep Yaacoub away', riled her further. 'A real man doesn't need to hint that he's got a gun, a real man uses words,' she said. 'You're weak if you think that just because you're ready to shoot someone you have the right to destroy other people's peace of mind, just because, forgive me for my choice of words, but because their own lives suck.'

Then she said something that I'd heard more times than I could count from other Södertälje residents, who emphasised it over and over, that in Sweden, in contrast to, for example, the US, education is free, health care is free … the cradle-to-grave system might not be perfect but there were fewer excuses here than in other places to choose a life of crime.

'They live in a country that offers all possibilities but they choose [this life],' she said.

Contract

ONE OF Yaacoub's old acquaintances, the owner of a store selling personal protection gear and surveillance equipment which attracted a mixed clientele, warned Yaacoub in early summer 2010 that someone had taken out a contract on his life.

With a price on his head, Yaacoub started to wear a protective vest at Eddie's games. At one match, he complained to a friend that the weight of the vest hurt his back. Things had been going downhill for a while. After the drive-by, Yaacoub had stayed awake for two nights straight, gazing out of the window, standing guard over his family.

Then one evening, Yaacoub did something he had never done before: he held a business meeting at home. This caught his wife off guard because Yaacoub had never mixed his private life with the outside world; it was not his style, she would later tell the police, and she had always taken it for granted that he considered their home a sanctuary.

Yet on that evening she watched as several men arrived on their doorstep. She greeted her brother-in-law Dany and also Bülent Aslanoglu, an old friend of Yaacoub who had spent time in jail.

Then she retreated upstairs – the kids were sleeping – but she stayed on the landing, trying to listen to the conversation downstairs. A few months later, she'd be asked to recall every word she had overheard, once the police started to try and piece together what had been going on after the drive-by.

'It was pretty clear that Dany only has Yaacoub, that Yaacoub was the only one stopping them from doing something to Dany,' she told them. 'I didn't understand everything that they were saying, because I was upstairs, but they probably wanted Dany to take off his X-Team vest and break ties with [X-Team]. There were raised voices, and a lot of it was in Assyrian, and I'm not great at Assyrian, but it wasn't a particularly calm discussion, there were a lot of angry emotions.'

Assyrians are expressive people, she added, but this night had been different. The tone had been different. 'I have wondered why Yaacoub took them home when I was there and the kids were sleeping. I mean, they must have held meetings many times but I'd never seen or been part of it. That he took them home with him that night made me really, really angry. I was so angry with him for doing that. Because our home was holy. No shit was allowed to enter.'

Looking back to that odd evening, she arrived at a conclusion, that her husband had made her into a witness: 'He wanted me to see them.'

Vehicle theft

AFTER THE meeting at his big brother's house, Dany did not take off his X-Team vest. But why not, given what had appeared to be both warnings and pleas overheard by his sister-in-law? That was a question only he could answer but he didn't write back to me when I sent him a letter requesting an interview. I had to get others to describe him instead.

It was no hard task to gather descriptions of Dany from his childhood friends. But their observations about him were contradictory, so contradictory that the contrasts lent themselves to the bizarre, as though he, as a boy, had had two faces:

… he was always crazy … a joker … that fucking retard … the sweetest guy … terrified … troubled … a full-time job …

Nor was it difficult to access his criminal record, and see how it all began.

By 1994 Dany had already been convicted of assault, assisting aggravated assault, attempted theft, assisting aggravated theft, vehicular theft, attempted vehicular theft, threatening an officer of the law, driving without a licence. Of course it had been illegal for him to drive, he had only been 15, three years off the legal age to take a driving test.

As for the rest, it begged the question: what had been wrong from such an early age?

The second charge against him back then, assisting aggravated assault, concerned the incident when Dany gave his kid brother George a knife, the knife used to stab another boy in the neck.

In the strange stilted legalese used by the Swedish courts, the verdict summarised the incident:

The victim knows both the Moussa brothers. The day before the incident, he had met George Moussa. They had then had a fight. When he came to the schoolyard, the Moussa brothers were there. Dany Moussa, who had a knife in his hand, called him over, asked him why he'd fought with George, and slapped him a couple of times. Then Dany told George and another youth to hit the victim.

In the ensuing tussle, the victim had gotten the better of George. Instead of continuing the fight, the victim had called it quits and been about to walk away.

The victim saw Dany hand the knife to George [...] He did not have time to shield himself when George stabbed him with the knife. The second stab cut him in the shoulder. He was taken to hospital where he had to stay five days, being cared for in the intensive care unit.

In court, Dany had defended himself by saying it was never his intention for his little brother to put the knife to use. He had just handed the knife, which he said belonged to his brother, back to George. And Dany had done so because he'd thought the fight was over. The court, however, had had little faith in Dany's protestations.

Dany has clearly understood that there was a high risk that George in his agitated state would seriously injure the victim with the knife. With the circumstances taken into consideration, it can safely be concluded that Dany handed the knife to George knowing the outcome [...] He can therefore not avoid responsibility for assisting aggravated assault.

The verdict then ran through the other charges against Dany, citing the boy's attempts to explain himself. 'Dany says he didn't know' was a frequent phrase.

He had, however, confessed to vehicular theft. A talent for stealing mopeds had been a valued asset back then, and remained so 16 years later. Shortly after the 2010 drive-by, Dany's old childhood friend Bernard Khouri was about to send errand boys to steal some mopeds[3]. And while such thefts were commonplace, Khouri issuing this order would be a bit different – these mopeds were going to be part of a bigger plan.

---

3 According to Appeals Court Verdict in case B 8076-13

Civil war

AT FIRST Hosep didn't notice the tension rising inside The Parrot café, because the argument was taking place in the kitchen; the raised voices didn't penetrate the din of gossip and the visitors' occasional gentle whoop of triumph when someone won a hand of cards.

But then a café employee came up to him and said that he needed to come and help, that a man Hosep knew had gotten into a fight.

'Who?' queried Hosep.

'Elie, Elie Maalouf, Khouri's guy,' the employee told him.

'Who's he fighting with?' said Hosep, a man known for being fearless and calm, and curious too, which his light-green eyes communicated in an unflinching, yet never aggressive, gaze.

'The football player, you know, the youngest Moussa brother, Eddie,' the rattled employee told him.

As a man who took pride in knowing everyone and, crucially, in helping everyone, Hosep didn't hesitate to get involved. He got up from his chair. Of average height, broad-shouldered and stout, Hosep was a solid breadth of a man who had once, in a different lifetime altogether, been a combatant in the Lebanese civil war, before he'd fled north. That was a long time ago. He had over the years become a gentler kind of man, he even owned a toy poodle. That didn't mean he had gone soft though.

Hosep abandoned his table and walked towards the kitchen. He noticed that the atmosphere in the café was changing, that there was movement en masse as the other café-goers made their way to the exit, spilling into the car park outside.

136

Hosep, moving against the stream, entered the kitchen, where he saw the café manager, Milad's brother Bahnan, trying to hold Elie back. Elie was staring at Eddie.

In the periphery of Hosep's vision, Eddie came hurtling across the space towards the two men, and Milad's brother stepped aside, presumably in fear because there was a madness to Eddie, a ferocity and vengeful purpose contorting his face that left an indelible impression on Hosep that he would remember for the rest of his life. Eddie was crazed, he'd gone mad.

Hosep saw a flash of metal. It was not a knife in Eddie's hand, it was a kebab skewer, and when Eddie – as fast as he ever was on the pitch – reached Khouri's friend Elie, he channelled his fury into that slim piece of metal, stabbing Elie over and over in a flurry of force and intent.

Hosep didn't lose another second, realising that if the attack forced Elie to the ground, he would be exposed. It didn't matter that these men wore protective vests, the vests left the neck exposed. There was too big a risk of fatal violence, so Hosep dived into the fight. He had seen too many men die already; that's why he fled the civil war all those years ago.

Hosep pried them apart, pushed Eddie away, then, as he spotted an emergency exit sign, he yelled at Elie 'Get out of here!' As Elie fled, Eddie disappeared out of the other door, heading through the café towards the car park.

As Hosep followed Eddie outside, he was met by a throng of onlookers. A throng so large it wouldn't surprise him if they had numbered well over 100, and there, in the middle, stood Khouri. And Eddie's no-good brother Dany was there too. That's when Hosep realised he was no longer sure he could calm the fight down – these were young men infamous for violence.

Hosep knew what it was to be young, with every muscle steeped in testosterone, your body aching for a fight, but these boys were out of control.

He knew it, everybody knew it. They were the kind of boys that mothers weep over.

Khouri looked down at the much-shorter Eddie, who, unde-terred by the difference in size, returned his gaze and unleashed a torrent of abuse.

'You fucking cunt, you're behind the murder of Mohaned,' he roared in earshot of 100 witnesses. 'I'm going to fucking hire people to take you out,' he screamed at Khouri. 'I'm going to pay so much fucking money to teach you a lesson.'

Khouri remained calm. He took his eyes off Eddie and turned to Hosep, asking him to go fetch Eddie's big brother Yaacoub from The Oasis, which was just around the corner.

'I don't know Yaacoub,' Hosep protested. 'And I have nothing to do with this.'

Another man instead left to fetch Yaacoub.

If Khouri expected Yaacoub to stay true to his reputation as a calm and fair mediator, he was about to be disappointed. When the eldest Moussa brother arrived, he turned to his little brothers Eddie and Dany and said, despite the crowd listening to his every word, that they should have killed Khouri's friend 'when you had the chance, you shouldn't have let him leave the café alive'.

Yaacoub then faced off with Khouri. Yaacoub, who was approaching 40, had filled out in recent years – not fat, just solid – and could fight Khouri. But instead, as the two men conversed, the tone started to soften. After a few more exchanges, Khouri, Yaacoub and Dany went back into the café to talk things through. Khouri's friend tried to join them, but they wouldn't let him; Khouri told him to stay away. Eddie was barred from the café too, as though the grown-ups needed to talk about their kids having a schoolyard spat.

Milad wasn't at The Parrot that day, but he eventually heard all about it. He was not surprised that it was Hosep who broke up the fight. Hosep was not the kind of guy, Milad told me, to ever be frightened, not even of Khouri. Because Hosep had seen much worse in the civil war back in the 1980s. 'He is not scared of anything, Hosep doesn't care, he saw a thousand guys like Khouri in Lebanon,' Milad told me.

Standing outside the café with the other onlookers, Hosep remembered something that Dany once told him – that Eddie was the source of all his troubles, that every time someone failed to repay a debt to Eddie, he would get Dany involved. He'd send Dany off to collect the outstanding debt.

While I didn't end up looking in any detail into Eddie's alleged loan sharking, another investigative journalist later found out that Eddie's forte was lending money to gamblers during the games. Small amounts at times, to keep them going after a loss, but lending someone 1,000 kronor to get into the next round with the understanding that the gambler would have to pay back twice that … that kind of ad-hoc interest rate added up.

In the crowd outside The Parrot café, Hosep turned to some of the other men for more information. 'Khouri's friend Elie and Dany were talking, but then Eddie got involved,' one of the men said. 'It went downhill from there.'

They, in turn, asked Hosep what had happened in the kitchen. 'Eddie was crazy,' Hosep told them. 'I think I saved Elie, because it could have ended really badly. He was just about to fall, you know, towards the floor, you understand, and if he'd fallen Eddie could have stabbed him in the neck.'

The assembled men shook their heads. 'The vest, it leaves no protection there,' Hosep added by way of explanation, gesturing towards his throat. 'He could have died.'

Later, Hosep told me that 'when you stab someone like that … I mean, Eddie wasn't just out to hurt him, he was out to kill.'

Fuck you, fuck you

THAT THE police were circling Khouri after the drive-by, once it became known, did not come as a surprise to anyone in Södertälje who had fallen prey to or witnessed his rampages. But good luck finding witnesses who were courageous enough to testify.

A person with strong opinions about the matter was Khouri's and Yaacoub's acquaintance Philip, the gambler. 'Let me tell you something about this police investigation into The Network,' Philip told me. 'In one of our home countries, this investigation would have been over and done with in 24 hours. Everyone would have squealed straight away, they'd confess to everything. Everything. 24 hours. Okay?' Philip finished off his treatise of effective police work with a characteristic deadpan stare. 'If you electrocute someone's cock, of course they will talk, 100 per cent,' he offered as an example.

Philip continued: 'I don't think the Swedish system works well for my kind of people. You can't use love to talk with these people, they don't understand it, because they come from countries where everything is regulated with violence. And people need it, that style of rule. You know, when Saddam was alive, Iraq was a great place, you can agree with me on that, right?'

'We're talking about the entire Middle East,' Philip continued. 'They need strong people in charge. If you give these people too much, they will take too [many liberties]. They'd don't understand the point when the police come to them and, what you call it, question them, and, fine, maybe the cop talks to you and sounds sort of tough, but he can't do anything.'

Philip paused, then added, 'So all you've got to do is deny, deny, deny, which is more or less a "fuck you, fuck you", and then you walk.'

Harassment

WHILE PHILIP was taking a step back from Khouri and the Moussas, other Södertälje residents kept living their lives as they always had.

Small-fry gambler Issa kept on going to his usual joint to play some cards with his acquaintances, although he had started to wonder if he should go back. In rapid succession since the first raid, he had endured the same ordeal a few times more. It was unheard of.

No one quite knew what the police were looking for. It couldn't be bootleg booze, even though the beat cops nagged local café owners about the need to apply for a licence to serve alcohol. Even if the law was still being flouted, the police would never send officers wearing additional protective gear to hunt for a few bottles of vodka. So what were they up to?

Regardless, Issa had started to feel that the police were picking on him and his friends.

'It's degrading, making old men lie on the floor,' he reflected.

Although he also realised that something bigger was going on. The police had started to stop and search cars ever more frequently, and it was always the same cars, mostly driven by Khouri's friends, although lately Khouri himself hadn't been around much in town.

'Okay, so maybe there's a serious situation going on,' Issa told me. 'But it's affecting us, we get caught in the middle. [The raids have] happened three or four times now. You never know when they'll show up.'

Issa was not about to give up his bantamweight gambling habit just yet, though, so one summer evening in 2010 he headed over to his club.

As soon as he stepped through the door, everything unfolded much as it always used to. He did the rounds, said hi, how are you, shook hands, enquired after people's health. He sat down, had a drink poured, and was dealt a hand of cards.

But then, as if on cue, the police showed up again.

'Oh, here we go again ...' he thought with an inward sigh.

He was told to get down on the floor, which he did grudgingly, and watched the black-clad police approach a door at the back of the venue. He knew they would kick the door in if they couldn't get it open, that's what they had done before, which he thought was unnecessary.

'I know where the key is,' Issa told one of the officers. 'Please let me just help you.'

The police let him stand up, and he walked over to help. The officers then gestured at him to get back down on the floor.

'Look, I've got a sore neck, and I can't lie on the floor. I'm just going to sit on this chair, all right?' he asked them.

The police let him sit on a chair instead, and Issa was glad for it, because, to be frank, he was fed up. He had never done anything wrong, he had nothing to do with this so-called mafia that the town had been wagging its tongues about ever since the drive-by some two months before.

Issa didn't deserve this. He looked at his friends splayed out across the floor like spilled matchsticks. Many were elderly. Some of them had grey hair. They didn't deserve this either. It was demeaning and cruel.

'That's it,' Issa decided. 'I have to change clubs.'

Even though Mohaned had been killed in The Oasis just six months earlier, Issa decided to give it a try; the venue was just a couple of kilometres away.

Job descriptions

'WE ONLY wear extra protective gear if we're looking for weapons,' beat cop Alice Ekengren told me, who neither confirmed nor denied Issa's claim that the raids were becoming more frequent in the spring and summer of 2010.

Ekengren had taken part in her fair share of run-of-the-mill raids, usually looking for drugs or booze. At the very start of her posting in Södertälje, almost fresh out the police academy, her colleagues had taken her on a tour of the gambling joints as soon as she'd hit the ground.

She had requested specifically to be posted in Södertälje, somewhat to the surprise of her superior officers. 'We've had to forcibly assign people here before,' a colleague had told her.

In the Ronna neighbourhood, her colleagues pointed out the main gathering points, The Oasis and The Parrot.

Almost from the outset, Ekengren had realised that the clubs were full of men, and men only. That was still the case.

'Where are your wives? Maybe they want to play cards?' she asked one evening.

'No, no, no,' an older gentleman responded.

Ekengren decided to press the issue with several men, but to no avail.

'No no, it's not possible,' they all said.

'But why?' asked Ekengren, who, like most Swedish women, had been raised to value gender equality, and to question gender separatism.

'No, no, no,' was the men's invariable reply.

'But what if your wife needs you for something?' she asked. 'Is she allowed to come in?'

'Then she has to ask someone to come in and get me,' one of the men replied.

She wasn't there to enforce mainstream society's gender-equality values, however, but to enforce the law, and from time to time explain that, no, the cops weren't making up laws as they went along just to annoy people, because 'Sveriges Rikes Lag' – The Lawbook of the Realm of Sweden – applied to everyone.

Most of her work, she'd realised almost from the get-go, wouldn't take place here in the informal gambling joints, instead she'd be out on the street doing classic beat policing and keeping an eye on the known troublemakers. And keeping the police log up to date in meticulous detail with special attention paid to the alleged members of The Network.

'We're mapping their movements,' she said. 'What persons, which cars, in which places, at what hour. We're being overzealous. It was made clear from the start that there were certain people that you always [have to] stop.'

In late June 2010, the police noted that Khouri was back in town. What they didn't know was that The Network, soon after his return, had ordered two errand boys to steal a couple of mopeds. Nor that The Network had picked up some free sim cards for their pay-as-you-go mobiles, known as 'burner phones' and put to use to make it more difficult for the police to tie a mobile to its user. Among the phones The Network had at their disposal was a decade-old model of an Ericsson mobile, no longer used to any great extent in Sweden – not a smart move, because with so few people using them it'd be easier to identify it.

The beat cops had noticed that Khouri had been gone for a while, and that he had just returned to Södertälje. He was a familiar face to all of them.

'Khouri is quite polite,' Ekengren told me. 'That's what happens when they rise a bit in the ranks, they learn how to behave towards the police. It's the junior ones who have the attitude, because they haven't learnt the rules of the game yet. I've never had any problems with Khouri,' she added. 'I'm doing my job, he's doing his.'

Not again

SÖDERTÄLJE WAS boiling, June had been unmerciful. People would complain to me that the heat was worse here than in the Middle East because of the humidity – and with storms brewing, the air at times felt like a pressure cooker. Not deterred by the heat, just waiting for the cooler evening air, Issa stuck to his decision to find a new club to hang out in in the evenings.

He couldn't go back to his old joint, the police raids were insufferable, so he made his way instead to Ronna, to Yaacoub's place, The Oasis. It was a larger space than his old joint, tucked into a corner of the odd-shaped Ronna Mall, with an assortment of shops tucked into the courtyard of a towering block of flats.

In the local betting shop, with its small screens showing horse races and football games, older men were buying cigarettes and taking bets. Outside, the ground was still hot under foot and while the sun had dipped below the forest, just a few metres behind The Oasis, the peculiar light of summer-solstice dusk had not faded.

Quite a few people had found their way to The Oasis in the evening of 30 June 2010. Inside, posters of Wayne Rooney and Michael Ballack adorned the wall. As he entered, Issa noticed, because it was odd, that there was a young woman there, seated at one of the handful of felt-clad tables. Issa sat down and lit a cigarette. The evening turned into night; this club wasn't bad, he thought, it was quite cosy.

An older woman showed up; it was clear she was Yaacoub's mother as they had the same nose, the same facial structure. The Moussa matriarch had brought bread and vegetables from her allotment – older Assyrians love their allotments, one man had once explained to me, because 'they represent the dream of having land to call one's own'.

In the club, Eddie praised his mother loudly, saying so everyone could hear that she grew the best organic vegetables.

As she prepared to leave, Eddie made sure she had money for the bus ride home.

Several hours passed. A couple of kids sauntered in; Issa reckoned they were out to score under-the-table booze. He couldn't have known that they'd end up being suspected for acting as scouts, sent to make sure the Moussa brothers were still in the venue. The boys disappeared as fast as they'd arrived.

A man at Issa's table pointed out Philip to him, whispering, 'That boy's a poker genius.'

'What's he doing here with us?' Issa joked.

The minutes snaked past midnight, the clock struck one, then started to ease towards two in the morning. The club stayed open. But it was time for Yaacoub to go home, and Issa watched as he picked up his keys and grabbed a black bag, it looked like a laptop bag, which he slung over his shoulder. But before Yaacoub had had time to exit the club, the door opened. Issa didn't see it, but noticed the change in demeanour and gaze of the man sitting opposite, a man who had a clear view of the door. Issa turned around to look too, and what he saw infuriated him. Two men, clad head to toe in black.

'Oh for God's sake! Not again, not the goddamned police!' was Issa's immediate thought.

'Those idiots are persecuting me. I came here to get away from those assholes.'

But there was no shouting. No one shouted at them to get down on the floor. And unlike the police, the two men were wearing some kind of black masks over their faces and goggles covering their eyes.

Then Eddie looked up at the two men, and he cursed. Issa didn't understand why the young footballer was swearing.

There was a split second of calm, then a sharp crack, and yet another crack.

There was pandemonium, but this time it wasn't the raised voices of a police raid, it was physical pandemonium. All of a sudden there was chaos. Confusion gripped Issa as he was dragged up to standing more by a contagious, emotional momentum than by any physical force, as though pulled and shoved about by a tidal wave of fear.

He and the others ran, and they ran as fast as they could. The cadence of the cracks puzzled Issa. It was rhythmic, evenly spaced out. Rapid bursts – clack, clack, clack. It sounded like firecrackers, but why were they all running away from people throwing firecrackers, Issa asked himself? What was happening? As Issa emerged into the summer's night, it dawned on on him that those weren't firecrackers.

Seconds passed, or was it minutes … Issa couldn't tell because adrenaline-tinged chaos had perverted his perception of time. From the other side of the building, Issa heard the trill of a moped or two. The trill changed frequency as the mopeds accelerated. Issa suspected that the attackers – because what had just happened could not have been anything but an attack – had headed towards the forest, criss-crossed with walking paths that made a quick escape easy.

In shock, Issa walked around the building. He was not alone. Older men had flung themselves from another club that lay wall-to-wall with The Oasis. Having had no way to exit their venue without passing through The Oasis, they had opened the window and thrown themselves the half-storey down to safety.

Yet again, Issa thought, black-clad men had robbed old men of their dignity. As more and more people arrived at the scene, Issa wondered where the Moussa brothers were. Had they escaped too?

Radiator

AS THE police started to arrive, patrol car after patrol car, one of the first responders stepped into The Oasis and saw the carnage. The brothers had not escaped. A stray bullet had punctured a radiator next to Yaacoub's body and the police officer's efforts to plug the hole failed. The water from the radiator mixed with blood, and with the dust from the bullets ripping into the floor, which created a greyish-pink sludge that was threatening to wipe out evidence. Fearing the crime scene would be destroyed, an officer fished out his phone and started to film what he saw, adding a blow-by-blow narrative as he bent down to catch details, including bullet casings.

At first, he filmed Eddie who lay on his back with his right leg curled backwards; a curious sight, as though he'd been ready to take a penalty shot. A gash several inches long had flayed open his right thigh, looking more like a wound from a switchblade than from a Kalashnikov. In previous criminal cases involving automatic rifles, a cop later told me, victims had had similar wounds, caused by ricocheting bullets slicing flesh open, but whether that had happened to Eddie wasn't clear.

The first responder kept filming. Eddie's skin was pale, but not just the pale of the dead; he was shrouded in grey dust from the floor, which showcased veritable craters where bullets had struck.

The officer pointed at a few bullet casings on the floor, explaining what he was seeing so the video could be used as evidence, then stepped deeper into the boxy room. Playing cards and cigarettes still lay on the tables, chairs lay knocked over on their sides, tell-tale signs of the witnesses having fled in panic.

The officer walked towards the opposite end of the venue and reached Yaacoub, whose body lay by the radiator. The radiator was leaking with such force, I'd note when I later watched the video, that the hiss drowned out the narrative; the officer's descriptions were inaudible.

What I'd be able to see clearly were the keys in Yaacoub's hand, indicating that he had been on his way home to his wife and kids just moments before the double murder.

Tidier ways to kill someone

UPON RECEIVING news of the shooting, Detective Superintendent Gunnar Appelgren could not believe what had just happened. While fearing retaliation after the drive-by, the police hadn't picked up any specific warning signs. It irritated Appelgren that they hadn't known and it also embarrassed him because they should have known.

And he felt anger. Not with his team but with himself, because no matter how complex this investigation, the buck stopped with him. How the hell had they not had a clue that this had been coming?

All the effort they had put in: wiretaps, bugged cars, surveillance. They'd even established a special hotline, and anonymous tips had started to come in; not many but a few. They had been getting a grip on the situation, they had started to sort through the nicknames.

They had employed a league of translators who'd been working overtime. All the investigators and analysts had learned that 'naknemo' meant 'fuck your mother' in Aramean, because the insult peppered the thousands upon thousands of phone calls the police had recorded.

When the high-level text message alerting him of the incident had pinged his phone, he would have been forgiven for screaming 'naknemo' himself, but as team leader he couldn't lose his cool. He needed to get to work straight away, but where the hell was his briefcase? Shit, he realised the colleague who had dropped him off at the pub the night before, straight after work, had taken the briefcase, filled with confidential documents, so that Appelgren wouldn't have to keep an eye on it while enjoying a beer.

Appelgren managed to get hold of his colleague, waking him, then jumped into his car, swinging by his colleague's house in the dead of night, then, briefcase in hand, he finally headed to work, delayed by an hour.

Over in Södertälje, Eddie and Yaacoub's brother Dany showed up outside The Oasis, howling in grief and fury. The police frisked him, found narcotics and detained him, but their true intent was not to arrest him for possession, the police just wanted to lock him up for his own safety – the killers could still be out there and intent on taking him out too – and furthermore, the police didn't want Dany going on a revenge rampage. An arrest cell was the best option for everyone.

Even though officers outside The Oasis had identified Dany, many of their colleagues, who'd been too busy to notice them arresting him, were working on the assumption that Dany was one of the murder victims lying inside The Oasis. They assumed as much because Dany was notorious for kicking up trouble, and it seemed logical that he'd at long last been killed. They'd quickly identified Yaacoub, but it took a bit longer to identify the second victim as Eddie. And once they'd recognised him, several of the police officers were confused. Including Appelgren, who like them wondered why anyone would take out the golden boy of Assyriska? The local boy done good, the star striker beloved by friends and team-mates.

Apart from confusion, Appelgren was beset by frustration. Not only had the police failed to stop the attack, they had failed to stop an attack that had clearly been planned meticulously in advance. This hadn't been, like in the case of Mohaned six months prior, a spur-of-the-moment shooting. In contrast, the double murder felt theatrical. Stage managed for maximum effect. Someone had bought masks and goggles for the gunmen to wear, someone had stolen mopeds to use as get-away vehicles. 'We had so much information. I can't stop asking myself how the hell we missed this,' he told me. Appelgren vowed to re-listen to the hours upon hours of recordings. He would find the clue that they had missed.

Once he'd been informed about the first responder who'd filmed the crime scene, Appelgren was grateful. 'He was on his toes,' said Appelgren, noting, however, that the water from the radiator had likely destroyed 'some evidence because blood and DNA and whatever else was being mixed together.'

A question played on repeat in Appelgren's mind. Who would go to this much trouble just to kill someone? The gear, the timing, the choice to execute the brothers in front of so many witnesses. It had to be personal, which the injuries on Eddie's body proved: they shot him 18 times. 'It's degrading to shoot that many bullets into a body. It's so obvious that they were making a statement,' Appelgren said. 'There are a hell of a lot tidier, and more effective, ways to kill someone. And you could do it somewhere else. Here, they've gone on to the victims' home turf and they've degraded them, it's making a statement.'

f*ucking 'Arameans'

AS THE police cleared the crowd that had formed outside The Oasis, dawn approached. A phone call at 6:30am. That was how Eddie's friend Andreas Haddad learned the brothers had been shot. Haddad's wife saw straight away that something was wrong, as the shock and pain gripped her husband's face. When she asked him what was wrong, Haddad started to cry. It hurt, but it also felt unreal.

He started to pray, hoping that they were still alive, that they were only injured, that they were fighting for their lives in hospital. They couldn't be dead. The police had yet to issue an official statement. Haddad turned on the television to check the headlines on Ceefax – 'Football player shot' – and as he read on, a few scant preliminary details of the event started to unravel. For him, the news began to move from unreal to real; his emotions from shocked confusion to desperation once he set off for the arena later in the morning. Everyone was there. And then the club managers confirmed what they all most feared: Eddie and his brother hadn't just been shot, they were dead.

Across Södertälje, people were shocked. And it wasn't just in Södertälje, Assyrians across the world went on online chat forums to discuss the murders. On the English-language *AssyrianVoice. net*, sorrow was forced to share space with the ugly feelings some Assyrians were expressing about Arameans ('syrianer' in Swedish).

the_dave:
[Eddie] will be forever missed, a pure assyrian [sic] fighter...

Knight:

R.I.P...very sad news indeed.

When will idiots who get into gangs ever realise that they ruin the lives of everyone around them?

Free_Assyria:

'The number 18-jersey has been worn for the last time by a player in Assyriska'

this just sent me over [the edge]

davidb:

Still can't believe it.

It's just something you'd never expect to happen to a footballer, especially to one of our own.

the_dave:

The murder motivation seems to have been revenge. A lot of witnesses know who might be involved in the murder but many are not willing to work with the police and many don't dare to say anything. Although there are some people who might want to say who did it even if it might be dangerous for them ...

The police has suspicions that 3 gang members from the gang in Sodertalje called (Södertäljenätverket aka Syrianska brödraskapet 'Arameean brotherhood') are behind the murder. The gang has been acting against Assyriska and their association before, example the burning of a Assyriska building in Sodertalje ...

Danny Moussa, Eddie's brother is a leader of the gang called X-team in Sodertalje, they are rivals of the Syrianska brödraskapet, both gangs have been fighting each other many times ...

The gang Syrianska brödraskapet planned the murder on Eddie and his brother Yaacoub because they had threatened to harm Dany's family if he does not leave the area and as a revenge for earlier incidents between the two gangs.

Micho:

I'm starting to hate a big part of my own people, the f*cking 'Arameans!' I hate their f*cking monkey behaviour, they act like little bastards who think they are Tony Montana and I hate their f*cking 'SURYOYE OROMOYE' – chanting. F*CK THEM TRAITORS!

Hanuni:

Their mother is still alive. But worst of all, Yaacoub had four children.

Tambur:

That's sad, may they rest in peace.

The killers should either get life or executed, but knowing Sweden's wussy law they will probably get off easy.

Zelge fans

LATER THAT day, the Assyriska fan club Zelge Fans released an official statement. They also provided a translation in English:

It was with great sadness and shock that we received the news that the most beloved player of Assyriska tragically and suddenly passed away. Words is a bad tool to describe the immense sorrow we're in right now and for a very long time will find ourselves in.

The circumstances surrounding the incident are still an unclear matter and we leave it to police investigators. What we surely know is that Eddie Moussa and his older brother Yaacoub Moussa, a former player for the club, were killed in a manner that is similar to an execution.

What we also know is that Eddie has been heavily injured throughout the beginning of the season following the brutal tackle he suffered in the Swedish Cup match against Hammarby TFF. For this reason he was not selected for the away game against Ängelholm that was supposed to be played tonight.

Eddie Moussa has played in Assyriska since childhood and is one of the players in the club history that has shown the most heart and fighting spirit throughout his time in the club. Therefore, he naturally became a big favourite in the stands. Not just because he was raised in the club, but mainly because of his outstanding technical skills on the pitch. The speed he showed up at his edge is unparalleled in Swedish football series. Last season, he moved up as a striker and then found the target in a superb way many times. Who does not remember his excellent lob in the crucial game against Häcken, or his two goals against Jönköping that sent the club for the qualifying stage against Djurgården last year? His success last season lead to many contract offers from the upper series, but he showed where he had his heart and signed a new contract with Assyriska.

Eddie has not just meant a lot for the fans in the matter of sports. He has been a great role model for young people in Södertälje and in particular the suburb Ronna, where he demonstrated that you can succeed in football if you just have the will to do so. He has always had a warm and open dialogue with the fans and to be able to accept that our mini-Maradona with the number 18 on his back never will run in to Södertälje Football Arena again is an impossibility.

The grief has no limits. The team has lost two burning souls, and the emptiness created will stay empty for a long future ahead. Right now, football means nothing. The contrasts created aches on our soul. Words don't do justice to even try to explain. All our thoughts go directly to Eddie and Yaacoub's families. We ask those who have the possibility to join in the grief to try to process the tragedy that occurred together. We need each other right now. In the next home game against Sundsvall, Zelge Fans will celebrate and honour the memory of our two dear brothers. The number 18-jersey has been worn for the last time by a player in Assyriska. Nobody will ever wear the white jersey again with more pride than Eddie did.

Rest in peace.

[sic]

Widowed

ON THE night of the murders Ekengren, the young beat cop, had been working until 1am, clocking off shortly before the gunmen had entered The Oasis. When she woke up the next day and went to work, taking the elevator to the seventh floor of the police station downtown, she found that the office was packed, everyone nursing their morning cups of coffee as they waited for a debrief from their senior officers. Ekengren was thrown into the throng of curious colleagues, all trying to find out more details.

'Who's died?' someone asked.

'It's the Moussa brothers,' a colleague responded.

It was *which* Moussa brothers that surprised Ekengren the most, as just like so many others she had been working on an assumption that Dany the troublemaker had at last paid his dues, so to speak.

'They took out Yaacoub Moussa?' she asked her colleagues in disbelief.

From here on, there would be no rest for the police. For the next two weeks, every hour of Ekengren's working day related to the shooting in some way or another. Their superiors assigned duties while the heat rose outside headquarters.

There was no sign of the July heat abating. As Ekengren headed out on the streets, her colleagues scheduled interviews with all the witnesses and the family. At six o'clock that evening, less than 24 hours after Yaacoub's death, the police met up with his widow at a local church.

'Yaacoub was meant to come home early last night', she told them, 'because he had an early start the day after.' He had been meant to join the other Assyriska supporters flying down to the small southern Swedish town of Ängelholm to attend a match. His decision to stay longer at The Oasis appeared to have cost him his life.

They had spoken on the phone a couple of hours before the shooting. She had told him about the wild boar roaming their garden; she had been filming the animal while talking to him. She told the police that her husband hadn't sounded worried during the phone call, even though he had been on edge for months. When Yaacoub had found out that the suspects in the drive-by investigation were connected to his brother Dany, he'd feared retaliation. Yaacoub would hover by the window, standing guard over his family. He had asked her to make sure that the children weren't sleeping too close to their bedroom windows, which, if there was an attack, would rain glass shards over them.

When the widow thought back a bit further into the past, she admitted that Yaacoub's worries had started earlier than finding out about the drive-by suspects. Ever since Mohaned had died six months earlier, her husband had grown distracted and absent-minded. Yet life had been ticking along much like usual. Talk of a vacation in Turkey. Making weekend plans to take the kids to the amusement park Gröna Lund up in Stockholm.

Yaacoub had been a man who took responsibility, she told the police. Ever since his father had died two years before, Yaacoub, as the eldest son, had taken on the role as head of the family, as per Middle Eastern tradition. Because it had been his job to keep them safe, Yaacoub had asked Dany to stay away from Södertälje.

A few days after the widow had given her first statement, the police called her in for another interview. She told them about the kids, that now that Yaacoub was gone, their seven-year-old was trying to fill the role of man of the house, and be brave, trying to care for her as she grieved. The five-year-old had asked who would take care of them if they killed *mamma* too? And one of the young twins wouldn't stop staring out of the window, waiting for *pappa* to come home.

Yaacoub's widow told the police she had a pretty clear picture of who was behind her husband's death. She couldn't tell them, though. Too dangerous. She had to protect her kids. But she did say that Mohaned, as he lay dying, had told Yaacoub that Abraham 'The Torpedo' Aho, AKA 'Pingu', had been the gunman.

The police again asked about the alleged contract and the price on her husband's head.

'Yaacoub told me that he'd received a phone call from someone, a Yugoslavian, he didn't mention the name, who told him they'd managed to stall it, but a contract's a contract. And the name of the person who ordered the hit was Bülent.'

'Sorry?' the police said, not catching the name of the man, alleged to be Khouri's predecessor, who'd been at the meeting at Yaacoub's house when they'd tried to convince Dany to take off his X-Team vest.

'Bülent,' the widow repeated.

'Bülent …?'

'Bülent Aslanoglu.'

'Aslanoglu?'

'Yes.'

The day I died

ABOUT A week later, the forensic pathologists finished the autopsies and released Eddie and Yaacoub's bodies, which were then being kept at Södertälje hospital until the funeral.

Ekengren, the beat cop, was given orders to go stand guard at the hospital because the brothers' family would be making their way there with a priest. 'Some sort of religious ritual, I think,' Ekengren would later tell me.

As she and her colleagues prepared for their assignment, they added a second layer of protection: two vests, not just one, and their standard-issue service weapons were replaced with MP5 submachine guns. Then they travelled to the hospital. When the family arrived, the officers stood to one side to let them pass.

Ekengren knew, of course she knew, who was behind these murders – Khouri, and his friends.

After months of on-the-ground work, mapping their movements, she knew them all by name, not least the three men whom the police believed were just one tier below Khouri on the mafia ladder, his deputies, so to speak; not just Pingu, but also the wheelchair-bound Sherbel Said and the other drive-by victim, Metin Ok, who had been shot in the stomach, a man with an unusually light complexion and a face wiped clean of all emotional expressions.

Outside the hospital, Ekengren strained against the weight of the protective gear, heavy enough on a normal day, but it wasn't a normal day, not even for July. The heat was profound and cloying. She was sweating and tired, and still bewildered by the events.

She wondered what it all meant, what it would entail, the causes and the effects.

She had been put on a four-day rotation, which would include the impending funeral, followed by patrolling the football arena at Assyriska's upcoming home game.

A car pulled up to the hospital. Ekengren couldn't see the face of the man who climbed out of the vehicle, but a colleague much closer to the car identified the fair, blank-faced man. Ekengren's earpiece crackled as the other officer uttered his name: 'Metin Ok.' It was just two little words, but as she connected the name to Khouri's right-hand man, those two words were more than enough for Ekengren's body to release a panicked infusion of adrenaline into her bloodstream. A high-level Network member ... 'He must be here to attack the Moussa family,' she thought, looking around and frantically scanning the parking lot, the hospital entrance, asking herself where she could take cover if he began shooting. Even a plant pot would do. But nothing was fit for the job.

She was frontline security; if he was here to kill, he would have to kill her first to get past the police. A thought struck her: 'Well, I guess this could be the day that I die.'

But Metin Ok didn't even look at her. And he didn't walk towards the part of the hospital where the Moussas had gathered; he instead disappeared into the main hospital building. The security detail decided to call in a regular patrol car, just in case, whose officers did a quick sweep of the building. When they found Metin Ok, who'd suffered from anxiety since the drive-by, the officer learned that he had a routine appointment with his doctor.

Later that night, when Ekengren returned home to her husband – a former ice hockey player turned police officer just like her – she peeled out of her undershirt, so drenched in sweat that the fabric was glued to her body. She wrung out the moisture, sweat dropping on to the floor. Her every muscle ached.

Funeral

THE DAY of the funeral arrived. Scores upon scores of mourners attended, including the motorcycle gang Bandidos. The growl of their bikes punctuated the otherwise silent cortege of cars led by a police motorcycle past the football arena. There the following halted for a moment, a final brief goodbye to the sport that Eddie and his brother so loved.

Eddie's team-mate Andreas Haddad arrived at the church, joining friends, family, neighbours. He saw skinny young players from the club clad in the beloved white uniform and he saw the vest-clad bikers, all bulging muscle and black leather. One of the bikers, with a huge beer belly and a goatee, walked past the church carrying a wreath of flowers with a red sash. The sunshine made the man's slick-backed hair gleam.

Several of the national newspapers had sent reporters.

'Bandidos have the same right to go to funerals as everyone else does,' police spokesperson Kjell Lindgren told the *Aftonbladet* newspaper. Lindgren confirmed that the police were keeping an eye on Bandidos, but they kept their eyes on all types of gangs, and in this context the police did not consider them a threat.

Uniformed police, including Ekengren, stood by in the heat to keep the peace. A police helicopter hovered above them.

Haddad also spotted plain-clothes officers, adding a surreal touch to the scene because as far as he could tell some of them, half-hidden behind trees, were filming the mourners as they carried the white coffins covered in red roses.

'The funeral became a spectacle,' one of the mourners told me afterwards. 'I felt sorry for the family.'

When I later asked Haddad about Bandidos' presence, he offered a cryptic answer about Yaacoub knowing a lot of people, adding that 'Yaacoub was always a good guy; many of his problems came from being a good guy, because he always wanted to solve problems without violence. He was a peacemaker, that was the Yaacoub that I knew.'

Eddie's last goal

IN THE weeks that followed, Eddie's sister Alexandra helped their mother to sort through his things. 'We found a diary where he had made notes every day about how far he'd gone running, and what he had eaten. He had been really strict with his food and running,' she told me. 'I think football was everything to him.'

Alexandra decided with the rest of the family that Eddie's beloved Rottweilers, Aurora and Edgar, needed new homes. 'They're too big and mum isn't used to dogs,' Alexandra explained.

The dogs had stopped eating; they returned over and over to a sports bag Eddie had left behind, just before he died. The Rottweilers sniffed at it, waiting for their master to come home. Aurora went to live with the neighbours; Edgar found a new home with family friends.

Over at Assyriska, the managers pleaded with Andreas Haddad to come back from his club abroad. He said he'd give them six months 'for Eddie'. 'Assyriska don't have any forwards,' Haddad told me when explaining his decision. 'I will play for Eddie's sake.'

When a derby against Syrianska FC approached, he made a decision. He had seen it so many times, and videos of it littered YouTube: he was going to copy Eddie's signature victory move.

On the day, when Haddad scored the second of his team's two goals in a match that ended 2-0, he copied the backward trot, and Haddad thought to himself, 'this goal is for you, Eddie.'

No arrests

EDDIE'S MOTHER decided to find a new allotment. The walk to the one she had took her straight past The Oasis where her boys had died, and she couldn't bear it.

Several of her friends and neighbours told the police that she had spent more and more time at The Oasis in the days and weeks running up to the murders. When the police asked her why, her answer was curt: 'My heart, my feelings told me to go.'

Eddie had offered to drive her home that night, then bought her a bus ticket, but she wanted to walk, it was not far. At 2am, as she rested on the sofa back home, a friend who lived just next to The Oasis had phoned her. There were people shouting, there must have been some fight at her son's place, the friend told her. She left her house, not even stopping to put on shoes, instead running in her indoor slippers along the sloping road towards The Oasis. A police officer spotted her and stopped her, pleading with her not to try to make her way to the crime scene; he had been debriefed by colleagues about the carnage that no mother should have to see.

The police couldn't tell her for certain which of her sons had been shot. She was convinced it must be Dany. Yaacoub had tried so hard to quell this conflict between Dany and The Network. It must have been them, they must have shot Dany. And then she learned it wasn't Dany, but her eldest, Yaacoub, and her baby, Eddie – 'He was my favourite,' she told the police.

The police had so many questions, but the family had just one question for them: they asked the police, although it was more of an accusation than a question, why they weren't doing anything to find the murderers. No one had been arrested.

Weeks would turn into months, the police kept asking questions and the grieving mother didn't rein in her accusations. High-up members of the Aramean church 'sit behind the scenes' on their 'invisible thrones', she said – how else did the killers have the money to buy such guns? And one of The Network members, she added – don't the police know that his father is the Aramean bishop's driver? They want to rule, she said.

When the police tried to question Eddie's sister Atie, she spat rancour. 'It's not my job to solve this. In any other country they would have caught them by now,' she told the officers.

Dany was calmer. He told the police not to get involved in a conflict that 'doesn't concern you'.

'Are you considering taking revenge on them?' the police asked.

'I don't know who "them" are,' Dany answered. 'It's difficult to take revenge on people you don't know. But I feel hatred for these people. Every church from here to Damascus will condemn them.'

'Do you think you are in danger?'

'I don't know,' Dany said.

'Do you think you are more or less in danger now, after these murders?' the police asked him.

'I'm still wearing the [X-Team] vest.'

Not that kind of wife

IN AUGUST 2010, about a month after the murders, Yaacoub's widow returned for another round of police questioning. She was fearful. She'd heard rumours that her husband's family had tried to find out how much her house was worth. And she said she was scared they'd break in and take Yaacoub's things.

She would stay awake until sunrise at 5am, then get a few hours' sleep. 'In a strange way they think that Yaacoub belongs to them,' she told the police. 'I don't exist in their eyes, the kids don't exist. There are so many rumours right now that they're looking into how much things are worth.'

'Who are they? When you say "They are looking into everything", who are they?' a police officer asked.

'The family. Yaacoub's family,' she said. 'They have moved so fast to take our life away from us. Because all we – me and the kids – have, is our home. I don't know what they want to achieve, if they want to make me have a breakdown and then take the children away.'

The widow explained that one of the staff members at her children's daycare warned her that another adult had tried to come and pick them up.

'What are you afraid will happen?' the police asked.

'If they get hold of my son and his passport, then perhaps they'll be in Syria by tomorrow. And then I don't stand a chance of getting him back.'

The widow had the impression that the few people who did bother to come by and check on her were there to see how much she knew and how much she had told the police. She felt she could trust no one. She felt abandoned.

The police asked her for help to understand the motive for the murders.

'What I don't understand is Eddie,' an officer said. 'Why shoot him?'

'I didn't have a close relationship to Eddie, but he kept busy with money, lending money with high interest rates, and I think he used Dany to get his money back,' she said.

'I was hoping that he'd go all in for the football and make something of himself, but it felt like cool cars and money were more important to him.'

They returned to the topic of Eddie's alleged loan sharking in a follow-up interview.

'Can you tell us about it?' the officer asked.

'It wasn't a secret that Eddie had money,' the widow said.

'For us it was a secret until all of this happened.'

'He wasn't exactly poor,' she responded.

'But he lived in a flat and his car was registered under another guy's name, that doesn't seem like a millionaire.'

'No, but he can't exactly walk around flashing cash when the only thing he does is play football in the Superettan league,' she responded.

'You mentioned high interest rates.'

'Yes, that's what I've heard now.'

'Now – afterwards?'

'Yes.'

'It's not something that you and Yaacoub discussed?'

'No, no, it's what I've heard now, afterwards, that he had a lot of money.'

'Did your husband lend money?'

'No, not in that way. Of course if a close friend turned up and needs a loan, he'd help as far as he could. But he wasn't a loan shark.'

The police asked her how Yaacoub made money. They knew how he had spent his time, managing The Oasis and helping at the football club, even flying to Brazil to check out potential recruits. But how did he make a living? It wasn't the first time they'd asked her that question, and the widow, time after time, had failed to give them an answer.

'He worked for that security company, he bet on the horses, I don't know. I'm not the kind of wife who sits there with my hand out waiting for money. I have my own job and we didn't discuss money. I paid the bills, I don't know anything about the rest of the money.'

She kept getting payment reminders from the owners of Ronna Mall who wanted her to pay the 18,000 kronor monthly rent for The Oasis. The invoices kept coming for six months after Yaacoub's death, even though she had asked their accountant to end the contract. 'Why should I pay rent for a place that I don't even have keys to?' she asked the police.

The world, it seems, had turned against her; a friend confirmed her suspicions that people were keeping their distance. It wouldn't be long before the situation became untenable for her and the kids.

During interviews, the police kept returning to one question over and over: why take out Yaacoub if the problem was Dany and Eddie?

'If they wanted to take out one of Yaacoub's brothers, then they had to take him out too,' she said. 'They knew that Yaacoub would never let them touch any of his brothers without taking revenge.'

PART FOUR

THE WITNESSES

Autumn 2010 to winter 2011

Holiday

ORITHA HAD been fond of Yaacoub, who was her father's godchild. 'Yaacoub was a respected man. There's a saying that no one is innocent, but I liked him. He was honest, straight and fair, he really was, I can't say that he wasn't. But you don't get rich standing by a door, as a bouncer, he had ways to supplement his income.'

As for Oritha, she, just like Yaacoub's widow, didn't think Yaacoub was the actual target. The gunmen simply took out a kind of life insurance by taking him out too. If they'd left Yaacoub alive, and only gone after Eddie and Dany, the gunmen would quickly have paid the ultimate price. 'Yaacoub would have left bodies scattered across all of Stockholm,' said Oritha.

After the murders, her father sank into depression. 'He's just completely broken. And he didn't even cry when my grandma died, but now he cries. I mean, to pepper someone to pieces, like they did with Eddie, was like a punch to the gut,' she said.

'Who are they to think they can take someone's life?' she added. 'The gunmen aren't particularly good Christians.'

Chief among her father's troubled thoughts was an obsessive question: whether the cash that their family had given Khouri, to repay Oritha's brother's debt, might have been used to pay for the murder weapons.

To get away from it all, Oritha booked a holiday to Egypt and flew south with her mum and two of her siblings. Oritha was pregnant with her third child; she carried the extra kilos in the sun, their hotel windows offered views of the sunset.

At home in Sweden, summer was ripening, the tree canopies turning a dark emerald. The period of late August to early September is called 'rötmånad' in Swedish, which means the 'month of rot', when food goes off fast and clothes never quite dry.

And for the police, another kind of rot had taken hold; they were advancing slowly in their investigation into the murders. No one had been arrested. Witness after witness told the police they either hadn't seen anything useful or that they wouldn't testify if the case went to court.

Oritha's father's generation had worked hard to build new lives for their families, to allow their children to grow up in security and prosperity, and Oritha would not let The Network undermine what her parents had achieved. She would testify, if called, no question about it. But she understood that the older people in town wouldn't.

She felt less empathy for members of the younger generation who were choosing to remain silent, and she was still angry at her brother for getting them into the mess with the debt to begin with. 'I know he'd lost his way, but it's no excuse,' she said.

She was hoping that as long as her brother kept out of trouble, the family would be left alone. But the calm turned out to be deceptive, and the ripples reached all the way to Egypt when her husband called to say there was a new demand for money.

Oritha's first thought was that The Network felt the family hadn't paid 'enough' the first time around – 'As you know, my mum managed to negotiate with them,' she told me later. 'So the way I see it, there was probably not enough money to go around once Khouri had taken his share, so his friends felt they didn't get their share.'

Then, she added, one should never forget that extortion works, after all. Her family had paid up before, they could do it again, just like so many other families before them. 'They know that people will get money if they have to. In the past, people have done just about anything to pay them and then they've not even had enough money to buy food for their kids, and The Network don't give a shit. I know a lot of families who have ended up in that situation.'

On the phone, her husband explained that it was not about her brother getting into debt again, there was some kind of dispute between himself and some people with ties to The Network about a car, and that was why they were asking for money.

Oritha didn't buy it. Or rather, dispute or no dispute, the way she saw them, The Network would come up with any reason just to get their hands on money. 'The Network need money for their girlfriends, and one of them just recently bought a house even though he's never had a job,' she said.

Waiting for the flight home to Sweden, Oritha spent each day in agony because Leon was home with his father. Oritha phoned the police back home, explaining the situation and asking them to protect Leon, but she felt they did not understand the gravity.

'What are they waiting for?' her sister asked her. 'Why aren't the police doing anything, why don't they get things done and why don't they take what you say seriously?'

For years, her sister would remember this as the moment she realised that 'the police are useless'.

At they flew home, the only thing they could think of was Leon's safety. Then the sisters discussed what strings to pull in order to come up with the cash. They still had some money in their savings accounts. If push came to shove they would have to take a loan from the bank. They knew from experience, from last time, that most of their relatives would be unsupportive. People didn't want to get involved.

Whatever happened, they would not borrow money from people they didn't trust, from people who might sell their debt. Because that would just lead back to Khouri. In a never-ending cycle, it would lead back to him.

Oritha worried about how far The Network would go to get the money. On the plane she thought only of six-year-old Leon. She had protected her eldest son his entire life, keeping him alive despite his grave illness, and now she was hurrying home from thousands of miles away to keep him safe from another kind of threat.

Heron City

BY 3 October 2010, Mohaned had been dead for nine months, Yaacoub and Eddie for three.

A young man called Georges Abo and his brother were eating at a restaurant in the suburban mall Heron City, perched by the motorway between Södertälje and Stockholm.

Around them, moviegoers headed to the 18-screen cinema, the biggest cinema in the country, to the evening's entertainment of *Inception*, *Salt*, *Resident Evil: Afterlife*, *Predators* and *Wall Street 2*. Only a few Swedish films nudged their way on to the Heron City screens; it was an American list of films for an American-inspired mall. Indie flicks were shown in town, not here in the car-culture suburbs. Families dined in the food court. In the atrium, the fountain's light-and-water shows added a constant whoosh and pitter-patter to the din.

Moments earlier, a grey Mercedes and a red wheelchair-adapted Chrysler had arrived at the mall. Khouri and his friends were on the hunt for Georges, who was not only a friend of Dany Moussa, but at one point had owned the car used in the drive-by shooting.

When someone had tipped Khouri off that Georges was spending an evening at Heron City, the hunting party had set off from Södertälje. Later, when the prosecutors pieced together evidence of what had happened at the mall, they found out that emergency services received two anonymous calls warning them that the 'Arameans' were on their way to Heron City. Whoever made those calls also told them that The Network was on its way.

In the restaurant, Khouri walked up to Georges and asked to speak with him in private. Georges followed him, only to realise that Khouri was not alone. He'd brought a posse, including the man paralysed in the drive-by. Also Abraham Aho, AKA 'Pingu' or 'The Torpedo' depending on whom you ask, who had been detained by the police as a suspect for killing Mohaned but had never been charged.

The Torpedo stayed back to keep an eye on Georges's brother, while the rest walked off with Georges. After a while Georges's brother thought that he had been gone too long.

'Where's my brother?' he asked.

'Give me your mobile! Don't fuck with my brains,' The Torpedo ordered him, patting him down and telling him to empty his pockets. Georges's brother knew better than to put up a fight and risk provoking him. He later told the police that once, at a party when they'd been younger, The Torpedo had stabbed him in the arm with a screwdriver 'as a joke'.

'Where is my brother?' he tried again.

'He is talking to us, and he'll be back soon,' was the reply.

Khouri's friends shunted Georges towards the kitchen of one of the restaurants. Once inside, they accused Georges of having helped plan the drive-by five months before.

Khouri punched Georges in the face. Joni Khado, a young skittish man whom I'd later give the nickname 'Travolta' because of his *Saturday Night Fever* hair style, joined in too. As did Elie Maalouf, the man Eddie had almost killed with a kebab skewer.

Georges lost his footing and fell to the floor, but still the blows kept coming. So did the kicks to his head and body. He tried to shield himself, bringing his arms up to cover his face. Then Georges lost consciousness. Khouri grabbed a hose tap from a sink and used it to soak Georges in water to wake him up, but then Khouri decided it was time to take a break – he was hungry – and he walked out of the kitchen to order food.

'What kind of person orders food in the middle of a vicious assault as though it is nothing out of the ordinary?' the prosecutor,

Björn Frithiof, would later ask me rhetorically. 'It says something about what kind of man Khouri is.'

As Georges stood up, the remaining men tried to take his phone, and when he protested Travolta took aim and head-butted him. He was dizzy and pain was shooting through his skull. Georges could feel a cut in his mouth.

Outside, his brother had managed to get ahold of another phone – he never explained how he'd shaken off The Torpedo – and sent a message to Georges trying to find out if he was okay. He got a reply, but had a feeling that someone else was using Georges's phone. And he was none the wiser as to where he could find Georges to help him.

In the kitchen, a chef walked in. He was taken by surprise by the gaggle of men having taken up residence in his kitchen, and noticed that one of the young men had swelling in his face. Then Khouri returned, allowing the chef to later identify him from a selection of police line-up photos – 'That one, the tall one.'

The men left his kitchen, heading for the garage where they forced Georges into the back seat of Khouri's Merc. They drove south, home to Södertälje. By leaving his phone on – savvy criminals know to turn them off when committing a crime – one of the suspects left a perfect trail of crumbs that would allow the police to reconstruct his movements. For anyone familiar with the names of Stockholm's southern suburbs, the location of the phone masts connecting to his mobile would paint a glaringly obvious picture of the entourage heading from Heron City straight to their victim's home. Further and further south. Mast data doesn't lie.

When the victim's brother, who'd failed to find him back at the mall, called Georges, the kidnappers allowed Georges to pick up the phone to say that everything was fine. His brother knew that he was lying.

For each kilometre the gang put behind them, their hostage's sense of panic rose. And it got worse when they arrived in Södertälje, where a small army of men – although some were too young to be called men – met up with them. One of them handed over an object that Khouri tucked into the waistband of his trousers. They had taken Georges home and forced him to call his parents who, not knowing what situation he had found himself in, threw down a house key so they could get in.

The Network grabbed the key and frogmarched Georges into the flat. As his parents let them in, one of Khouri's men forced the mother into the kitchen, making her stay put – a clear act of illegal coercion. They searched the entire house, looking for any spare phones that could be used to call the police.

In the living room, the stage was being set but it was theatre without any spectators, apart from Georges and his father, as The Network pulled the curtains shut to prevent the neighbours from seeing what was going on. Khouri sat down in front of Georges's father and pulled out a gun.

'You don't recognise me?' he asked. 'My name is Berno.'

Georges watched his father's face crumple in fear at the mention of the name he had heard so many times. Then Khouri cocked the gun and placed it on the table.

Khouri and his men repeated one and the same question, asking Georges over and over: 'Where are Dany's weapons?'

That The Network were asking about weapons indicated, the police woudl later tell me, that they were scared that Dany was planning to avenge the murders of his brothers. Convinced that Georges was storing weapons for Dany, Khouri and his men decided to look for themselves, forcing Georges to go down to the cellar.

They found nothing, so they marched Georges across the parking lot to the family's garage. Even as they walked, they kept hitting him from the sides and from behind, invisible fists peppering his path with stabs of pain. Once in the garage, Khouri's boys found a toolbox containing a saw: 'Should we take his ear off?' one asked Khouri.

The men kept telling Georges that actually they'd been nice to him, they'd treated him well given the circumstances. And Georges just had to help them find Dany, who'd gone underground: 'You've got two weeks to bring us Dany.'

As Khouri and the others again forced Georges into a car, Travolta, the jittery errand boy who'd head-butted Georges at Heron City, underlined how serious their threats were by pointing out that 'Khouri is a psychopath, which means that he keeps his word.'

When they at long last let Georges go, he went home and crawled into bed. He stayed there, silent, for days. His mother lifted the blanket to inspect the bruises across her son's neck and back, and along his arms. She took him to a doctor, who wrote in his journal:

A haematoma around the left eye, a small bleed on the conjuctiva of the same eye [...] a small injury on the eardrum of the left ear.

When the family reported the assault to the police, Georges's mother described his injuries, saying that 'it looked like monsters had hurt him'.

Goldsmith

A YEAR into his 7,000 kronor monthly payments to Khouri, Milad hit another low. He had an old outstanding debt to the goldsmith whom he'd borrowed money from back when The Network first demanded he pay protection money. Given the never-ending demands for money, Milad hadn't been able to repay him, and now that the goldsmith had passed away his family called and wanted the money back so they could pay for a decent funeral. Milad said he'd try, but later had to admit that he couldn't deliver.

The goldsmith's family tasked Khouri with getting the money back. In total, Milad would now have to pay 200,000 kronor.

Once the police had taken the goldsmith's son in for questioning, he denied that he'd sold the debt on to Khouri, or anyone else. The police didn't believe him, noting in their case file that the son had been 'polite and accommodating, but his alleged ignorance of a situation that should be clear to the eldest son in the family was neither truthful nor genuine. That was [our] resounding impression.'

'The explanation closest to hand is that he's afraid either to say too much or to risk being implicated,' the police concluded.

Even when the police showed him phone records proving he'd been in contact with one of Khouri's men – one call lasting 33 minutes – the goldsmith's son said, 'that's odd, I don't know how that could have happened'.

In Södertälje, Khouri's men gave Milad a deadline to pay, a Sunday like any other, about a year after that first murder in The Oasis that had triggered the turf war and led to the double murder.

On deadline day, Milad took his wife and daughter to have Sunday lunch with his parents. He told his parents nothing of the 8pm drop-off. He'd told Khouri's men that he had the money, but he'd been lying. He had no money to give them.

The sun set on the second-to-last day of a mild January, this winter not a scratch on the wolf winter of the previous year when the shootings had begun. There had been so much violence since.

Although in Milad's case, the violence had begun many years before the murders. He remembered it all: apart from the verbal threats, the casual name-dropping of Khouri's nickname, he had come home one evening to find bullet holes in his front door. And after he'd made sure that Khouri's middleman was sentenced for his role in the captive bolt pistol assault, someone had fired shots at Milad's car. A cycle of violence was the wrong way to describe it, it was an endless road. Milad hadn't been able to sleep, at times he hadn't been able to feed his family because he was so broke.

He stared down that endless road and decided that he couldn't take it any more. After lunch, Milad left his parents' home, and then left Södertälje. Khouri's men kept on calling him, Milad kept stalling, telling them that his car had broken down. That he was delayed, he didn't know for how long, but he promised that he would meet them soon, yes, back home in Södertälje, he promised, just another half an hour, at most 45 minutes, okay, see you soon.

Then Milad turned off his phone for good.

When his pursuers realised that their prey had slipped the net, they sniffed the air for fresh meat and found an easy target. They contacted Milad's brother, the manager of the café known as The Parrot. If Milad wouldn't pay his debts, his brother would. He wouldn't be given a choice.

'I have nothing to do with this,' Milad's brother protested over the phone, 'but I swear on the cross that I don't know what this is about, do you understand me?'

'Milad told me that he'd have the money ready,' the man informed him.

'My brother's fallen on rough times,' he replied. 'I swear on the body of Christ that he doesn't have the money.'

The Network's phones were being tapped by the police, who were recording the call to Milad's brother. The Network contacted him several more times. During one call, the conversation hit a frantic note as the men kept on interrupting each other. There were expletives and insults – 'Fuck him in the eye, my cock in his mother, fuck his mother.'

In a subsequent call between two of Khouri's associates, who were comparing notes on how their extortion was going, the cussing kept going – 'Son of a whore, son of a slut, faggot.'

In the end, one of Khouri's men showed up at The Parrot and asked to speak with Milad's brother in private. He handed him a phone. Khouri, who was abroad, was waiting on the other end of the line.

'Do you know who I am?'

'Yes,' said Milad's brother.

'Don't say my name!' Khouri interrupted. 'You've got two days.'

'What do you mean, two days?'

'You've got two days – and don't interrupt me! You will find your brother and fetch him for me and pay 200,000. If not, you know what will happen to you, what has happened to other people before you.'

When Milad's brother understood how serious the situation had become, fear flooded his body. He started to shiver, his head hurt. He knew exactly what he was up against. As the evening grew late, he tried to keep up appearances, but one of his colleagues at the café saw that something was wrong.

'Let's close the café early, we need to talk,' his colleague told him. Once he had been debriefed, he said, 'You have to go to the police and tell them everything.'

'But you yourself have paid money to them,' Milad's brother countered. 'When your son had those problems with The Network a few years ago, you didn't go to the police.'

'I was worried about my family.'

'And I'm worried about my family,' he said. 'I can't go to the police and tell them what's happening.'

Black eye

THE BRUISES, the swelling, the damage to his eardrum … Georges had lay silent in his bed for days, his father telling him that they needed to go to the police and report what The Network had done. Their family could move and leave Södertälje behind, he told him, or he'd send Georges abroad, and he could support him financially.

Eight days after the kidnapping at Heron City and the repeated beatings, Georges had to go to the District Court to testify because the investigation into the drive-by had gone to trial. He was not a suspect, he had only sold the car that was later used by the gunmen. And thus he made his heavy-hearted way to the court building.

The police officers on duty noticed that something was wrong. One asked if that was a black eye turning yellow? Georges told her that he had fallen and hit himself.

The officers didn't buy his explanation. So they opened an investigation into 'perversion of justice' – which beating up a person who's about to testify falls under – and managed to secure security-camera footage from Heron City. Georges's kidnappers were visible on the tape, and the footage was good enough quality for the police to identify several of them.

To get a better picture of what had happened after Heron City, the police called in Georges's father who told them, 'I wanted to go to the police from day one. We swung back and forth, there was also this fear.'

Shortly after The Network had assaulted his son, the van he used for work had been destroyed in a fire. The police asked if someone could have set it on fire on purpose to take out revenge, or to send a message. 'It's hard to tell,' he answered. 'We live in the Ronna neighbourhood, cars burn every day. It is routine.'

Beirut

IN DECEMBER 2010, six months after the murders at The Oasis and about two months after he had kidnapped Georges from Heron City, Khouri landed at Rafik Hariri International Airport in Beirut. He travelled on a 'Foreigner's Passport' because Khouri was stateless, neither a citizen of Sweden nor Lebanon. Khouri had just recently got engaged to be married to his new girlfriend, Claudia, who had taken time off from work as a receptionist at a hair salon and joined him to spend all of January in Lebanon.

They'd brought their mothers along too. Khouri's mother spent most of her time visiting churches while the couple looked at places to live. When I later on ended up speaking to Khouri about the trip, we spoke about shopping for an expensive wedding dress. 'You know,' Khouri said, 'women don't want a man, they want three animals. A donkey to work and bring home the cash, a Jaguar in the garage, and a tiger in bed.'

'And you fit all three, I presume?'

A question provocative enough to earn me a 'well aren't you cheeky' smile from Khouri.

In Beirut, his fiancée never left his side – shopping, restaurants, visits with his uncle, time spent with Khouri's friend Elie, the one Eddie had attacked with a kebab skewer the year before.

When night fell they retreated to their lodgings. Claudia shared a room with their mothers. As the light faded over the Mediterranean, did Khouri suspect what was coming? That the prosecutor had issued a European Arrest Warrant with his name on it? Did Khouri know that he was a wanted man?

He sent his fiancée back home. Khouri was set to return to Europe soon after, too; he and Elie needed to wrap up some business. The business was with Milad, that little motherfucker of a snitch, who still owed them money.

Uncle Tony

AT HOME in Södertälje, Khouri's Uncle Tony found out what Khouri and his friends were up to, specifically that they were trying to force Milad's brother to pay the money.

Tony called one of Khouri's intermediates, a man called Gabi. Yet again, the police wiretap caught the conversation:

'Hi, Gabi, how are you?'

'Good, praise God.'

'Gabi, this business has to stop here and now! Milad's brother has nothing to do with this.'

In response, Gabi wound himself up into a long complicated 'he said, then he said' monologue, until Tony interrupted him.

'Milad is a devil and his brother doesn't know where he has gone to hide. What has he got to do with this?'

'I agree with you, uncle, I swear on the cross that I agree with you,' said Gabi, who had a thought … perhaps Tony could call Khouri directly, maybe Khouri would listen to his uncle?

'Oh dear Gabi, I don't want to call him from here to Beirut and end up in a conversation with me saying inappropriate things. Tell him that you're busy looking, that I will help Bahnan look for his brother Milad, and things will pass and cool down, and then we'll find a solution.'

'I will do everything I can, I swear on the cross,' said Gabi.

'Okay, and this Network, you should keep away from it for a little bit,' Tony cautioned.

'What, uncle?'

'This gang, I mean, you should stay away.'

In the end, Tony's uncharacteristic intervention was of no use, the debt still stood. Milad's brother had to cough up the money, which he did in painfully large instalments. He came up with 30,000 kronor, then another 50,000, and finally 40,000.

But 80,000 kronor was still outstanding. Which meant the feud was not over.

Uncle Tony grew ever more displeased, eventually speaking to the police: 'We don't live in a jungle with no rules. They're conspiring and trying to get Bahnan involved in something that he has nothing to do with. It's Milad who's the cause of this problem,' he told them, before complaining specifically about Khouri, whom he referred to as Berno. 'I have even told my nephew, "Don't set foot on the street where I live." He's not allowed to talk to me,' he said.

'Berno's mother and I are siblings, she's my sister. I've broken contact with her and she's not allowed in my home. I've built a wall. Berno grew up without a dad, without a real father figure to look up to. That's why things have turned out like this for him.'

Khouri's ever more frequent absences from Södertälje had made things worse, Uncle Tony argued, because as soon as he'd started to travel abroad for longer stretches of time, it had created a power vacuum. 'Berno had several right-hand men, that's the problem. Without him all these right hands became the boss all of a sudden, and were supposed to lead the others. Things actually became rather tumultuous. Everyone wanted to steal from everyone and everyone wanted to shoot each other.'

'I'm tired of my family. They don't listen. What you say goes in one ear and out the other. My other sister's son is also involved,' Tony said, referring to The Torpedo, and then mentioned that the man that'd been paralysed in the drive-by was a cousin of his. 'Nobody listens.'

Two years earlier Khouri had promised his uncle to toe the line. Khouri had lied. Or been unable to deliver. Yet despite his anger, Tony refused to place all the blame on his nephew – as he saw it, Dany Moussa had a lot to answer for.

'He brings with him trouble, problems, gangs, and Kurds to the left and right,' he said, in reference to the first murder victim, Mohaned, having been Kurdish.

'Berno and [Dany] are on the same set of scales,' the old man continued. 'It's the two of them balancing against each other. Dany and Berno used to be best friends, like brothers. Berno started to slide, and the problems started. They started to compete. Berno told Dany not to go get Kurds into the neighbourhood because we don't want trouble. But Dany went and got the Kurds.'

Then Tony told the police that Eddie was also to blame for the turf war, due to his and Dany's loan sharking. 'And when people couldn't afford to pay, they'd go fetch the Kurds to get the money back. The interest rates were extortionate. One time, I was sitting counting my cigarettes, and I saw Eddie in a new Mercedes, and I thought, "How the hell can he drive that kind of car?" Where's the money coming from?'

Wedding prep

BÜLENT ASLANOGLU – the man nicknamed 'The Godfather', the one who had visited Yaacoub's house with Dany to persuade Dany to leave the X-Team – had agreed to be Khouri's best man.

Wedding preparations were taking shape when Khouri's fiancée, in early February 2011, once again joined Khouri, this time travelling to Paris where his father lived – Khouri's old classmates had been right, his dad was not actually dead, but living in another country.

Khouri's presence in Paris set off alarm bells at Europol up in the Hague where the incoming piece of intelligence coincided with a visit from Bo Eliasson, a detective superintendent from Sweden's national police, who was involved in the investigation in The Network.

Eliasson, a handsome and somewhat dour policeman from the north of Sweden, had already formed a pretty clear impression of Khouri. The investigation so far had painted a picture of him as the undisputed leader of The Network.

'I don't think there's a "godfather" higher up that gives orders,' Eliasson said. 'But I think that maybe, and I underline that I'm saying *maybe*, they have taken on assignments from others who have more clout but aren't members of The Network.'

As befitted a detective in the middle of an investigation, and rather befitting the stereotype of Swedish northeners, Eliasson was quite taciturn when talking about the case.

Yet he did explain why the national police – at the time called 'Rikskrim' – was involved in a case that, at first glance, seemed so local and which was speerheaded by the county police in Stockholm. 'Because there are some persons, crimes, and money that move across borders, and Rikskrim has the best channels to act across borders,' he said, adding that they and 'Säpo', Sweden's intelligence agency, had access to more advanced investigation methods than county police did. Eliasson declined to explain what those methods were.

When news of Khouri's presence in Paris reached him, Eliasson and his Hague-based colleagues realised that the moment had come. Khouri couldn't be allowed to slip the net, not now after all the investigatory work, which Eliasson called 'methodical and extensive'.

He couldn't say if there had been one last piece of the jigsaw, if something specific had made the prosecutor issue the European Arrest Warrant. 'It's often a case of "the full picture as we see it now",' he noted.

Eliasson spoke to the Swedish desk at Europol, who in turn held a brief meeting with their French colleagues to set the arrest in motion.

Within a few days, Khouri and his fiancée were intercepted at Roissy Airport. He was detained, and she flew home alone. When the police asked Khouri why he'd been carrying more than 7,000 euros on him when he was arrested, he said, 'It's money for the wedding dress.'

While the arrest left Eliasson with a sense of a job well done, he didn't think catching Khouri was any cause for celebration.

'No,' he said. 'Because this entire case is just tragic.'

Bridesmaids

THE IMPORTANCE of lavish weddings in Aramean and Assyrian culture came to pop-cultural attention in Sweden with the 2011 reality TV series *Mitt stora feta syrianska bröllop* – *'My big fat Aramean wedding.'* The glamour made for easy watching, but Assyrian–Swedish politician Robert Hannah, at the time a rising star in the Liberal Party, told me he believed the cultural phenomenon could also be seen through a political lens. He credited what he called 'clan mentality' for the elaborate celebrations, and said the weddings provided a way to measure just how much of a clan mentality the families had.

'The more bridesmaids, the more clan mentality,' the young politician said. 'It's about the façade. The more bridesmaids you have, the more money you have, so the more bling you can be, the bigger ring you can buy your fiancée … it's about gold, about how much money you give to your relatives. We've kept our traditions from our home countries but it's as though it's been turned into some kind of deluxe variety here, as though it has accelerated.'

Having recently come out as a gay man, Hannah had had ample time to dissect some of his community's conservative views.

'And it's very macho in the way that you should be as masculine as possible,' Hannah continued. 'There are certain criteria to what a good man is, and they go like this: Beautiful wife, expensive car … in actual fact, your car should be nicer than your home, because where you live isn't as important as driving a Merc.'

He continued to talk about status: 'Being a football player gives more status than being a lawyer,' he continued. As Hannah had

196

studied law at university, he'd been lovingly given the nickname 'The Professor' by his family.

Hannah, an Assyrian from Gothenburg, did see some differences between the Assyrian and the Aramean communities, despite them living side by side. I was keen to hear his explanation, because for outsiders, such as myself, a concise explanation of the difference between the two groups had proved hard to come by. The local paper in Södertälje had gone as far as always writing the two community names together, with a slash – 'assyrier/syrianer'.

At one of the derbies, I had asked an Assyriska fan what the Syrianska FC fans were chanting on the other side of the turf. He hadn't really answered my question, instead stating with an irritated shrug, 'We're the same people!'

Hannah, however, said he saw some key differences between the groups. 'Compared to Assyrians, a huge clan mentality has developed among Arameans who stick together because everyone is family or related to one another,' he attempted as explanation. 'Even though we Assyrians are religious, our identity has as much to do with culture and nationalism and the religion is just one part of our identity.'

'Among Arameans, religion is the glue,' he continued. 'That's why you see those huge crosses, the tattoos, and it's funny because most of them don't go to church that often yet they wear huge fat crosses.'

'Most of them originally come from peasant communities in Turkey and they fled genocide and many of them ended up in Syria, others in Lebanon. So they're scarred from being a people that were subjected to genocide and to violence because they were Christians,' he said. 'You see the result in Sweden because they close ranks. It's of the utmost importance that you keep your identity alive and that you've got each other's backs, which is more important than having Swedish society's back.'

He summarised: 'You support each other, you help each other. You don't snitch.'

Lazy eye

'YOU CAN write as many books as you want,' Khouri wrote to me from his cell in response to my first letter. More letters from Khouri followed. I was already quite well read-up on the case, but he filled me in on how he'd been treated since his arrest. For example, one of the prosecutors had informed him that he was now suspected of an additional murder, not specifying which one, even though the investigators had not questioned him about that alleged crime. About the prosecutor he wrote:

'And then she doesn't have the intention to question Me! It isn't reasonable to make a person an official suspect for Murder, & not have any questions for the Suspect! They've breached My Rights as per the [European Convention of Human Rights], articles 5 & 6!'

In preparation for meeting Khouri in the detention centre, I had re-read all his letters, but once there, he told me he wouldn't talk. I didn't know where to go from here. We'd been given 20 minutes for our interview. So I just had to trust my own curiosity; which had become one of my own guiding principles in journalism because if I want to know more about something, then there are other people who want the same thing.

And for some reason, maybe because I'm a woman, I was very curious about his fiancée.

So an interview about three murders ended up being a conversation about the wedding dress they'd picked out in Beirut before his arrest.

'Elie Saab?' I asked, referring to the only Lebanese designer whose work I was familiar with.

'No. We did go to his house,' he said, and I assumed he might mean showroom rather than house but didn't interrupt. 'But my fiancée didn't like the dresses.'

'Why not?' I queried. 'I mean Saab has designed dresses for the Swedish Crown Princess.'

'Women want what they want,' he said calmly, as though it was a law of nature or an incontestable fact.

The couple had been looking for flats before the police arrested him. Giving him the benefit of the doubt, it had looked as though he was going to start over, turn over a new leaf. Not giving him the benefit of the doubt, his plans looked like a way to escape justice in Sweden after the turf war turned deadly.

In one of my letters, I had asked him why he wanted to leave Södertälje, and he'd written back that 'people should live where they belong'. A cryptic statement, although I knew, from a previous letter, that he considered Sweden to be a racist country and claimed that the police investigation was a way to harass an ethnic community.

It was one of my questions, what he meant about where people belong, that I'd brought with me, but our allotted 20 minutes were being eaten up by wedding chat. Khouri seemed to be relaxing somewhat in my company.

I've got a bad habit of closing my eyes when I ask a complicated question, which I at one point ended up doing, and when I opened them again, Khouri was no longer in front of me, having moved at what seemed like lightning speed across the room to the small wash basin where he was drinking water from a disposable cup. I got an eerie sense that he'd moved with supernatural speed, 'like a vampire', I thought to myself, and wondered if the fever I'd been suffering for days was playing tricks on me.

But my mind also wandered to a surveillance video showing Khouri speaking to a group of younger men, well, boys really, where it was clear that his long legs meant that he was built for speed. So he was fast, but probably not supernaturally so.

Khouri sat down again, and even though he had said he wouldn't talk, he was talking. I guess he must have been bored after spending such a long time in a cell. Who wouldn't be bored? Locked up while life goes on on the outside.

The investigation was growing and growing as the prosecution added charge after charge.

Yet Khouri was confident that the court would find him not guilty in the end.

'And if they don't?' I asked.

Khouri looked at me with a steady gaze. One eye was borderline lazy, a droop to the lower lid, which added a cool insouciance to his demeanour.

'They will,' he said.

I glanced at the clock, our time was nearly up, but I was determined to squeeze in a few more questions. But which ones?

A declaration of love

AN INCIDENT took place outside the detention centre that the prosecution would come to cite as yet more proof of Khouri's leadership role in The Network. The Moussa family's lawyer called the stunt 'unbelievable'.

At first, when Khouri's fiancée paid regular visits, bringing him razors and a Bible, the couple didn't yet know that it would be months until he was charged. But for every passing week, their dreams of a new life in Beirut grew fainter, a mirage in the rear-view mirror.

The relationship had started to stall.

During one of her visits, Khouri mentioned he could see the corner of the local police station through his cell window, that she could stand there in between visits and wave to him.

The officers in the room with them – who never left Khouri's side during the visits – took note of the conversation. The police decided to keep an eye on the street outside Khouri's cell. Their vigilance soon paid off, because some of the younger members of The Network turned up. The police took photos of them and of Khouri in the window.

Khouri had prepared a handwritten sign in stark capital letters. As the bars on the window prevented him from making the entire sign visible, he had to reveal his message to the boys on the ground in segments:

'Let media,' the first row read.

'Write about,' the next line read as he shifted the sign, 'police dirty play.'

When the police passed the information on to the prosecutors, they filed it as evidence.

'Maybe [his fiancée] would just walk by and wave to him,' Frithiof said about receiving the piece of intel. 'The police had no way of knowing, they had to be on their toes. I believe they just wanted to check if there was going to be a simple declaration of love.'

None of the investigators were entirely surprised by the event. A quick scan of interrogation transcripts revealed to me that Khouri had grown ever more taciturn, aggressive even, during questioning.

He often told the police off for asking him 'irrelevant' questions. And at the end of interrogations, when the police must give a suspect the chance to approve the summary of what they had said during questioning, Khouri didn't play along.

'Do you accept this summary?' the police asked.

Khouri said nothing.

'Answer!' the officers barked.

'I don't accept anything,' Khouri said.

Eventually, Khouri was transferred from the detention centre in Stockholm. He ended up in the maximum-security facility 'Fenix', known simply as 'The Bunker'.

Fenix

THE ENGAGEMENT was eventually broken, and the wedding was off. Khouri was consigned to staring at the cell walls.

Whatever people in Södertälje thought about the Swedish justice system's lack of balls, this time, the investigators were playing hardball. The prosecution had asked the court to impose severe remand restrictions on Khouri, which, when granted, meant their prime suspect couldn't communicate with any other detained suspects while he awaited trial. In essence, it was the modern-day equivalent to being held incommunicado. After restrictions had been approved and put in place, his visits were monitored, as were his phone calls. The police read through all his letters.

'It has been so clear from the beginning that [none of the witnesses] dare to tell us anything. If we are to get people to talk we have to keep him locked up,' Frithiof, the prosecutor, explained.

It was not just Khouri. His cousin, 'The Torpedo', had restrictions imposed on him. 'You can't even phone your mother without someone listening in,' his lawyer, Jan Karlsson, pointed out.

But the prosecution were adamant they were justified in their restriction requests, which a judge had to approve once every two weeks.

'It would be enough for [The Torpedo] to make just one phone call,' Frithiof countered. 'Just knowing that he could communicate [with the outside world] would make a person ready to retract everything they had said.'

Frithiof and his colleagues didn't just need restrictions, his team needed time. As the investigation material swelled,

Aramean translators picked through the wiretapped conversations.

It wasn't just a question of resources, it was a question of patience and attention to detail in order to make the case against the suspects watertight. There was no deadline in sight, the work would have to take the time it needed, which meant that Khouri could not be allowed to speak with other suspects being held in their cells.

'This will take a long time, and the others could be set free and communicate messages for him,' Frithiof explained.

The judge approved each renewed application for restrictions.

'I'm in total isolation,' Khouri pointed out in a letter to me.

In international comparisons, Sweden had long used extensive restrictions and protracted pre-trial detention – a UN torture committee ended up criticising the system – but up until the investigation into The Network, it had usually been a matter of sitting in a cell for weeks or months, not years. And everything was pointing towards this case going on for several years, because if it went to trial it'd likely also then be passed on to the Appeals Court for a second round.

International criticism of the remand system aside, Frithiof stood by his decision, calling the use of restrictions 'one of the obvious keys to prove what we have to prove', by giving them time to amass evidence and witness statements.

Pre-trial detentions and restrictions also had their domestic critics. Olle Eriksson, the editor of *Filen– 'The File'* – a newspaper for inmates, had a thing or two to say about the matter.

At a café, the *Searching for Sugarman* soundtrack playing in the background, Eriksson showed up with his daughter; ahead of the interview, he gave her crayons and paper to keep her occupied. With her big eyes and white-blonde hair, she was the spitting image of her father.

Eriksson had just returned to Stockholm from interviewing an inmate, unrelated to Khouri's case, in one of the Fenix facilities – 'The Bunker' in criminal circles' common parlance.

'*Pappa*, I heard what you said, did you mention someone called Fenix?' the five-year-old queried.

'No, it's a prison,' he said matter-of-factly.

'But I've heard, at my other friend's house, that they said something about Fenix.'

'I'll tell you a little more about that later,' he said.

He handed her a carton of juice.

'Anyone who has kids knows how fundamental they are to your life,' he said. 'In Fenix, if someone wants to hug their kid during a visit, they need to apply for permission ahead of time.'

'*Pappa, pappa*, I dropped my orange juice,' his five-year-old interjected.

'Here, there's still some left in it,' he said, picking the carton up. 'Finish it if you want to.'

During his visit to Fenix, the barren and bewildering walk into the 'prison within a prison' had made him lose track of both time and direction. In the visiting room, the wardens had pointed out his chair. The inmate had been told to face him. There was a window. Through the bars Eriksson had been able to see the inside of the wall around The Bunker, and a slice of sky through a double-netting cover that made the outside area look like an aviary.

'Fenix is incredibly destructive. [The inmates] don't hesitate to use the word torture because they are so isolated,' Eriksson said.

When the Fenix system was introduced, the Prison Service had built three units – spread out over three separate prisons – with space for 72 prisoners in total. The system, Eriksson argued, had proved to be everything that a normal prison could be at its worst, but worse still. Former inmates Eriksson had spoken to said it was common to have just one bunkmate – some albeit restricted company. That Khouri was being detained in total social isolation was rare, perhaps even unique, he said, but Eriksson didn't have the statistics at hand.

'*Pappa, pappa*, what comes first in the alphabet, I or J?'

'I comes first, then J.'

'A B C D E F G,' the child started to hum, reaching as far as H before losing momentum.

Recreation was usually limited, Eriksson said, and the inmates returned to their cells at 8pm.

'Many people are broken by sitting there,' Eriksson said. 'Fenix is awful, it's extreme, it's like a bad American action film.'

Apart from social limitations, the long pre-trial detentions – one of Khouri's main gripes – was another issue.

'There is no upper limit for how long a person can be detained,' Eriksson explained.

'*Pappa* …'

'Sweden sticks out [internationally] by not having laws that regulate how long you can keep people in these extreme conditions, when all the research …'

'*Pappa!*'

'… shows how dangerous and destructive they are.'

'*PAPPA*, I'm hungry.'

'Do you want a cinnamon bun?'

'No … I think I want a chocolate ball.'

'Okay, let's order a chocolate ball.'

Tax

LOYALTY. The young Assyrian politician Robert Hannah was not afraid to say it, there were some Assyrians and Arameans who had allegiance only to their extended family; the Swedish state was an abstract concept at best, a thing to plunder at worst.

The prosecutor, as befitted a public servant, picked his words with more diplomacy.

'We know they have a fundamental distrust of the authorities, which is easy to understand, in a way, and I think it can take a generation or two before they let go of that,' said Frithiof.

'And it becomes more complicated if the kids don't attend school as much as they should and if they don't let Swedish culture in at all, then it's really difficult to explain why one should even bother to pay tax at all.'

An intelligence report entitled 'Serious and organised crime among criminal Arameans and Assyrians in Södertälje' ('*Grov och organiserad brottslighet bland kriminella syrianer och assyrier i Södertälje*') was being passed from one government agency to the next; in paper form only, according to my sources, as they couldn't risk a digital document being leaked as it contained names of the key players.

The police carried the report around like a secret weapon for each debriefing with the agencies and key social actors now roped in to help: among others the tax agency, the debt enforcement authority, customs and excise, the police financial crimes unit, border police, and the social benefits agency.

While the report did not leak, people started talking; even my beautician had heard from a friend of hers that the hairdressers' association had been asked to help; while I didn't double-check this information, I knew that the police believed beauty salons and other businesses that handle cash were being used to launder money.

The intelligence report had an ambitious scope, stretching back to the 1970s, when Assyrians and Arameans were forced to close ranks because their stores and cafés were targeted in attacks by 'raggare' – members of Sweden's greaser subculture. Which meant that the Assyrians and Arameans had to go on the defensive, and to stick together even more just to keep themselves safe.

While unclear if he read the actual report, a *Fokus* magazine reporter summarised the contents, noting that the report wound back the clock even further to explain the community's history:

To the Babylonian/Assyrian realm around the Euphrates and the Tigris a couple of thousand years before Christ, to [later become] a people living without a country that despite being a minority for millennia have managed to keep their identity, their religion. Subjected to persecution and genocide, still surviving as a people.

While the police and prosecution were not saying that all members of the community committed crime, they were saying that the culture of silence – still intact four decades after the first Assyrians and Arameans migrated to Sweden – permitted far too many to do so.

One aim of the newly created 'Operative Council', where the police and other state agencies compared notes once a week to draw up an action plan, was to bring all kinds of misdeed to the surface.

Once they were done with Khouri's gang, the police wanted to move on to investigate several suspected cases of welfare fraud. In Sweden, the municipalities pay for some services, including personal assistance and elder care, and Town Hall in Södertälje had expressed concern about rising costs.

Soon after the national government allowed private companies to enter the welfare sector, Södertälje's public servants and politicians noticed that the number of people applying for personal assistance at home was increasing. While new welfare companies, set up by local entrepreneurs, were expected to access new clients – as they could explain the welfare system to clients who had not understood that they were entitled to help, and often do so in the client's native language – Södertälje Town Hall thought the increase looked too big. And they forwarded their suspicions of fraud to the police.

Elitism

IN SÖDERTÄLJE, many people were growing weary of being associated with the mafia turf war and also, as migration to Sweden increased, with being held up by immigration critics as a poster child for failed integration. That was not to say that people downplayed the challenges of welcoming immigrants. Including just helping them find their footing socially.

In the early 2010s, a few years after the large number of Christian refugees arrived from Iraq, Assyriska's club director, Aydin Aho, told me that the football club had become a gateway for newly arrived immigrant children to make friends. And, he added, football could provide the children with positive role models. 'We know that a ten-year-old boy will listen more to his football coach than to his teachers, or to his mum and dad,' Aho said.

Aho and I met at the club house, tucked under the stands at the new arena; in the venue's common area, a group of men were having a 'fika', the Swedish word for a coffee break. There was not a woman in sight; the club did not have a top-league women's team, and fewer girls than boys in the junior teams.

'There's a tradition that girls should do some things and not do others, they shouldn't be outgoing and stuff like that, and especially when they reach a certain age,' Aho said by way of explanation. 'That's something we've had to battle, of course, and we see it every day.'

The club was founded the same year that the then two-year-old Aho came to Sweden with his family. For many new arrivals, football was a lifeline. That had been true then, and was still true.

'We're a huge club today,' Aho said. 'More than 550 girls and boys, which means that you're in touch with all the families and their day-to-day challenges, not just the youths but their families … and that means we have a huge responsibility to take care of these youngsters.'

The kids were adaptable, and learned about Swedish society fast, but their parents, in some circumstances, needed a bit more coaching. Almost all sports clubs in Sweden are run as civil-society associations – Assyriska FF is short for 'Assyriska fotbollsföreningen' and 'förening' simply means association. And these voluntary organisations rely on the children's parents to help out. Which, Aho pointed out, often came as a surprise to parents who had just moved there from the Middle East, where parenting was more *laissez-faire*.

'It's a fight, telling parents that they have to volunteer and drive the kids to matches. Or that they have to sell lottery tickets to help the club finances, they just don't get it,' Aho gave as examples.

'They don't really get what a "*förening*" is. They ask, "I have to give up two hours of my time?" and I think, well, how we view parenting is quite different in Sweden. We raise our children in one way, but in the Middle East kids are more independent,' he said. 'Their parents used to tell them to go out into the yard and play, and to come back when they wanted to go to bed, but here at the club we place demands on the parents because otherwise we can't make the club work.'

They had also placed demands on certain players. In 2010, promising talent Mikael Ishak told Aho and then coach Rikard Norling that he was going to drop out of school. Aho and Norling had put their heads together and decided to tell the 17-year-old that if he quit school, the club would kick him out.

Aho remembered Ishak's response: 'I'm gonna be a professional player now, I don't give a damn about this!' Then he had walked out, slamming the door in their faces. Aho and Norling had known that their hard stance was a gamble. The young player could, after all, just go and join another club that would let him play regardless of whether he had finished school or not. Their gamble had paid off.

'The day after, Mikael came back and apologised. We signed a contract, then we helped him get into the senior high school we've got here [in Södertälje] that has a sports-focussed curriculum.'

Ishak would end up a pro in Italy, Germany and Denmark, eventually joining Sweden's national team. The club has taken pride in such success stories and also expressed pride at being available to so many children in town. By 2010, their youngest members were just six years old. 'Everyone is welcome, you don't have to be good. If you're in a team, everyone gets to play equally, we're not elitist at all,' Aho said.

Passion

ONE PERSON who very much wanted Assyriska to be more elitist was Conny Chamas, who as a boy had come to idolise Eddie after falling in love with 'the national team'. As a teenager, Chamas had trained briefly with Assyriska, but only grumbled about it looking back. Especially about one of his team-mates who, according to him, shouldn't have been allowed to play at all. 'I don't know how many matches we lost because of him,' Chamas complained. 'That guy in my team, he was really not fit, I mean, he was *really* overweight, and he got to play every match, every minute because his dad was on the board.'

While the club chief had said with pride that the club was not elitist – fast-tracking the talents only when the kids had turned 13 – Chamas yearned for the club to produce more stars. Nepotism, which he saw it as, wouldn't help them do that.

'It was really frustrating that the rest of us had to share the match time that was left over,' he remembered.

After just a year in the Assyriska youth team, Chamas had left, but he could never be rid of his love for Assyriska. Even now their recruitments annoyed him. 'They've started to buy non-Assyrian players. Why don't they use [the money] to get the best coaches and nurture the talents properly from the ground up instead?' he said.

Eddie was a good example of how good the local players could be. Chamas also pointed to Kennedy Bakirçioglü, who played for Hammarby, Ajax and Racing Santander, and whose portrait was later added to the Famous Swedes gallery at Stockholm Arlanda International Airport.

'They've started to buy in new players instead of investing in the players they have,' Chamas told me. 'Assyrians have a passion that is unparalleled. Few clubs can match that passion, and if you can harness that passion earlier on ... look at Kennedy, there could be an unlimited number of Kennedys.'

Girl germs

THE RULES of the game, when it comes to journalism, were as far as I saw it pretty straightforward. Such as explaining that everything's on record unless specifically stating otherwise. Before seeing Khouri, I had tried to lay down these rules with him.

When he had called me the first time, I first had to accept the call. Over the faint line, a prison warden had informed me, 'You have a phone call from Bernard Khouri at Kronoberg Detention Centre' – he'd been moved from Fenix to The Crown ahead of trial.

After a few prelim questions, Khouri had laughed at my offer to talk *off the record*, saying there was no such thing.

So when we sat there in the cell at The Crown – me looking at the clock to note how many minutes were left – I tried to memorise every single thing he was saying so I could put it in print. During our first quarter-hour conversation, his body language had changed. At first he'd seemed almost delighted to speak with a new person, and he'd sat facing me full-on, leaning forward across the table, but after talking about his fiancée, the drive-by, and the 'follow fucking orders' quote – he had started to turn his body away from me. As though he was taking shelter.

Did he feel he was talking too much? At first his knees had faced more towards the police sitting to the side on the narrow single bed than towards me (one of the cops had fallen asleep). Now he sat with his arms defensively crossed.

When I coughed, he shot his chair away from me with exaggerated urgency, exclaiming 'girl germs' – an ironic imitation of the middle-school riff uttered by boys scared of getting too close to girls. Irony that might have been charming if one could ignore the crimes Khouri stood accused of.

A thought struck me: with his theatrical bent, he would have been much better off in life as a stage actor than as a gangster – imagine his Othello – than here in this tiny cell, ready to fight for his freedom in the impending trial. But instead of going to auditions he was stuck there in his cell holding auditions for journalists – which reporter could help him be found not guilty? He was vetting us.

When the wardens outside at last opened the door, the stout woman in her 40s, who had ushered me here 20 minutes before, told us that time was up. She and the other warden, the tiny and quiet man who'd plodded alongside us on my way to Khouri's cell, led me out of the room. I was still coughing, and I could feel my temperature rising. On arrival at the lift, after coughing and coughing, I cracked a feeble joke that all writers had tuberculosis.

'We don't have tuberculosis in Sweden,' the man said softly – his first words to me – with an accent that revealed he had Finnish heritage.

His colleague retorted: 'I think there are one or two people locked up in this building who *do* have tuberculosis.'

Her comment could be interpreted in one of two ways: either the class aspect of crime meant prisons weren't much different from the poor houses of old with all their attendant health problems, or that, given that immigrants were over-represented in the crime stats, some of the people locked up there might have brought tuberculosis from abroad. I didn't ask because I just wanted to get out of the detention centre.

Thankfully, the warden leant forward to hit the lift button. Reversing my steps from cell to reception, grabbing my things from the locker, I stepped outside and found a restaurant where I feverishly wrote down everything from the interview. It wouldn't be verbatim, as quotes should be, but I'd memorised everything I could.

Exile

SILENCE HAS many faces, but when a woman chooses 'the wrong man' she is not punished with silence, she's punished with gossip. Even though the engagement was off, Khouri's ex-fiancée couldn't shake her past, saying so herself to me over Facebook Messenger when I asked her to give me an interview. 'I'm so tired of being associated with him, I only knew him for a few months,' she wrote, annoyed that I'd reached out to her.

She had left the country. Why was a topic of gossip in town. 'Her father told me she's off the marriage market,' a friend of her family divulged. 'Nobody dares go near her because even with Khouri locked up they are frightened he will hurt them.'

In my last attempt to get her to speak with me, I mentioned what the family friend had said. She had, so far, been both upset and irritated with me, as I was just another person in the long line of people who'd brought up Khouri, and she wanted to be left alone.

'What do I get out of talking to you?' she asked.

'Nothing,' I replied, 'apart from giving your side of the story.'

That didn't sway her. But that question stuck in my mind, because I had heard it so many times … what's in it for me?

One of the younger men who'd been arrested for his role in kidnapping Georges at Heron City asked me, 'Whose side are you on?' When I said 'no one's' he said he wouldn't talk about his friends, but might consider talking about being detained with the same incommunicado restrictions as Khouri.

While 'What's in it for me?' wasn't something I'd been asked only in Södertälje, I had often heard another one-liner unique in

Södertälje: 'The Network is old news.' The fiancée told me so, and, when reaching out to Aramean acquaintances to ask for their opinion on the investigation into The Network, one told me to go write about 'persecution in the Middle East instead', AKA do something worthwhile with your journalism, focus on something important. While I thought that logic was invalid, because I was neither a foreign correspondent nor a Middle East expert, I didn't press the issue. And I understood that the unwillingness to speak with me about The Network in part stemmed from the fear that the entire Aramean community would be tarnished by their crimes, from the worry that an investigation with such an emphasis on one ethnicity would open the floodgates to generalise about all its members.

So I was just another journalist focussing on the 'wrong things'.

Perhaps trying to get Khouri's fiancée to speak with me was a brilliant example of focussing on the wrong things, but if I wanted to know more about her, so would others. She told me once and for all that there would be no interview. My curiosity didn't wane, so I browsed her social media accounts. Shopping at Michael Kors, glamorous parties. The photos revealed an Instagram-beautiful blonde with big eyes and tiny waist. 'Fake tits,' one of her old classmates told me *en passant*. In one picture, a Chihuahua was nestled in her bare-legged lap. In another she sucked a finger with a Lolita gaze.

But there weren't just party and glamour pictures. As the Arab Spring descended into chaos, and the persecution in her community's old countries worsened, she posted a picture with the Arabic letter ن – an N that stands for Nazarenes in reference to Christians as Jesus Christ's family came from Nazareth.

The dream was of a better future for her people, but what about her future?

'Maybe,' the family friend continued, 'she could marry some blue-eyed naïve Swedish boy who doesn't know who Khouri is.'

Mafia wives

'THEIR WOMEN are the worst!' exclaimed Oritha when we met. 'They've never worked a day, they've done nothing. They walk around with the [most expensive] stuff while I work like an animal and can only afford a brand-label pair of jeans once every four years.'

Oritha lifted an eyebrow to accentuate her disgust. 'And then they come along and take everything from you.'

Oritha – a pretty and tiny woman who in winter was swallowed up by her down jacket – was no stranger to make-up, but she felt no mafia-wife need to always leave the house looking a million dollars. 'In my eyes, their women just look so cheap,' she said. 'I want to tell them, "You buy your make-up with other people's money, other people's savings that they worked hard to earn so they can take care of their children. You feed your children with other people's money!"'

The working mother-of-three said that the women of her generation had no excuse to stay home with the kids. 'Get a job!' she hollered, continuing her monologue against the mafia wives.

'I've worked for more than ten years, I've paid everything myself, my car, my house, my furniture. Some people think that being a housewife is such a nice thing, but eh … No!'

The pursuit of nice material things irked her when it went over the top, and she said that many Arameans in Södertälje were obsessed with putting their wealth on display. 'Look at my car! Look at my house! Look at how rich we are!' she ranted. 'My family is better than yours!'

To be fair, I thought to myself as she continued, quite a lot of people like nice things, but I didn't interrupt as she was on a money-quote roll.

'The only thing they care about is money and filling their houses with stuff,' she wrapped up. 'And the mafia wives, they're the worst!'

Embassy

DESPITE KHOURI having been arrested, his business had taken care of itself in the custodial hands of his cousin in the wheelchair, Sherbel Said, who had taken it upon himself to get Milad's money back. Said met with Milad's brother, Bahnan, and found out that their mother still owned property in Syria. The brothers would have to sell it. That would bring in enough money to settle Milad's debt. Again, a deadline was set.

A few days later, an older man with ties to The Network accompanied Bahnan to the Syrian embassy in Stockholm. A notary transferred the right of sale to Bahnan, who then flew into Aleppo in late March 2011, travelling on from there to the town of Qamishli where he sold the flat, below market value, to clear his brother's debt.

When Bahnan returned to Sweden on 4 April – a year after the drive-by shooting in Södertälje – the money transfer had yet to go through so in haste he borrowed 13,000 kronor from a friend, making up the remaining 17,000 with his own money. That made 30,000, allowing him to pay the first instalment. Then as the money from the flat came, he made further payments.

But even though his brother was transferring tens of thousands of kronor to The Network, Milad, who'd gone into hiding, was weary. 'I knew even when we sold the flat that they would never leave us alone.' Milad had no trust in Khouri ever being satisfied.

'Even if you pay him so many millions, even if you want to kill yourself, even if you want to rob a bank, they don't care, [they say] just bring money.'

Milad was tired, and he told me that the older man who took his brother to the embassy, to get the notary signature, was once a friend of his. 'His mother, he can sell her for one krona, money is everything to him,' Milad said.

I had had a very brief chat with the man in question in another context; he stood close to me, invading my personal space in order to communicate in a whisper. I asked him about the rumour that he used to work for the *mukhabarat* as an informant for the Syrian government, back in Qamishli. The man just shook his head, then complained about the police investigation.

When I asked the lead detective, Gunnar Appelgren, about the *mukhabarat* rumour, he said he couldn't confirm it, but pointed out that whether or not it was true, just having that reputation would make others scared of him.

'But he's such a short and slight man,' I said, comparing the man in my mind to the imposing Khouri.

'When you have that kind of reputation, you don't need to be tall,' Appelgren countered. 'You don't even need to be violent because people still fear you.'

Despite the money that Milad's brother had already paid, there was 80,000 left; the family were given yet another deadline: 19 May at 4pm. The brothers reached breaking point. Bahnan went to speak with his parents and Milad also emerged from hiding to explain the situation to their family. They told their parents everything that had happened, with Milad's side of the story stretching back many years.

The brothers' decision started to take shape. This couldn't continue. Milad called a police officer he knew and said he wanted to file a complaint against Khouri. Within hours, officers picked Milad up and took him to county police headquarters on the Stockholm island of Kungsholmen.

After a first round of questioning, the police contacted the prosecutor, Björn Frithiof, and passed Milad's information on to him. A few phone calls later, it was decided to pick up the rest of Milad's family and put them in a safe house. Milad's brother and his family were also spirited away from Södertälje within 24 hours. They didn't know whether they'd ever again see their parents, who had been supportive of their decision to go to the police.

'They just said "Be careful",' Milad told me.

The brothers' decision gave the prosecution not one but two key witnesses, and not just that, their new witnesses gave them an insider view into the grey-loans market, The Network's bread and butter.

Bahnan explained to them how insidious the mafia were. 'You have to understand that everyone who lives in Södertälje lives with this so-called network every day,' he said. 'The Network works in Ronna, Geneta, and Hovsjö where many Arameans live. Whenever they show up, it's not one person but many, they always operate in a group, and everyone knows that they are running Khouri's errands.'

At times, Bahnan forced the police officers to turn off the microphone, giving them information that put him in danger, and he refused to talk about the double murder, saying only, 'I don't want to make more enemies in Södertälje. After the murders of Yaacoub and Eddie, everyone in Södertälje knows you have to turn to Khouri.'

Khouri had won the turf war. But when he was confronted with the accusations of usury, extortion and illegal threats of violence, he said 'no no no' and explained that he was a mediator, not a mob boss. 'I'm known for being modest,' Khouri told the police. 'If you have to pay but aren't able to, and you ask for another week, I say "No problem". You solve it in a peaceful way [...] you have to be a bit humane.'

When the police pressed him with questions about who his associates were, Khouri refused to answer, saying he didn't want to betray their trust.

When I recounted Khouri's description of himself to Milad, who'd no reason to consider him modest nor humane, Milad gave me one of those knowing 'Khouri's so deluded' smiles.

Fuck the law

TRAVOLTA, THE errand boy who had helped kidnap Georges from Heron City and then told him that Khouri was a psychopath who didn't issue empty threats, had added me on Facebook. He posted a link that caught my eye. It led to an article citing research about the effects of being held in custody long-term. Isolation, that Swedish remand restrictions have been likened to, could cause cognitive decline. The ability to concentrate and pay attention thus suffers, possibly affecting a suspect's ability to defend him- or herself in court, the article said.

Travolta had posted the link with a short comment, 'FTL and the rest of the justice system who are torturing my brothers.' FTL stands for 'fuck the law'.

Khouri's lawyer, Fredrik Ungerfält, pointed out that Swedish prosecutors apply for and are granted remand restrictions far more often than their colleagues abroad. 'Why can the rest of Europe make do without restrictions?' asked Ungerfält, who was based in the port city of Gothenburg on the west coast. 'There's a saying in Gothenburg that it's easier to be remanded with restrictions than to find good prawns.'

Frithiof, the prosecutor, defended his decision to repeatedly request restrictions. When they started the case, the prosecutors had nowhere near enough evidence to go on. 'We needed a lot more,' Frithiof said. 'When it came to the murders the case was quite weak at the start. A lot of the evidence pointed towards these dangerous individuals, and we noticed how scared people were [of testifying].'

When the police had started making more arrests, putting not just Khouri in a detention cell, the prosecution had hoped that maybe people would start to talk. Frithiof admitted he hadn't been sure at first if he and his colleagues could tie the case together. Yet against all odds, the pieces had started to fall in place.

When Georges had showed up at the drive-by trial, when the police officers had spotted his bruises from being beaten up by The Network, it had given the investigators another lead to follow up. 'We knew he'd been the victim of crime, the police saw he had a huge black eye when he came to testify. We started to secure evidence, such as the CCTV from Heron City,' Frithiof explained.

When Georges had finally decided to file a report about the kidnapping and beating, he told them that Khouri had called him a 'cunt' and a 'dog' on that evening.

'Khouri hit me the hardest,' Georges told the police, who also asked his father to speak with them about what he knew. They showed his father a series of pictures, asking if he recognised any of the men: 'No. No. No. No. No,' he replied as he went through the first five pictures. Then they hit upon picture number six.

'Yes, I know him, I think that's Khouri. When he came to [our home] he had long hair and a long coat,' Georges's father said.

Armed with this new knowledge, the police brought up the incident with The Torpedo, who was by then also in custody. The transcript of the interrogation ended up looking like a parody of hardened criminals' attitude towards law enforcement:

Do you have any knowledge of the event at Heron City on 3 October 2010?
No comment.
Which mobile phone number were you using at that time?
No comment
Did you have mobile number 073-7356079?
No comment.
This number was wiretapped. Have you been informed of that?

That it was wired?

Are you aware of this?

Yes, Frithiof gave me a list.

We're gonna listen to some of the conversations later during questioning.

No comment.

Do you know Georges? He's the injured party.

No comment.

Do you know this man [the officer holds up picture of Georges]? How old is he?

I don't know.

Do you recognise Georges?

No comment.

[Police officer holds up picture of Georges's brother, who had claimed The Torpedo frisked him]

No comment.

Do you recognise him?

No comment.

[...]

Were you at Heron City on 3 October 2010?

No comment.

[...]

Who were you with around 8:30pm that Sunday night?

No comment.

There were a large number of people there from the 'Södertälje Network'. If you were there do you want to tell ...

No comment.

Was Bernard Khouri there?

No comment.

Regardless of the suspects' unwillingness to talk about that evening, there were parts of Georges's statements that proved to be invaluable to the prosecution – including their attempt to pin the double murder on Khouri. 'It's a jigsaw puzzle,' Frithiof said. 'Different parts [of the case] started to bleed into each other, such as the kidnapping when they threaten Georges and say stuff such as "Like what we did to the Moussa brothers".'

'The names [Georges gave us] fit the information we already had. That's when I felt that we were on the right track.'

In the end, Georges tried to pull out of the case. He sent a text message to one of the police officers he was in touch with.

Hej mickael i cant face testifying because i know how my people how they work when it comes to revenge of that kind i have so much anxiety over this and worried about my family because we have been threatened already so i'm asking you to close down my testimony [...] I'm asking you to take this into consideration kind regards, GEORGE [sic]

At that point, however, Georges was far from alone in having spoken to the police. So while he was valuable to the case, there were others who were equally valuable. Frithiof mentioned Milad and his brother. 'They'd reached a point where it didn't matter which road they went down because they were doomed either way. For us it was an ice-breaker because it taught us how The Network operated,' Frithiof said. 'We had been told they made money off aggravated extortion, that it was the foundation of their business, but [after speaking to Milad and his brother] we knew how it was done.'

Finally, they had Oritha, who had refused to back down even when her parents and brother had tried to retract their statements to the police. Frithiof described her as 'the only one left standing', and said she had given them 'good information that was important to the double murder, about how [The Network] stored and transported weapons.'

As for Appelgren, the lead detective, he called Oritha 'an extraordinary woman' and praised her courage and determination. Not least in the face of her family not wanting her to testify. Oritha told me that her brother was furious with her, and they'd had fights where they were standing inches from each other shouting. She had no intention of budging.

And she didn't budge, not even when the police told her they could not guarantee her safety if she stayed in Södertälje. If she decided to move, they would help her.

As simply as Oritha could, she explained what was going on to her eldest son, Leon, who communicated to her that he was worried about her, but not worried he would get hurt. Leon was a fighter too, he was still alive even though the doctors had warned Oritha that his illness meant he was not likely to survive childhood.

Leon communicated to Oritha that despite his worries for her safety, he wanted her to stand tall and do what was right.

No vodka

WITH KHOURI behind bars, things had started to change in Södertälje. The police told the media they were starting to see a drop in crime.

Other things had changed too in poker whiz-kid Philip's beloved gambling world; but not for the better and Philip was no longer a kid. He again brought up how, 'Nowadays the clubs are full of 16-year-olds, they're members of different gangs, they shout insults about each other's mothers, insult each other's gangs, and I don't know what else.'

While no longer fresh off the block, I thought he was rather young to sound like a grumpy old man, but then Philip had already used up so many of his nine lives. He had survived his use of drugs and the booze, he had survived that night at The Oasis when he had fled from the gunmen. A ricochet had injured one of the other witnesses and it had just been providence that saved Philip and the others from being hurt as bullets flew through the air.

It was a clear-eyed and healthier-looking Philip who showed up to our interview. And he was no longer fat. 'No vodka,' he said to explain his weight loss. 'My girlfriend started to get worried, she said I was getting aggressive, something had to change.' So he had gotten clean, got professional help. Yet still he missed gambling.

'I know I was technically a criminal, hosting underworld gambling events is illegal. But now it's a different game, these kids think that being a criminal will make them rich.'

Although he was glad he had given it up, he was nostalgic, and still insisted that he, when he was a gambling host, had provided a public service. Philip might have had a point. Whatever one wanted to call Philip – criminal, addict, gambler – he had offered a place for people, mostly men, to vent the frustrations of the day.

Even the small-fry gamblers, they too had had a need and a place to socialise, he pointed out, a place to let the continuous flip of cards soothe them. 'Where are people supposed to go?' he said. 'They're gonna end up loitering on the streets, there will be more robberies, people are gonna gamble at home in front of the kids who won't be able to sleep, there will be problems with people running up and down the stairwells.'

And there was that other thing that had kept him gambling for so many years. That it was just so much fun, that it erased every worry; better than drugs, better than sex.

'What do you think about when you're playing cards?' he asked. 'Nothing, except the cards. So if you've got problems, it's a good way to sit down and relax, you give your brain a break. People could die right next to you and you wouldn't notice.'

But then someone did die, right next to him, and he did notice, because it broke his heart. 'I loved Yaacoub as a brother,' he said.

He wouldn't talk about the case but did say the police wouldn't be able to keep Khouri locked up forever. 'They have nothing on him,' he said.

Vilified

ÖZCAN KALDOYO, a commentator on Assyria TV, had always been an insistent yet gentle critic of his own community, not least the churches because he thought they had too much say over people's private lives.

A quick example, that churches were still mediating divorces around the time of the turf war. 'There's a document they use,' he explained, 'in which every question probes the wife's responsibility for the breakdown of the marriage. "Did she cheat? Did she fail her duties?" and so on.' The husbands weren't subjected to the same questioning, he told me, calling the question sheet 'sexist'.

For many years, long before the double murder, Kaldoyo had encouraged his friends and neighbours to go to the police and report usury, extortion and threats, but they'd always pulled out in the end. You couldn't wipe out a culture of minding your own business overnight, Kaldoyo told me.

'Those who have had their souls stolen are not able to make choices, nor to make evaluations or judgements,' he said.

And many thought the police couldn't do anything anyway, so why bother filing a report. And another deterrent was Sweden's short prison sentences. Better to pay up shut up, and then turn your face up to the sky and pray to God that The Network went away.

One morning, facing a busy day as usual, Kaldoyo opened *Dagens Nyheter*, Sweden's largest daily newspaper, and stumbled upon an op-ed written by Stockholm County Police Chief Carin Götblad.

In Södertälje, organised crime has become established across [all scales] of criminality. Big sums of money go into circulation in connection with property and business deals. This operation includes murder, extortion, assault, drug smuggling, refugee smuggling, money laundering, tax crimes and much else.

But she was not talking generally about Södertälje, she had singled out the Aramean/Assyrian community. The text soon made Kaldoyo's blood boil. He couldn't shake the feeling that she equated his entire community with criminals. He continued reading.

Götblad's text explained why so many different state agencies were involved in tackling the situation, and pleaded for help from politicians:

Lawmakers should also consider whether [it should be possible] to confiscate any possessions acquired through criminal activity. It's reasonable that the tax agency ask a person who lives in a palatial house but declares barely any income to explain the situation.

Kaldoyo was not the only one to feel singled out. A local Södertälje politician told me, 'I have friends who live in [those palatial houses], and they felt vilified.'

Götblad's text continued:

The worst kind of organised crime is when a parallel [social] structure is established, with [its own] laws, a separate taxation system, a separate justice system including sentencing and punishment.

She mentioned torture, attempts to pervert the course of justice, threats against public servants, police officers' private cars being vandalised, the intelligence the police were gathering about suspected drug smuggling, refugee smuggling, money laundering, tax evasion …

There were even suspicions of corruption at the Town Hall, she pointed out in the text, with cases where fees or fines had mysteriously been taken off the books. Senior public servants had asked independent auditors to go through the records because the Town Hall no longer trusted all its staff.

The op-ed left Kaldoyo with mixed feelings. He was grateful that the police were tackling these parallel structures, but the wording of the text made him ill at ease.

Kaldoyo was not naïve; he was well acquainted with his town's woes, and disliked profoundly the disinclination to get the police involved. And he half-joked that the favourite pastime of anyone from the Middle East, irrespective of religion, was never to take responsibility for anything – the grown-up version of the young Bülent Aslanoglu shrieking 'I wasn't here!' when a teacher caught him red-handed scrawling 'Scarface' on the walls of the nearby school.

Benzo

AS THE police had stepped up the fight against The Network, its leader was stepping up his rhetoric about the police in letters to me. They were trying to frame him, he said, and brought up the whole incident with him telling his fiancée to wave at him from the street outside his cell. At a later date, once Khouri realised things were not going his way, he wrote an 80-page letter of fury addressed to the court judges. He wrote about the officers who had monitored his fiancée's visit and who had then handed the information over to the prosecutor:

It was entrapment. The police could have told us, 'That's not allowed'. Instead, they help us by giving my girlfriend instructions on how to get [to that spot], they also give her the street address.

In his letters to me, he said it was a case of miscarriage of justice from start to finish. He accused Frithiof of being a 'kamikaze' prosecutor who would end up sabotaging his own career by not playing by the rules. The case was a 'parody', he wrote, adding that the prosecutor 'won't even look me in the eye because he is ashamed'. He continued:

There is a lot of political prestige connected to this case, and a lot of prestige for the police, who have hated me since the early 1990s. I've fought and assaulted them several times and in 2001–02 I was even charged and convicted of attempted murder/aggravated assault! They shot at me out in the open, but I'm the one who was convicted!

I checked the dates, and they corresponded with the incident outside the furniture store, many years before, when he had trapped a police officer by the arm, by rolling up his car window, and then dragged him about 200 metres.

Khouri's letter went on to lambast the justice minister, Beatrice Ask. 'That hairdresser Beatrice Ask has poured money over the police and wants to make an example out of this case,' he wrote.

Chief among his criticism, Khouri was furious at being locked up ahead of the trial, and being locked up with 'remand restrictions' that limited his ability to communicate with friends and family.

He compared his treatment to an infamous miscarriage of justice: the case of self-professed 'cannibal serial killer' Thomas Quick. Quick had confessed to a string of heinous murders, but several years after being convicted he claimed that heavy medication, including Benzodiazepines or 'Benzos', had so impaired his judgment at the time that he had confessed to crimes he had never committed. As there had been no strong forensic evidence against him, retracting the confessions was enough for him to be set free.

While nothing like Khouri's case, Khouri took it up as an example that miscarriages of justice had happened in the past.

Parts of the case against me are more dirty even than the Quick case. I usually say that with Quick, they used Benzos to keep the lid on, & in this case, it's [remand] Restrictions.

Lunch boxes

ON A Wednesday evening in September 2011, more than a year after Khouri's visit to her parents' house, Oritha received a phone call. The person on the other end of the line kept it brief. This was business, after all; brevity saved time and time was money. The man told her to back out of testifying in the upcoming trial, to retract all her accusations, because if she didn't – the man rattled the repercussions like a simple to-do list – they would kill her brother, place a bomb in her parents' house and take out her husband.

There were rumours that The Network believed her testimony and her testimony alone was the lynchpin of the police investigation, that without her testimony, the case against them would fall apart like a house of cards.

When Oritha told the police about the phone call, they assigned a security detail to the flat. Personal-protection officers showed up at her front door. They came carrying guns. And they brought lunch boxes too. From then on, whenever she came home, an officer bobbed their head out of the living-room door to check who it was. They asked her to please knock first, so they'd be expecting her and not have to spring into action every time the door opened to check if any bad guys were incoming.

'It's over the top,' she told me, although she credited the police for not being obtrusive. 'Even when they're changing shifts, when the new batch turns up with their lunch boxes, they're not in the way.'

Leon's personal assistant, who had worked for the family for a long time, was happy that the police were finally protecting them.

Sometimes she also helped Oritha out with household chores and one day, as she tidied the kitchen, she saw that the bin needed emptying. She tied the plastic bag together, heaved it up from its container and walked towards the front door.

'Wait wait wait,' an officer blurted out.

Perplexed – had she done something wrong? – she turned to him.

'Let me check the stairwell before you go out,' he said.

She thought to herself 'it's like a movie', but didn't protest. She knew she should be grateful that the police were finally taking Oritha's situation seriously, but she also suspected something bigger was going on, that her employer's steely stance came at an opportune moment. Given the town's culture of silence, getting enough witnesses to step forward must have been a nightmare for the police. Lucky for them that Khouri's crew pushed Oritha too far.

The stairwell was clear, the officer let her out, and she turned the old metal handle to the disposal chute and chucked the refuse through the hole. The assistant wondered if the family were truly in danger. She didn't think so – because making threats was easy, but following up on them was another thing entirely – but over time she grew paranoid also about her own safety. As she got into her car, she started to look over her shoulder. Then glanced more times than usual in the rear-view mirror as she drove home to see if there was a car following her.

Whenever she accompanied Oritha's children to any kind of activity, the officers went with them. One evening they took Leon's younger brothers to Heron City.

Freestanding elevators carried them from the huge atrium to the upper level where there was a kids' playground. It was just above the jungle-themed entrance to the restaurant where Georges had been beaten up by The Network. At the top of the atrium, above the cinema, photos of film stars covered an entire wall, the faces of Brad Pitt and Marilyn Monroe gazing down on them. They weren't the only ones who were looking at her, Oritha and the kids, because the police officers caught the attention of passers-by. The assistant felt embarrassed, she was used to keeping a low profile and didn't like people staring at her, but the kids soon cheered her up.

That same month, a series of raids led to an additional four arrests across Södertälje. It had been six months since Khouri had been detained and by now the number of arrests had crept up to over a dozen.

Charges

ORITHA AND her family's information, along with Milad and his brother's statements, helped the prosecution secure enough evidence to take The Network to court.

On 16 November 2011, the prosecution brought charges against 17 defendants, including Khouri who was to stand trial for ordering the murders of Mohaned, Yaacoub and Eddie. Several but not all of the suspects were charged with aiding and abetting the murders at The Oasis, while others would be tried only for extortion.

The trial date was set for 22 November 2011.

While Khouri's defence lawyer dismissed all the evidence as circumstantial, the police had gathered so much of it that they believed the sheer weight would make up for the lack of a smoking gun – there was no one piece of evidence tying Khouri to The Oasis.

The burner phones used to coordinate the attack, according to the prosecution, were prime evidence. The police had proof that The Network had acquired pay-as-you-go sim cards, that had been handed out for free in a marketing drive in central Södertälje not long before the double murder. And the police had secured the telephone numbers of the sim cards.

Not long after the murders, the police had pulled Khouri's car over, in connection with another case, and found a plastic card that sim cards come in, which fitted one of the numbers.

As for the suspects' movements in the days leading up to the murders, their phones had connected to several local mobile masts.

To get a picture of where they had been at any given time, the police had used the triangulation method: as a mobile mast covers a circular area, just one mast can't pinpoint the phone's location (it could be north of the mast, or south, or anywhere within the circle's radius). But when a phone pings off several masts in quick succession, each mast's radius overlaps with the others, creating a Venn diagram – and within that overlap, the suspect's location becomes more precise.

The police had also spoken with witnesses who'd seen the get-away mopeds being stolen before the double murder. The get-away mopeds had also been found, but they had been torched, making much of the evidence worthless. However, forensics had retrieved the remnants of an unusual phone: the sturdy Ericsson R310, which, due to its unique chubby antenna, was referred to as 'the shark-fin phone'. Despite sending the phone to a specialist forensic team in Norway, the police couldn't get any information from it as it was too damaged. They could, however, see that one of the burner-phone sim cards had been used with a 'shark-fin phone', and that model, released many years before, was no longer popular. Its rarity meant the police considered the connection a strong, albeit circumstantial, piece of evidence.

The prosecution were also set to bring up that Khouri had returned to Sweden just 12 days before the double murder, which in their view could not be mere coincidence. To them, it was clear that he had come home to oversee the murder preparations.

There was also all the intel from the beat cops as well as the never-ending wiretap transcripts that showed, according to the prosecution, that The Network had a hierarchy – it was that kind of line of command that put the word 'organised' into the term 'organised crime' – with Khouri at the very top.

And, of course, yet more proof that Khouri was top dog – the police had the recording of him shouting at The Torpedo to 'follow fucking orders'.

The Moussas

DURING THIS drawn-out acquisition of evidence, the Moussa family had made changes to their legal counsel. The family's first lawyer had recused himself from the assignment due to a potential conflict of interest. The case was so big, the suspects so many, and Sweden so small, that it had been hard to find lawyers who were 100 per cent clear of potential bias.

They had been put in contact with Claes Borgström, the closest there was to a Swedish celebrity lawyer, and the lawyer representing one of the women who had accused Julian Assange of sex crimes. When it came to representing the Moussas in the upcoming trial against The Network, Borgström had come into the process rather late, but despite a fair deal of time having passed since the double murder, he had found that very little, if any, of the family's pain had subsided.

'They were still more or less in some kind of state of shock,' he recalled. 'It's part of my profession to meet people who are incredibly vulnerable. You come into contact with human tragedy of the kind of magnitude that most people will never encounter. Once, just as a parenthesis to this, I came home to my wife and said, "I feel like I wallow in human tragedies." That's one way to describe it, and it's not least true when it comes to the Moussa family.

'Furthermore, [the murders] took place at The Oasis, which was not [the brothers'] home, obviously, but a place where they felt at home and where they felt safe,' he continued. '[Their mother] went there at night just to spend time with her children, Yaacoub and Eddie spent a lot of time there, it was a gathering point. So it wasn't a murder out on the street, which would have been bad enough, but there, at The Oasis, it was almost like shooting them in their own home.'

'Did it matter that Yaacoub was the oldest?' I asked.

'Yes, of course it did,' he said. 'There's a strong sense of family. It's partly cultural. I mean, the importance of family exists in all cultures but I think that sense of family becomes more important when you belong to a smaller group in a society that has problems with segregation, which brings up questions such as, "How can I feel I have value? That I matter?" And one way to answer that is to find your place in these groups where you've already got a base.'

'Like a microcosm?' I suggested.

'Yes, and it's a good example of this hidden problem in Swedish society that the people who [migrate] here can't quite get into society properly.'

'The family seemed angry at the police just after the murders,' I pointed out.

'The family weren't given that much information in the beginning,' Borgström replied. 'But there were a lot of rumours, some of which were well founded – not all rumours are wrong. So quite early on they had quite a clear picture of who was responsible and there was an immense anger at the police for not doing anything.'

'Then later on, they realised that wasn't the case, that the investigation and the resources going into it were extremely extensive. But there is still a sense, and the police have hinted at this, that there could be more people involved, but they don't have enough [evidence] to press charges against them. So the [family] feel that some people got away with it.'

Borgström brought up the level of violence that made these murders stand out; that it wasn't just Eddie's career as a football player that made sure the murders made national newspaper headlines, but the way he was killed.

'It's sort of unusual, almost like a movie, this business of shooting someone 18 times,' Borgström said. 'It's horrendous. That type of violence is unusual in Sweden. It sounds more like some kind of drug war you'd associate with Colombia or something like that.'

'The police say that the hit was so complex,' I interjected, talking about the pre-planning involved, 'that someone with experience, like, for example, robbing value transport vans, was probably involved.'

'This wasn't an amateur job,' Borgström said. 'The people who did this had knowledge and experience. It was planned in advance, with these [get-away] mopeds. And no one leaked information ahead of time, which hints at a strong organisation and a strong respect [for the orchestrators].'

Unhappy

MILAD HAD once again been set adrift, not unlike the lonely years he had spent in the US – 'too far from my people' – before moving to Södertälje. Yet again he had to deal with his own isolation. As the head of investigation pointed out, witness protection had the same innate flaw as the system for dealing with schoolyard bullies, or with those whose lives had been laid to waste by domestic violence. You move the victim, not the attacker; effectively a sort of double punishment.

At least Milad had his wife and child with him. He had tried to keep his daughter out of things, he didn't tell her too much. She was too young, she had the right to a normal life. And he didn't want to scare her. He had enough fear for the two of them. Milad hadn't slept a full night, he said, since that day when the extortionist came into his office and demanded 27,000 kronor a month.

Some nights Milad lay awake thinking of all the people he knew back home who were victims of extortion. The entrepreneurs who had had to pay protection money or ended up owing money that needed to be repaid not just in full but with extortionate interest.

He counted them, family after family after family. One, two, three, he didn't stop there, the list grew ever longer. I asked him how long. At least 70 people, Milad told me.

When I told one of the beat cops about Milad's tally, he reacted with a certain aloof disbelief. It was easy, he countered, with the benefit of hindsight, to slap an extortion label on informal loans with high interest. He called Milad's estimate 'inflated'.

Which I then told Milad, who responded that the police still had no idea of the scale of the grey-loans market. When a late instalment can be paid in blood, what does it matter if the loan was 'informal' or not?

His number was 70, he stood by it. Yet despite such a high number, so few were now standing up alongside him and Bahnan to testify against Khouri. Even his brother was not happy about the upcoming trial, and felt he had been tricked by the police into taking the stand. He had just wanted help, to give them information off the record without sacrificing his entire life in Södertälje. But he, just like Milad, had had to move with his entire family.

The same was almost true for Milad. For while he didn't regret his decision to testify, he said it with little conviction. To me it sounded like a tired mantra, used to convince himself that he had no regrets, even though he had to face the daily sorrow of being separated, once again, from his family and his people.

'You know, I don't know how to tell you about the last few years. Yes, I get help from the police and I appreciate that … the first year, you know, when I was [in hiding], it was so bad, believe me. In the night-time, I never sleep.'

He still lived with the fear that one day The Network would catch up with them, and he swore he saw one of them on the road just recently, one of the ones that the police hadn't arrested. The one he thought was going to take over from Khouri if Khouri ended up being convicted. He prayed the man didn't see his face behind the rosary that hung from his rear-view mirror. Sweden is small. He'd like to move abroad, but Milad had no money left.

Milad tried not to think about Khouri, but sometimes he was there in his nightmares, the tall figure looming over him as he lay in bed, half-awake, sweating out his angst.

'Every time I feel tired I can't sleep. I think they will break my door down, I don't know from where they will know my address, [but] I know that kind of group, they are looking for someone all over, all over Sweden.'

His name was no longer Milad, but what did that matter when criminal gangs could pass his photo around until copies of his face had spread across Sweden? He'd never be safe.

'The psychologist gave me medicine to sleep, to relax, but I couldn't use it every day, because I don't want to feel tired and I don't like so much medicine. Sometimes I'm so tired I want to sleep a few hours, I use it.'

Milad was setting his hope on the court awarding him damages so that he could leave Sweden after the trial and start over. Yet Södertälje – his haven, his home, his family – still tugged at his heart. 'I cry sometimes, because, think of someone who is close to their family, it's not easy. We Arameans don't leave people behind in different countries; we bring everyone.'

Some nights, he told me, when the insomnia became too hard to bear, he would grow reckless, jump in the car and start to drive towards Södertälje. He'd always stop at a certain point. It was like a silent barrier, 100km away from his own private Jerusalem. No red Scania griffin to guide his path towards the turn-off, no iron girder bridge hanging over the canal, overlooking the docks and truck yards lying like a silent reminder to all that had made Södertälje into the thriving industrial town.

He couldn't go home so he relied on phone calls to his friends, always telling them nothing about his new town, instead asking them to tell him everything about his old town. That way, he could keep in touch and find out what was happening.

'How would you describe Södertälje today?' I asked him. Milad was quiet for a few seconds. 'I don't know what I'm going to tell you,' he said. 'I hate it so much now, it's not like before.'

'What's changed?' I asked.

'A lot of things. The people, they are not happy. I know many people, not all, but not only me, they're scared to do something. If you work and get money they try to break you, if you get a new car they try to break your new car, if you try to make your life better they don't let you, you have to pay. So how are you going to be happy?'

'Who are "they"?' I said.

'The people, the same people that I've got a problem with. Yeah, the gangsters,' he said, explaining that even now, with so many Network members having been arrested, his friends in Södertälje never bad-mouthed them. 'They still have a lot of people on the outside,' Milad said.

'So you think they're still in control?'

'Yeah.'

Princess Oritha

THE LONG, dark nights of winter had descended once again, turning urban areas into ghost towns. As soon as people got home from work, they stayed there; the streets emptied of life.

Oritha's mother, Jamila, hated the darkness. It made the burden of having to testify feel heavier – even with the suspects locked up and about to face trial, the fear of The Network lingered and soon her resolve started to crumble.

So did her husband's resolve. He'd come to regret that he ever reported Khouri for extorting them of hundreds of thousands of kronor.

In the run-up to the trial, the police kept in touch with Oritha's parents, in part to make sure they were still on course to testify despite their fears. After a phone call with Oritha's father, Samir, the police filed an official memo:

10 November 2011: Samir Chabo called and said he wanted to 'withdraw' his complaint. Chabo says he doesn't want to get involved and what he has [previously] said isn't correct [...] Chabo did not want to say why he gave the information he gave and then he said that he'd like the police to come visit him at home to talk more. This information has been forwarded to relevant officers on the case for further action.

Another internal police memo, filed five days later:

The married couple Samir Chabo and Jamila Marraha and their son Hedro Chabo have several times asked that the complaint they filed and the questions they answered 'be removed'[...] They will not take part in a trial and they will not stand for the information they have given during questioning. Hedro claims that most of what he said the two times we questioned him was a lie.

Oritha was still living in Södertälje with her children, despite the threatening phone call two months earlier, but as the trial neared the police were getting ready to move her to a secret location.

Oritha spent New Year's Eve at home with her sister and two police officers despatched to the flat to protect them. The atmosphere was stiff at first, but then the officers relaxed a bit and chatted about all manner of topics.

It was not just her family who needed help moving. Apart from Milad and his brother, who'd been given new names to make them impossible to track down, the police were protecting members of more than 20 families – some 40 individuals in total – who were either victims of crime or key witnesses. The police told the media they had never before had to protect so many people in connection with one single investigation.

Apart from the threatening phone call that led to the police moving into her house, Oritha had also been dealing with other kinds of attempts to sway her. At an inter-generational party, she'd bumped into Khouri's father, who'd been reunited with his son a few years before. As Khouri's mother declined to give me an interview, I'd never know why she'd told Khouri that his father was dead. Shortly after being reunited, Khouri had been arrested and his father was trying to be there for his son.

At the party, upon meeting Oritha, he asked if she would consider withdrawing the charges against Khouri. 'He was sucking up to me,' she told me at a later date. 'He even called me "Princess Oritha" and then I told him that I couldn't NOT press charges, because [unlawful threats] falls under public prosecution.'

When she told me this story, Oritha looked both proudly defiant and amused at having dealt him a legal punch-to-the-face. 'Basically,' she said, 'it was a way to tell him to go to hell.'

Ahead of her participation in the trial as a key witness, it had become time for Oritha to move. Even though she and her sister, who was helping her pack, had known for so long that the move was coming, still they managed, somehow, not to be well-prepared. Oritha focussed on Leon's things, including all the medical supplies, while her sister packed his little brothers' bags. But, they realised afterwards, they were both packing as though they were going on holiday. That they were actually moving had not, on some level, registered, nor had the fact that Oritha could never return. The sisters forgot pillows and blankets, important omissions that they didn't notice until later at the new house.

Finally, they left. And while the Hovsjö neighbourhood's no metropolis, Södertälje's no capital city, their safe house was out in the sticks. Oritha looked out at the agricultural land and horse paddocks as they drove into the modest town centre.

The town wasn't tiny. The community was neither well-appointed nor downtrodden; it was a typical middle-class, typical outer-suburb sprawl on the outskirts of a typical mid-sized Swedish town. But their heart constricted, and her sister later told me her first thought was 'Really? Here? It's in the middle of nowhere.'

PART FIVE

THE TRIAL

November 2011 to September 2014

Fuck your mother

THE PAPERWORK, UPON joining the police every recruit knew they'd signed up for it as part of the job, but what lead detective Gunnar Appelgren was facing was more akin to choreography. He was advising the District Court on what order to usher a rough dozen defendants into the courtroom to avoid skirmishes, because there was some bad blood even within The Network itself. 'With one guy, there are a lot of opinions among the defendants that he shouldn't have run his mouth off so much in the car,' Appelgren said, explaining that the car in question had a wiretap and that the other defendants' attitude was that any worth-his-salt gangster should have known there was a risk that a car had been bugged.

'You have meetings in a café or in the forest, not in the car,' Appelgren summed up.

He sat down with the District Court chairwoman, the Swedish equivalent to a presiding judge; she told him how she'd like the day to unfold; he told her how they'd best achieve a smooth trial. They drew up a blow-by-blow schedule to allow everyone to enter and exit the courtroom as fast as possible, including breaking for lunch and mid-afternoon 'fika', the coffee break that's integral to Swedish workplace culture, even in the courts.

After a two-hour planning session, the detective and the chairwoman had their action plan. 'It is just a relief to finally get going, because it is going to be a long trial,' Appelgren said.

On the first day of the trial, the courtroom filled up fast. Prison wardens brought the defendants into the courtroom where they joined their defence lawyers on the rows of seats opposite the chairwoman's bench. She was flanked by lay judges – Sweden has no jury system – and a notary. To the left, the prosecution took their seats. To the right there was a desk for the injured parties and their legal counsellors. As well as the wardens who had remained in the courtroom, there were police officers on duty as an extra security measure.

Appelgren was there, keeping an eye on things. He noticed that the defendants kept looking up at the viewing gallery, not just to see which friends and family members had showed up to support them, but to take in the number of journalists present.

The trial began with the prosecution summarising the case they'd built against the defendants, an opening statement known as 'sakframställan'. Then they went through each charge one by one in meticulous detail. Because it was such a large case, they had given the different parts code names. The murders were categorised as 'Oasis 1' for Mohaned and 'Oasis 2' for Eddie and Yaacoub. Oritha's part of the case had been nicknamed 'The Living Room' because Khouri had made his demand for money in her parents' living room. The section called 'Heron' referred to Georges, who was assaulted and then kidnapped from the Heron City mall. As for Milad and his brother, the extortion and threats were now referred to as 'The Purse'.

For both practical and security reasons, many of the injured parties, including Milad, did not attend court in person, instead testifying via video link. When it was Milad's time to take the stand, so to speak, the court could see him on the screens on the courtroom walls and Milad in turn had a live feed from the courtroom in front of him at the undisclosed location. The quality was good enough for him to see one of Khouri's men, the one in the wheelchair, mouthing insults at him.

Milad pointed out to me afterwards that while 'a good Christian' shouldn't say bad things about 'invalids', that man was a 'piece of ****' and 'he shouldn't be saying stuff like that about my mother!'

White binders

AS MILAD told the court what he had been subjected to, the defence lawyers questioned him over and over, trying to find gaps in his story, but Milad knew the ins and the outs of his travails by heart.

Many of the lawyers looked like cookie-cutter stereotypes of their profession; slim, standing tall without ever slouching, holding their heads high and dressing discreetly in well-cut clothes. Only a few of the lawyers stuck out from the mould. As well as The Torpedo's young female defence lawyer, Elsa Svalsten, there was Khouri's defender Fredrik Ungerfält, a lawyer from Gothenburg whose mop of tight curls crowned a round face with a jovial expression.

And then there was the legal counsellor Claes Borgström, representing Yaacoub and Eddie's mother and siblings, who, while posh, exuded a working-class-boy-done-good air thanks to a somewhat flattened boxer's nose and a Stockholm drawl that sounded less formal than his colleagues' manner of speech.

Borgström kept calm throughout the trial, but as the days went by Khouri started to lose his patience with all the cross-examinations.

'He feels threatened by my questions, quite simply,' Borgström said as he recalled that specific day in court. 'In one of the first cross-examinations he kind of ended up getting lost when I questioned him and he felt cornered and thought I was being mean, which I don't ... I always keep a nice tone, but of course I have a certain type of experience. So now he refuses to answer any questions from me.'

Over time, Khouri's resentment led to his refusal to answer questions from anyone, Borgström noted, even from the prosecutor. 'Khouri just makes a long statement, then he says, "Boom, that's that!" and the prosecutor just sits there saying, "But you haven't answered the question."'

In preparation for the trial. Borgström had printed out the police case file in its entirety to read up; his assistants had sorted the pages into white binders. When I interviewed Borgström one afternoon, he turned around in his chair and pointed.

'This is the investigation,' he said, gazing at an entire bookshelf filled from top to bottom with white binders. Borgström then looked towards the ceiling, where an extra shelf lined the top of the wall; more white binders. As he turned back to face me, he then pointed at an additional stack of ten or so binders next to my chair. 'There's some more here on the floor. We're talking in excess of 20,000 pages,' he said.

Later on, I tried to put that in context by looking up *The Lord of the Rings* trilogy – about 1,000 pages long – and Homer's *Odyssey*, that came in at some 500 pages.

'A lot of it are transcripts of wire-tapped telephone conversations and the conversations from [the defendants'] homes,' Borgström explained.

'What's the strongest evidence that Khouri ordered these murders?' I asked.

'The telephone conversations, and that Khouri has some kind of leadership role. He tells people on the phone what to do. I think the prosecutors have described and supported with evidence that there is a hierarchy with Khouri at the top, [The Torpedo] next in line, then a few more people,' Borgström said. 'It is very clear that Khouri calls the shots.'

'Are there any weaknesses in the case?' I asked.

'Of course there's a certain weakness because there aren't any immediate or absolute pieces of information that tie him to the crimes,' he answered. 'We don't have a conversation in which he tells [The Torpedo], "Go over there and shoot him."'

'Instead it's sort of the big picture,' he continued, 'and in terms of the value of that as evidence, well it's precarious. Yet the very strong feeling I get is, "Who could it be but Khouri?"'

Borgström said that in cases where there's no one piece of evidence that could make or break a case, the court would instead assess the value of all individual pieces in relation to each other.

'There's a type of evidentiary valuation – the exact legal term slips my mind at the moment – that states that if a pattern becomes clear and distinct enough, and it's difficult to see any alternative, then that is adequate,' Borgström told me.

During the trial, Khouri's defence pressed the point about an alternative: that there could be others out there who'd had a motive for the murders. His line of defence reminded me of something Oritha had told me, that the police had focussed too much on Khouri as 'there are others out there'. And also of what Borgström told me earlier about Yaacoub and Eddie's mother hearing rumours about other people being involved in killing her sons.

'Do people who have worked on this case think that there are more people behind the scenes of these murders?' I asked Borgström.

'Not in the way that there's another leader, or something like that,' he replied, 'but there could be others who took part in planning or executing it. Who unlocked the door of The Oasis, for example?' he asked, pointing out that the two young boys who earlier that evening had tried to buy alcohol from Yaacoub might, according to the prosecution, have been scouts sent out to make sure he and Eddie hadn't gone home yet.

And Borgström brought up that the two gunmen, upon entering, seemed to know not just that both brothers were inside – 'Who told them that?' he said – but also their precise location inside the venue itself.

'They knew exactly what they were doing,' he said. 'The gunmen entered and then went after one victim each. They knew where they were sitting.'

Bernard Khouri, the alleged leader of The Network, in a prison-service visiting room. Photo: Lars Pehrson/SvD/TT

Assyriska FF placed photos of Yaacoub and Eddie Moussa at the clubhouse after the double murder. Photo: Annika af Klercker/SvD/TT

Assyriska players paid homage to Eddie Moussa and held up the Assyrian flag at a game against GIF Sundsvall ten days after Eddie was murdered. Photo: Niklas Larsson/TT

Eddie Moussa in action at an Assyriska FF-Syrianska FC derby at Södertälje football arena the year before his murder. Photo: Janerik Henriksson/TT

Young football players and members of the Bandidos motorcycle gang attended the funeral of Yaacoub and Eddie Moussa.

The police cordoned off the area outside the murder scene at The Oasis – 'Oasen' – in the centre of the Ronna neighbourhood of Södertälje.
Photo: Simon Paulin/TT

FOTOKONFRONTATION

Ärende: 0201-K 192693-10

BILD – 6

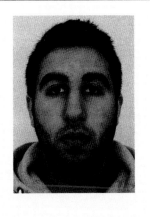

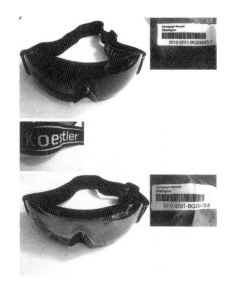

Abraham Aho AKA 'The Torpedo' in a mugshot used by the police for photo line-ups in order for witnesses to identify him. Photo: Police case file.

Ski googles, similar to those witnesses said the gunmen were wearing, found at the house of one of the suspects. Photo: Police case file.

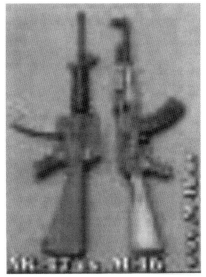

An image retrieved from a suspect's mobile phone. Photo: Police case file.

Another image retrieved from a suspect's mobile phone. Photo: Police case file.

Undersökning av brandrester

Vid undersökning av brandplatsen där två mopeder var uppeldade anträffades rester efter två mobiltelefoner. Bilda telefonerna låg nära varandra mitt i brandrestarna efter de två mopederna, endast några centimeter från de anträffade resterna från automatvapen (G001) och pistolen (G002). Telefonerna var kraftigt brandskadade och det fanns inte mycket kvar av dem. Mobiltelefonerna togs i beslag (2010-0201-BG16798).

Det bedömdes inte vara möjligt att undersöka mobiltelefonerna vidare gällande DNA eller fingeravtryck. Den enda möjliga undersökning som eventuellt kunde göras av mobiltelefonerna var att tömma dem på information. Därför förpackades de i papperspåsar och lämnades över till IT-tekniker, IT-forensiska gruppen/Strategiska sektionen/Länskriminalen Stockholm, på förmiddagen torsdagen den 1 juli.

Bild 1: Översikt av brandplats för de uppeldade mopederna.
1 = automatvapen 2010-0201-BG16764-3 (G001)
2 = pistol 2010-0201-BG16764-4 (G002)
3 = De två mobiltelefonerna 2010-0201-BG16798 (se bild 2)

2 (3)

The charred remains of the get-away mopeds. The arrows show where the police retrieved the remnants of mobile phones, a handgun and an automatic weapon. Photo: Police case file.

Bernard Khouri in a mugshot used by the police for photo line-ups in order for witnesses to identify him. Photo: Police case file.

Joni Khado AKA 'Travolta' with a friend. Photo: Police case file.

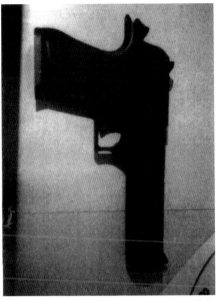

Oritha Chabo, a key witness and victim of extortion, who with her three young children went into the witness protection programme. Photo: Private.

An image retrieved from a suspect's mobile phone. Photo: Police case file.

Bild 1

Skyddsvästar fotograferade på Hyggesvägen 17 i Södertälje.

Bild 2   <Bildplats>

Protective vests found at a suspect's home. Photo: Police case file.

Ibas AS
Postboks 1250
Arkoveien 14
2206 Kongsvinger
Tel.: 62 81 01 00
www.ibas.no

Polismyndigheten i Stockholms län /LU/SIT
V/Tommy Nordström
Norra Agnegatan 33-37
106 75 STOCKHOLM
SVERIGE

Kongsvinger, 29. oktober 2010

Vår referanse: 542940   Deres referanse: K192693-10

Utvidet analys – brannskadede mobiltelefoner

Ref. bilder bilag 1.
Undertegnede har, ved hjelp av ressurser internt i Kroll Ontrack organisasjonen samt et eksternt service verksted, undersøkt kretskortet fra begge mobiltelefoner med hensyn på identifikasjon av fabrikat og modell. Vi har kommet frem til at den ene modellen (som vi har merket Item 2) med overveiende sannsynlighet kan være en Sony Ericsson R310. Dette er en gammel vanntett telefon med spesifikasjoner vist i bilag 2.

Bakgrunnen for at vi tror det kan være denne modellen kan sees fra bildene:

Antennefestet med metallplate (2 skruer i høyre kant) kan vise at det er lik innfesting av antenne. Fysisk mål viser omtrent samme (131x53x25mm). I tillegg kan vi se at skrueinnfesting med 2 skruer

A specialist lab in Norway could not retrieve anything forensically useful from the 'Shark Fin' phone found close to the crime scene, but noted that it was in all likelihood a Sony Eriksson R310. Photo: Police case file.

 KROLL ONTRACK*

Ibas AS
Postboks 1250
Arkoveien 14
2206 Kongsvinger
Tel.: 62 81 01 00
www.ibas.no

Polismyndigheten i Stockholms län /LU/SIT
V/Tommy Nordström
Norra Agnegatan 33-37
106 75 STOCKHOLM
SVERIGE

Kongsvinger, 11. november 2010

Vår referens: 542940   Er referens: K192693-10

Utvidgad analys – brännskadad mobiltelefon

Ref. Bilder i bilaga 2 i denna analys
Undertecknad har, med hjälp av resurser inom organisationen samt Kroll Ontrack Remote Service
Center, undersökt kretskortet på mobiltelefonen märkt *ITEM 2* för möjlig identifiering av märke och
modell. För den fysiska undersökningen av materialet har en intakt mobiltelefon av märket Ericsson
R310 använts som jämförelsematerial.

Undersökningen visar att telefonen (märkt *ITEM 2*) är en Ericsson R310. Detta är en äldre vattentät
mobiltelefon med specifikationer som visas i separat bilaga.

Bild 1 – Ericsson R310 – Den gula telefonen utgör fysiskt jämförelsematerial till den brandskadade
telefonen.

Typ	Samtal fran	Samtal till	Vidarkopplin	Tidsstampel	Tid(s	lmsi nr	Imei nr	Cellid	LAC	System Typ
31	0720252650	0722999983		100628 01:14:25		24007851106655703	357804011764140	10B0, Ronna *210 longitude: 17.591309691 latitude: 59.205302453	0034	UMTS
30	0722999983	0720252650		100628 01:15:36		24007851106655703	357804011764140	10B0, Ronna *210 longitude: 17.591309691 latitude: 59.205302453	0034	UMTS
31	0720252650	0722999983		100628 01:18:50		24007851106655703	357804011764140	10B0, Ronna *210 longitude: 17.591309691 latitude: 59.205302453	0034	UMTS
30	0722999983	0720252650		100628 01:19:59		24007851106655703	357804011764140	10B0, Ronna *210 longitude: 17.591309691 latitude: 59.205302453	0034	UMTS
31	0720252650	0722999983		100628 01:20:40		24007851106655703	357804011764140	10B0, Ronna *210 longitude: 17.591309691 latitude: 59.205302453	0034	UMTS
30	0720252650	0720068925		100628 01:20:50		24007851106655703	357804011764140	10B0, Ronna *210 longitude: 17.591309691 latitude: 59.205302453	0034	UMTS
31	0720252650	0720068925		100628 01:21:23		24007851106655703	357804011764140	10B0, Ronna *210 longitude: 17.591309691 latitude: 59.205302453	0034	UMTS
30	0722999983	0720252650		100628 01:21:26		24007851106655703	357804011764140	1985, Geneta *330 longitude: 17.591384502 latitude: 59.194661545	0034	UMTS
31	0720252650	0760559008		100628 01:21:36		24007851106655703	357804011764140	10B0, Ronna *210 longitude: 17.591309691 latitude: 59.205302453	0034	UMTS
31	0720252650	0722999983		100628 01:21:46		24007851106655703	357804011764140	10B0, Ronna *210 longitude: 17.591309691 latitude: 59.205302453	0034	UMTS
30	0720068925	0720252650		100628 01:21:47		24007851106655703	357804011764140	10B0, Ronna *210 longitude: 17.591309691 latitude: 59.205302453	0034	UMTS
30	0720252650	0720068925		100628 01:22:13		24007851106655703	357804011764140	10B0, Ronna *210 longitude: 17.591309691 latitude: 59.205302453	0034	UMTS
30	0760559008	0720252650		100628 01:22:38		24007851106655703	357804011764140	10B0, Ronna *210 longitude: 17.591309691 latitude: 59.205302453	0034	UMTS
30	0720068925	0720252650		100628 01:22:51		24007851106655703	357804011764140	10B0, Ronna *210 longitude: 17.591309691 latitude: 59.205302453	0034	UMTS
31	0720252650	0760559008		100628 01:22:54		24007851106655703	357804011764140	10B0, Ronna *210 longitude: 17.591309691 latitude: 59.205302453	0034	UMTS
30	0722999983	0720252650		100628 01:22:58		24007851106655703	357804011764140	10B0, Ronna *210 longitude: 17.591309691 latitude: 59.205302453	0034	UMTS
30	0760559008	0720252650		100628 01:23:11		24007851106655703	357804011764140	10B0, Ronna *210 longitude: 17.591309691 latitude: 59.205302453	0034	UMTS
31	0720252650	0720068925		100628 01:23:12		24007851106655703	357804011764140	10B0, Ronna *210 longitude: 17.591309691 latitude: 59.205302453	0034	UMTS
31	0720252650	0760559008		100628 01:23:25		24007851106655703	357804011764140	10B0, Ronna *210 longitude: 17.591309691 latitude: 59.205302453	0034	UMTS
30	0760559008	0720252650		100628 01:23:50		24007851106655703	357804011764140	10B0, Ronna *210 longitude: 17.591309691 latitude: 59.205302453	0034	UMTS
31	0720252650	0722999983		100628 01:24:05		24007851106655703	357804011764140	10B0, Ronna *210 longitude: 17.591309691 latitude: 59.205302453	0034	UMTS
31	0720252650	0760559008		100628 01:24:39		24007851106655703	357804011764140	10B0, Ronna *210 longitude: 17.591309691 latitude: 59.205302453	0034	UMTS
30	0760559008	0720252650		100628 01:24:57		24007851106655703	357804011764140	10B0, Ronna *210 longitude: 17.591309691 latitude: 59.205302453	0034	UMTS
30	0722999983	0720252650		100628 01:25:21		24007851106655703	357804011764140	10B0, Ronna *210 longitude: 17.591309691 latitude: 59.205302453	0034	UMTS
31	0720068925	0720252650		100628 01:25:29		24007851106655703	357804011764140	10B0, Ronna *210 longitude: 17.591309691 latitude: 59.205302453	0034	UMTS
31	0720252650	0722999983		100628 01:25:55		24007851106655703	357804011764140	10B0, Ronna *210 longitude: 17.591309691 latitude: 59.205302453	0034	UMTS
31	0720252650	0720068925		100628 01:26:08		24007851106655703	357804011764140	1985, Geneta *330 longitude: 17.591384502 latitude: 59.194661545	0034	UMTS
30	0722999983	0720252650		100628 01:26:59		24007851106655703	357804011764140	10B0, Ronna *210 longitude: 17.591309691 latitude: 59.205302453	0034	UMTS
30	0720068925	0720252650		100628 01:27:13		24007851106655703	357804011764140	10B0, Ronna *210 longitude: 17.591309691 latitude: 59.205302453	0034	UMTS
31	0720252650	0722999983		100628 01:27:19		24007851106655703	357804011764140	10B0, Ronna *210 longitude: 17.591309691 latitude: 59.205302453	0034	UMTS
30	0722999983	0720252650		100628 01:29:01		24007851106655703	357804011764140	10B0, Ronna *210 longitude: 17.591309691 latitude: 59.205302453	0C34	UMTS
31	0720252650	0722999983		100628 01:29:34		24007851106655703	357804011764140	10B0, Ronna *210 longitude: 17.591309691 latitude: 59.205302453	0034	UMTS
30	0722999983	0720252650		100628 01:30:19		24007851106655703	357804011764140	10B0, Ronna *210 longitude: 17.591309691 latitude: 59.205302453	0034	UMTS
31	0720252650	0722999983		100628 01:30:41		24007851106655703	357804011764140	10B0, Ronna *210 longitude: 17.591309691 latitude: 59.205302453	0034	UMTS
30	0722999983	0720252650		100628 01:31:10		24007851106655703	357804011764140	1985, Geneta *330 longitude: 17.591384502 latitude: 59.194661545	0034	UMTS

Mobile phone data showing incoming and outgoing calls of suspects and persons of interest, and the calls' durations. Photo: Police case file.

Burned-out cars in Södertälje, a common sight in the late 2010s. Often cases of suspected insurance fraud. Photo: TT

Abraham 'The Torpedo' Aho's defence lawyers Elsa Svalsten and Jan Karlsson after filing a conflict-of-interest petition against one of the District Court's lay judges. Photo: TT

The Kronoberg Detention Centre, known as 'The Crown', in central Stockholm.
Photo: TT

A courtroom sketch of the trial against The Network. Illustration: TT

The police erect barriers outside the entrance to the high-security courtroom during the trial. Photo: TT

Detective Superintendent Gunnar Appelgren during one of his signature 'on the one hand but on the other hand' interviews. Photo: TT

The Ronna neighbourhood of Södertälje where the double murder took place.
Photo: TT

Queen Silvia visits Södertälje on Swedish National Day. Photo: TT

Prosecutor Björn Frithiof holding a law book.
Photo: TT

The Hovsjö school in Södertälje was destroyed in a fire in 2009, the year before the double murder. Photo: TT

Justice Minister Beatrice Ask, who earmarked financing to fight organised crime, visits Södertälje.
Photo: TT

Satellite dishes in a residential neighbourhood of Södertälje.
Photo: TT

Children playing outside in Södertälje. Photo: TT

Verdict

ON 21 May 2012, the seven-month trial drew to a close. The bench needed almost two months to go through all the evidence and testimonies and on 1 August 2012 the Södertälje District Court found Khouri guilty of three counts of instigating murder, and also of kidnapping, unlawful coercion, unlawful threats, aggravated robbery, two counts of extortion and one count of attempted extortion, as well as aggravated unlawful possession of firearms.

The court sentenced 31-year-old Khouri to life imprisonment and ordered him to pay damages to Yaacoub's widow and four children as well as to Yaacoub and Eddie's mother and their siblings, including Dany.

Several of Khouri's associates were found guilty of aiding and abetting the double murder, including The Torpedo, who was also convicted of murdering Mohaned. He was sentenced to 12 years in prison. Because he'd been younger than 21 when he committed the crimes, his sentence had automatically been reduced due to the Swedish 'youth rebate' principle.

The rest of the defendants were all found guilty of various crimes including extortion.

The tab

LAUNCHING A targeted and long-term investigation into organised crime had come at a steep price. After the verdict, *Sveriges Radio*, the public-service broadcaster, went through what the case had cost the authorities in total:

The Police: 106.8 million kronor
The Prison Service: 23.8 million
The Prosecution Authority: 4.4 million
Södertälje District Court: 4.3 million
Lawyers' fees paid by the state: 68.9 million

Looking just at the cost of Khouri's defence, the District Court had awarded his defence lawyer, Fredrik Ungerfält, 4.3 million kronor in remuneration. Adding the 2.9 million kronor fee for Khouri's associate lawyer, his defence had cost the taxpayer almost £600,000.

Then there were impending costs. The Prison Service had already paid for keeping the defendants remanded in custody in the run-up to the trial and would now house them in prison, which, per inmate, costs 3,202 kronor a day[4].

In Sweden, a life sentence can be reduced to 28 years in jail, which means that even if Khouri were to be granted parole in the future, the cost for his imprisonment would end up at around 33 million kronor – £2.7 million.

---

4 *Source: The Prison and Probation Service 2019.

As the case had been making the news for years at this point, people had been asking me about the particulars. At a gathering for Columbia University alumni, I chatted to an older lawyer, not connected to the case, who said 'But did it have to cost that much?' I gave him a counter question: 'What would it have cost not to bring them to justice?'

And I didn't just mean in kronor, I meant for society as a whole and for the rule of law.

Down in Södertälje, a teacher told me that 'it would have been a catastrophe if they'd let Khouri go'. She pointed out that parents used to fear that their children would be recruited by The Network. 'Khouri played dice with their kids' souls,' she said.

The verdict had been announced in May 2012. Two months later the police could compare the first six months of 2012 with the same period the year before: The Södertälje police noted a seven per cent decrease in the overall number of reported crimes. When it came to violent crime, the change was even more noticeable with a decrease of ten per cent.

When *Sveriges Radio* spoke to Södertälje residents about the verdict, a woman said she had noticed a change. 'I no longer feel fear when I leave the house,' she said, although she had declined to give them her last name, which, as far as I saw it testified to lingering concerns about safety.

Yet the police suspected that the lull in crime would be short-lived. A new generation of wannabe gangsters could be waiting in the wings, having been too scared to take the reins until they knew whether or not Khouri would be coming back. And now that he'd been found guilty, at long last, and wasn't coming home to Södertälje, the police started to wonder what the wannabes had in store.

The Fire Finch

AFTER THE verdict, everyone expected Khouri and his associates to appeal.

Appeals are more the rule than the exception, because even if a verdict were not overturned, there was a chance of a reduced sentence. However, there'd also be a risk of getting a longer sentence, yet the potential reward of being freed of charges was often seen as outweighing the potential risk of a few more years in prison.

For the police, the verdict had proven that targeted operations against organised crime could be successful. Even though it was case closed for lead detective Gunnar Appelgren, who had moved on to other tasks, the case still felt very much alive to him. Questions lingered and there were details that still bothered him, in particular about the double murder. The police hadn't been able to prove the identities of the gunmen. Yes, five men had been brought to justice for the murders, but Khouri had gone down for instigation and the remaining four for aiding and abetting, none for actual murder.

Who had ordered and helped execute the murder was one thing, who had pulled the trigger was another. Some police officers told me that The Torpedo – who had killed before – was one of the gunmen, but there'd been no evidence to back that claim up in court.

Some evenings after work, Appelgren would walk down the gentle slope of Kungsholmen Island towards a bar called Amaranten (The Fire Finch), where he, now and then, would meet up with other high-level officers for a drink; it was a place where detectives could go to compare notes, and to gossip. I met him one midweek evening at the low-key but plush bar, with its dark-wood chairs upholstered in turquoise velvet. Eighty different kinds of beers on the drinks menu stood testimony to Stockholmers' burgeoning obsession with artisanal ale.

The bar's proximity to the District Court and the accompanying sprawl of law firms, as well as the Town Hall and Stockholm's Regional Government, meant that lawyers and bureaucrats were filing past on the pavement outside. At the close of the working day, it looked like pedestrian rush hour. Inside, the bar was almost full.

Despite the chatter, Appelgren had no problem checking out of his surroundings as we revisited the scene of double murder. There was one detail that bothered him, which should have been a key to figuring out who the gunmen were. Why did the gunmen not shoot the brothers in the head? At such close proximity, it would have been the easiest way to make sure the gunshots were fatal.

'The gunmen showed them respect,' Appelgren said. 'They peppered Yaacoub's torso with bullets, but they left his face intact to allow the family to bury him with an open casket.'

'Yaacoub was shot three times in the throat, the entry wounds all in one coin-sized spot,' he said.

At this point in his career, the calm and collected Appelgren had started wearing suits to work, but when he shaped his index and middle fingers into the barrel of a gun and leant his heavy-set frame forward to illustrate how Yaacoub was killed, he all of a sudden looked menacing. There was no way to tell, I thought to myself, if he was just getting carried away by the theatrics, or if what I was seeing gave a hint of his days in uniform out on the streets.

Then he sat up and transformed back into looking more like Father Christmas than a gangsta-film beat-cop bully. 'It was, in actual fact, an execution,' Appelgren said as he used his palm, in a swift, almost child-like motion, to push his glasses back, which had slipped down the bridge of his nose during the murder re-enactment.

'It bothers me,' he said. 'I think it means something and we haven't figured out what. If you look at a lot of other murders, you shoot people in places where you know it will kill them. ... The face, the head ... three shots to the head and you're dead.'

It was a perfunctory comment to describe a kind of violence that so jarred with the serene surroundings of The Fire Finch.

Appelgren pointed out that Yaacoub had already been wounded, which meant that by the time the gunman – or woman, but Appelgren believed that to be unlikely – walked over to fire the last trio of shots, Yaacoub would either have already fallen on to his knees or been slumped on the floor, defenceless. 'Why do you choose, in that situation, to shoot him in the throat?' Appelgren said. 'To show respect to the family? To make sure they can say goodbye to an intact face? Or does the gunman have a relationship to the victim, which means there is a psychological barrier to shooting him in the face?'

Appelgren knew he might never get an answer. These boys wouldn't snitch, they'd never allow the police to catch up if they could help it, and Appelgren knew that, he'd be a fool not to after doing this job for so long. Maybe too long. As he'd been wrapping up the investigation, he had started to put out feelers, scouting for new jobs; he'd even consider the private sector.

During the trial, Södertälje had made him sort of famous, in a flash-in-the-pan media-darling kind of way. He was the face of 'tidying up' Södertälje. Making him the spokesperson was a conscious decision because he had the bird's eye view of the entire investigation, and was experienced enough to not let details slip, even off record; a company man, through and through.

However, the beat cops didn't mind talking in more detail to me. After each interview or informal chat, I'd been left with the impression that they had to talk to sort through all their feelings. They'd seen first-hand how The Network had destroyed people's lives, not just their victims, but also the young boys recruited into the gang. Some of those boys had gotten into crime because their families were poor. 'You're not left unaffected,' a beat cop told me, 'when you bump into a boy carrying a jar of pickled vegetables and realise that's all his family has to eat for the rest of the month.'

The beat cops were the ones who knew. They understood. Alice Ekengren had also come to understand after years of trying to make a difference in one of Södertälje's poorer neighbourhoods. She was going to pay a price for her idealism, she just didn't know it yet. The local police were the foot soldiers, Appelgren was a commander. They had the details, he had the big picture. The media spokesperson for the Södertälje police, Lotta Thyni, answered most in-depth questions with the line, 'Appelgren's the one to ask, Appelgren knows best.' So Appelgren stepped in, stepped up, became an old-fashioned constable kind of poster child. He posed for the cameras and grew an old-fashioned moustache to fit the part. He was the face of a police operation that finally made a difference. Or at least that's what everyone was saying, and, even more important, it was now what everyone hoped would turn out to be true.

While Appelgren was expecting Khouri to appeal the verdict, he was not expecting what would come next.

Betrayal

THE RELIEF after the verdict turned out to be short-lived. In Sweden, political parties appoint lay judges – the system has its critics – and the Södertälje District Court discovered that one of the lay judges on the case had been attending police debriefings with town-hall politicians, who'd wanted updates on how the investigation was progressing.

As this attendance may have affected the lay judge's neutrality – the police's narrative etched on his mind – he had put the integrity of the verdict into question. It was ruled a mistrial, which meant the entire case had to go to court yet again.

Following the announcement that there would be a retrial, I wanted to know the police's reaction, but Appelgren didn't pick up his phone. He was in Paris on police business, but replied to my text messages: 'We'll just have to reload.'

'What were you doing down there?' I asked him when he got back to Sweden.

'Stuff,' he said, then veered off-topic, possibly to throw me off a confidential subject, by asking: 'Did you know that the French police don't have riot gear adapted for women?'

Which I didn't know (why would I?), but having tried on protective vests at work, I could empathise with ample-chested female officers. On 8 November 2011 the retrial began. Yaacoub's widow attended every day for the next six months. Each time I saw her, she was wearing black. As the exhaustive retrial drew to a close, she gave an interview to the local paper, *Länstidningen*, about why she and the children had had to move from Södertälje.

'It was impossible to take part in the investigation and the trial to the extent that I did and keep my old life,' she said, adding that it had hurt to leave behind the Assyrian community – referring to them as 'my people'.

'I had to make a choice,' she said. 'That the children and I are safe is the most important thing.'

In the time between her husband's murder and the case making it to court, several witnesses had withdrawn the information that they had given to the police. Oritha's family were a case in point, I thought to myself reading the interview, because they had tried to get Oritha to pull out. Other witnesses had claimed they lied in their initial statement. Or blamed the police or the translator for misunderstanding them.

Yaacoub's widow said it was time for people to stand up against the gangs; the people who kept quiet or refused to stand up for what they'd initially said, they'd 'betrayed Yaacoub, the children, and the entire justice system'.

'I understand that people are scared,' she said. 'But at the same time we can't have everyone sitting at home being scared. I'm scared too, but I never hesitated or regretted that I did the right thing and testified.'

Verdict number two

FROM THE train station it took less than ten minutes on foot to reach the Södertälje District Court, its lobby looking out over the main square and, to the left, the Lutheran church of Ragnhild, the town's patron saint. It was a sunny late-summer day, 29 August 2013, the air was muggy and it was yet again time for a verdict – three years had by now passed since the double murder back in summer 2010.

Outside the court building Khouri's cousin, who'd been paralysed in the drive-by shooting, wheeled his way across the cobblestones, parking his wheelchair in the middle of the square and gazing at the reporters going into the court building, a Brutalist-architecture building fronted by floor-to-ceiling windows. I was watching him from inside the lobby and got the feeling he was avoiding the press. Some of the younger defendants, however, had made their way into the court and now stood close to me in the huddle between a metal detector, some potted plants and a desk that the court staff had fetched to make it easier to hand out printed copies of the verdict. More reporters filed in, a few carrying TV cameras. Elsa Svalsten, the tall young lawyer defending The Torpedo, showed up; she was a head taller than the young teenage defendants in their tracksuits.

In the crush, I noticed a red-haired man, whose pristine white tracksuit did nothing to hide a bit of a beer belly and poor posture. He fished out his smartphone and started to film the journalists. He was not discreet about it, it was clear he was putting on a show. Then he grumbled, loud enough to be heard, 'I'm gonna make some money out of this too.'

I took note of his comment, thinking to myself that actually journalists really didn't earn a lot of money, but I didn't immediately recognise him as the local rapper whose 'Long Live Södertälje' music video had been posted on YouTube. His lyrics included lines such as 'There was drama and panic, when we dropped some dead bodies,' which rhymes in Swedish: 'Det blir dramatik panik, när vi lämnade nå'ra lik.'

He'd once given an interview to the local newspaper and told them that the trick to being a good gangster was knowing when to quit.

Next to him in the crush of people, I spotted the kid I'd nicknamed Travolta because of his hairstyle. He was doing less of a good job of keeping his cool than the calmly disdainful rapper, who, I'd find out afterwards, was Travolta's brother. Last time around, after the first trial, the court had sentenced Travolta to five years in prison for the kidnapping at Heron City and for perverting the course of justice. Now he'd find out within minutes if he had been found guilty this time around as well.

He looked nervous. He manoeuvred his slender frame through the media gaggle to get to the clerk's impromptu desk. Everyone had ordered copies of the verdict, either in print or on a DVD, or both – unlike in the US, Swedish judges don't read out the verdict in court.

The security guards had just wheeled a steel trolley stacked with a minor mountain of papers and DVDs out from the lift. Then they set to work. They asked for ID cards, scanned the name, then pivoted to pick up a copy of the verdict.

Travolta handed over his ID. When the guard read his name and turned to the trolley, without giving the card back, Travolta shrieked, 'What the hell, give my ID back!' He was shrill, on his tiptoes, his body wound so tight he looked like a coiled cobra, ready to strike, yet at the same time he looked so so young, and just so frightened. The guard stayed calm, not acknowledging the shout of protest, then picked up and handed over a print copy of the verdict along with the ID card.

Travolta grabbed the items and shot out of the building. A quick scan of the verdict revealed that he'd been found guilty this time too, but his sentence had been reduced from five years in prison to four years and six months.

Most of the charges against the rest of The Network stuck this time around too. And just like last time, the court had decided that Khouri would spend the rest of his life in prison.

Dreams

THE PERSONAL assistant who had worked with Oritha's son since he was born was one of many who welcomed the new verdict. She believed Khouri deserved his punishment. And one thing had always been clear to her: Khouri himself had never considered his conduct to be a breach of morality. The assistant brought up Khouri's behaviour when Oritha's father had handed over cash to pay off his son's debt; that Khouri had gifted the old man a bottle of liquor, then kissed him on the forehead.

'I think he gave him that bottle as some kind of sign of respect, like, "Arab respect", like "uncle", or whatever, "I respect you",' she said. 'Empty words, empty words.'

'One day Khouri's at a person's home issuing threats, demanding money, and pulling out a weapon. Then he's giving Oritha's dad a kiss and giving him a bottle of raki. It's creepy, that kiss on the forehead,' she said.

'Read between the lines. It means that Khouri feels justified in what he did.'

Now that the District Court had reached the same conclusion after the retrial, and found The Network guilty again, the assistant hoped it would be the end of the saga. But, she said, the trial hadn't, as far as she could tell, made people any more inclined to report crimes nor to testify – the culture of silence prevailed. And, she pointed out, she'd noticed and was infuriated by a culture of socially punishing those who did speak out. That had been very clear to her after the first trial, when Oritha's neighbours and friends in the Aramean community gossiped about her. The assistant, also an Aramean, had overheard several such conversations at parties. 'There's been so much chatter, like "Why did Oritha do it?" and "Why's Oritha making life difficult for everyone else?" And for those people, the easy way out was to stop socialising with Oritha and her family!' the assistant said angrily. 'I mean, seriously?!'

Psychopath

FOLLOWING THE second District Court verdict, a host of appeals started to take shape. Nobody was happy. The defendants proclaimed their innocence, while the victims wanted to be awarded more in damages.

Khouri's lawyers set to work writing his appeal, in which they accused the prosecution of a criminal lack of imagination. If the prosecution was so intent on proving the existence of The Network, the appeal argued, shouldn't they have considered the possibility that Bülent Aslanoglu might have been the leader?

Appelgren, the detective, didn't buy Khouri's argument, and in his opinion Bülent Aslanoglu – nicknamed The Godfather in the press – was not cut from the same cloth as Khouri. 'Neither is Bülent classified as a psychopath, at least not as I recall,' Appelgren said, in reference to a psychiatric diagnosis of Khouri that I'd not been able to access because medical records are classified.

'But what classifies a psychopath?' I asked.

'A certain kind of grandeur, that you have problems feeling empathy, that everything stems from your own needs in every single situation. They're often perceived as being strong leaders, they project that image of self-confidence.'

'Bülent is calmer,' Appelgren continued. 'We have questioned him and he said this conflict [between Khouri and Dany] razed everything he had built to the ground, just because they couldn't keep the peace. So without placing a halo over Bülent's head in any way, I'd say he's the better businessman.'

'Did the drugs influence Khouri's choices?' I asked.

'I can't remember if he was just doing coke at the time, or also hash, but yes, the drugs did influence his choices. Among other incidents when Bernard Khouri picks up a machine gun because he's pissed off at [The Torpedo] and walks down to the centre of town and starts shooting. That's an aggravated weapons crime that Khouri has actually confessed to. And we believe he was high when he did it. So, in short, that was a pretty bad choice on his part,' Appelgren said.

'Khouri is quite intelligent,' he added. 'That's what people who have spoken to him say. I've never met him, I have no interest in meeting him. I've heard that he's well-mannered, smart, conceptual.'

'Is he impulsive?' I asked.

'I think he does like to have things happen straight away, but when it came to this revenge hit [against Yaacoub and Eddie] we think they waited until the right opportunity. And he intimated as much in the case, in which Oritha testified,' Appelgren said, referring to the fact that Khouri had threatened Oritha's family a short time before the double murder. 'He said something like, "We'll see what happens" or "We'll sweep them away." That's a signal that he knows something big is in the works.'

'Khouri believes that the police have built a hypothesis on circumstantial evidence,' I said, summarising the appeal, 'and then you've thrown his name into the mix, but it could have just as well been Bülent.'

'I don't agree,' Appelgren said. 'If you compare The Network to some kind of company, then Bülent would be the chief executive, and Khouri would be the chief operating officer. Or Khouri's like the area manager, because Bülent's out travelling the world and needs someone to keep the business running at home in Södertälje.'

Crisps and dip

WHEN EKENGREN worked evenings, she tried to speak with
the boys hanging out on the square. The boys were playfully
talkative one moment, poisonously taciturn the next – even to
Ekengren who had been working in Hovsjö for so long. At least
when these boys were out in the open, Ekengren knew where they
were. They hadn't broken into a cellar, as they were prone to do,
to drink and scrawl the names of all the local police on the walls,
including rather graphic depictions of what the boys would like to
do to the cops, with specific mention of her. Slander was the least
of it; she was getting used to being called cop whore, cop cunt.
And being called a traitor when she tried to be their friend one day,
then finding herself forced to file a complaint against them the
next. She'd taken one of them to court. The worst thing about
working there, she'd come to realise, was when parents covered for
their sons, lying to her straight in the face. They weren't unknown
to claim, 'He was at home all night' when Ekengren had seen their
son commit a crime right in front of her eyes.

Ekengren had grown used to worrying about the boys. She
didn't know how much they would be paid for the grunt work of
being an aspiring small-town gangster, such as stealing a moped
or driving one back and forth in front of a shop until the owner
paid protection money just to get them to go away.

Sometimes they were ordered to torch a moped. They would
open the gas tank and turn the moped upside-down, letting the
petrol trickle down, to make it easy to set it alight. And then there

were the never-ending car fires, often suspected insurance fraud. Although there was also a growing fear that burning cars had become a way to send certain people certain messages.

One evening, Ekengren had stepped out to patrol her beat in heavy rain – 'Horrible weather, I mean truly horrible, it was cold too,' she said when later recalling that night – and bumped into a group of boys huddling together looking somewhat miserable.

'What are you doing here?' Ekengren asked the boys. 'Why aren't you at home?'

No one answered. Surely she didn't need to point out why she thought they should be indoors, where they'd be warm, dry, and safe?

Another evening shift. Friday. Again a group of boys outside. Ekengren thought they should be at home watching TV and relaxing with their families. Why weren't they doing *fredagsmys*? she thought to herself. The term *fredagsmys* – literally 'cosy Fridays' – appeared in the Swedish language in the 1990s. Used by potato crisp companies, among others, the term has become a Swedish catch line for domestic harmony and material welfare at the end of the working week. With that in mind, Ekengren addressed the boys again: 'Why aren't you at home enjoying *fredagsmys*?'

The boys looked at her in silence.

After a few years on the beat, after seeing how some families in Hovsjö had to live, Ekengren afterwards realised how stupid that *fredagsmys* question had been, because many of the boys' parents had no working week, they were unemployed. Or on salaries too low to rent a bigger flat that'd better fit their families' needs.

'Why should the boys be at home?' she asked me. 'Many of them live in a one-bedroom apartment with five other family members. They're poor, they don't have crisps and sour-cream dip. And the stress of poverty, she explained to me, affected their results in school. 'These guys don't have a vision for the future, they can't see that far. Just a thing like finishing school, that's not a given, that's not a vision; it's not something they count on doing.'

Ekengren connected the dots, explaining why the gangs thus had an easy time of it when they recruited new members. 'If you don't have all that, and if some other element comes into the picture and offers you status, easy money, attention, to make you into somebody [who matters], to give you confidence, of course you go for it,' she said. 'There's nothing else to tempt you, nothing to pull you in a different direction.'

'It makes me
feel like a cunt'

AT THE same time that Khouri was preparing to fight for his freedom in the Svea Appeals Court, his former best man-to-be Bülent Aslanoglu was languishing in a French remand cell awaiting charges for drug smuggling.

'Aslanoglu's far from being one of God's best children,' said detective Bo Eliasson at the national bureau of investigation. An apt choice of words, given that Aslanoglu used that exact phrase when Swedish media interviewed him about the impending criminal charges against him.

Two and a half years before, customs in Dunkerque had found 258 kilograms of 76 per cent pure cocaine aboard a ship carrying coal from Venezuela. Four men had been arrested immediately. In March 2013 the police, citing evidence from wiretaps, had come to the conclusion that Aslanoglu was the brains behind the failed attempt to import cocaine with a street value of 900 million kronor (£73 million). The cops had then brought him in. Aslanoglu denied being involved.

'I've sniffed a few lines of coke,' Aslanoglu protested in an article in the *Expressen* tabloid newspaper. 'I don't claim to be God's best child, but I've never sent as much as a gram of cocaine to Sweden or any other country. The drugs trade is dirty.'

Drugs, he pointed out, were taboo in his culture. And as for any insinuation that he was involved in the Moussa brothers' deaths, Aslanoglu wouldn't hear of it. He and Yaacoub once laid the foundations of what was now referred to as The Network. They did it together. It was different back then, he told the *Expressen* reporter, things were well-managed and cordial. But once Aslanoglu had served a stint in jail at home in Sweden he'd come back to a different Södertälje, a town where Dany had started to kick up dirt and cause trouble. He and Yaacoub had tried talking to Dany together, that evening Yaacoub's wife has been eavesdropping on them, but Dany, part of a new generation, hadn't listened.

'The young guys thought we were too soft,' he told *Expressen* about the generational shift.

The ensuing turf war reduced Aslanoglu to wearing a security vest.

'It doesn't befit a guy like Bülent, a father of four, to walk around with a vest on,' he said, slipping into third person, then back again to first. 'It's shameful, it makes me feel like a cunt.'

Church

WHEN I brought up the issue of parents who wouldn't cooperate with the police with Assyrian politician Robert Hannah, he said it was due to feeling shame. He told me that one institution could help them deal with shame: the church.

'The priests have informal power that goes above and beyond any others,' he said. 'I think [the priests] know what is happening and I think they're the ones who have the power to change things. They have a responsibility to get people to start talking.'

Down in Södertälje, not everyone was fond of the priests' power. Milad said they should have intervened and tried to speak with Khouri many years ago. When I asked the bishop for an interview about the case, he said no.

Oritha thought that when it came to private matters, the priests should keep their opinions to themselves.

She remembered when she had decided to divorce her husband – reminding me that on the night Khouri demanded money from her parents her husband had locked her in a room so she couldn't call the police – the priests had wanted her to reconsider her decision. 'Their attitude was that I shouldn't get divorced,' she said. 'I was heavily pregnant with our third child and went from one church to the next with the 12,000 kronor fee to get a divorce, yet the priests were running around trying to get me to change my mind.'

Oritha refused to feel ashamed. Her parents were scared the divorce would taint the family's reputation, which annoyed her, but they also expressed concern that she would not be able to find a new husband. 'My dad said, "You'll be a single mother of three and no one will want you",' Oritha recalled.

She had no plans to remarry, she called herself emotionally scarred from her marriage because he was controlling, ripping her skirts when she tried to leave the house, screaming, 'Whore, where are you going?' Just seeing her apply on mascara would set her husband off, Oritha told me.

Even though she refused to feel shame, she knew that her children might be teased about their parents' divorce, because when she was a kid she'd see children picking on single-parent kids and telling them, 'Your mother's a whore.'

'It wasn't that common back then to just have one parent,' Oritha said. 'It was really taboo to get divorced.'

Luckily for her own children, that attitude had started to fade. Even her own parents, once they'd come to terms with her divorce, had become 'kinder and more relaxed', she said. 'It changes from one generation to the next, nowadays people get divorced all the time, I mean look at us Arameans leading our "Svensson" lives.'

She said that, unlike many other immigrant groups, where parents become more rather than less conservative in order to preserve their culture, second- and also third-generation Arameans have a lot of freedom. 'I wouldn't change my life for all the money in the world,' she said. 'I can do what I want, date who I want.'

She was moving on with her life, even though the case against Khouri was now going to go to the appeals court.

Her legal counsel had told her the chance of Khouri being freed of the charges, including the extortion of her family, was slim to none. So she could relax and focus on her children.

Question mark

THE MOUSSA family's legal counsel, Claes Borgström, started to get ready again for a fresh round in court. The white binders with the police case files still lined the shelves of his office. A slightly wobbly stack stood on the floor.

'Khouri's appeal says that the prosecutor could substitute his name with Aslanoglu's and their argument would still hold,' I said.

'It's possible, sure, that Aslanoglu was involved, I think that's clear, but I don't agree that all you have to do is swap Khouri's name with Aslanoglu's and the situation would be the same.'

And his clients agreed. 'The Moussa family are convinced that the right people have been charged, despite thinking that one or two people have slipped the net,' Borgström said.

'Khouri's lawyer argues there's no criminal gang, just a group of friends dabbling in crime?' I said, summarising the appeal.

'These are very advanced cases of extortion, well-planned and ruthless in a way. They're not dabbling in minor crime,' Borgström said.

'Is it possible that the court of appeals will find Khouri not guilty?'

The old lawyer paused, obviously not 100 per cent certain.

'I feel there's a question mark,' he finally said, 'about the outcome.'

Scale

THE APPEALS trial began in November 2013. The sun had long gone. Instead the chill and the grey had invaded Stockholm.

Next to the rust-red building that houses county and national police HQ, sits an imposing black gate with barbed wire: the gates to 'The Crown'. Inside the detention centre, Khouri had been getting ready for court. He had settled for a simple black T-shirt and grabbed his rosary. The wardens had handcuffed him, ready to escort him through the passageways that led to the special high-security court.

Outside on the street, two heavily-armed police officers were guarding the court building's old wooden door. Their boots were laced up tight, semi-automatics slung over their shoulders.

Next to the guards, Fredrik Ungerfält, Khouri's lawyer, spoke with almost boyish animation with Borgström. Khouri had tried to replace his entire defence team before the appeals trial began; I heard from police and others close to the case that Khouri had had conflicts with Ungerfält because he 'won't do what Khouri tells him to do'. The court had denied Khouri's request to change lawyers so he and Ungerfält were stuck with each other, whether they liked it or not.

Apart from the officers eyeing passers-by with professional suspicion, everyone standing outside on the pavement seemed at ease; they had seen it all before: Ungerfält, Borgström, the steady stream of lawyers who entered through the wooden door then through a security lock to get into the court building.

The reporters, what few remained for this third round as even the media had grown tired of the story, had to go through airport-like security, including a metal detector and a pat-down.

Because the case had dragged on, several of the defendants – mostly the younger ones but also the old man who used to collect the money from Milad – who were charged with less serious crimes were now on free foot. If found guilty again, the time spent in custody would be deducted from the prison sentence, so in this case, where so many of them had been kept locked up in order not to intimidate witnesses, they had effectively already served their time.

Just like the journalists, these defendants had to go through the security check. Once inside, waiting for the court doors to open, they huddled in silent groups, shooting curious glances at me.

I spotted Travolta, a bit hyperactive as usual, like he was ready to strike a pose or sprint off into the distance. When he spotted one of the police officers who worked on the case – a middle-aged woman clad top-to-toe in denim and with blonde Rapunzel hair – he lunged towards her. They hugged.

'She's the best! Why are you so fine?' he said, with no hint of sarcasm. 'I swear I'm gonna marry her,' he added, half to himself, half to the other defendants who were making their way down the narrow corridor that led into the bunker-like courtroom.

Travolta appeared to be a natural-born actor, a showman. The policewoman asked him how he was getting along now that he was out. He told the truth, it was not going so well, it was difficult to find work and he felt he wasn't getting any help with moving on with his life.

Sherbel Said, the man paralysed in the drive-by, arrived. The former bodybuilder rarely smiled. The huge bulk of his torso and shoulders sat squarely in the wheelchair, which pinched his hips. He swivelled with ease on the back wheels; he had learnt how to manoeuvre the contraption to where he needed to go.

He was with his brother, a burly man whom I'd seen working the door at an Assyrian pizza joint in the less-than-affluent suburb where

I lived. I asked him why he was clutching a white pillow: 'He can't sit in that thing for long,' he answered, indicating Said's wheelchair.

The courtroom doors opened and everyone spilled in from the corridor. When everyone was in place and the doors were secured, it was time to fetch the defendants who were still in custody.

Khouri looked calm as he entered, flanked by several prison wardens. A large wooden cross hung around his neck. Khouri was still young, 33 by this time, but deathly pale, with a greenish tint to his skin. More than two years in lock-up without any sunshine will do that to a person.

Glass separated the viewing gallery from the courtroom. I was sitting next to a colleague behind Khouri, who turned around and looked at us. Afterwards, my colleague remarked, 'It felt like a lion looking straight at you.'

The prosecution, Björn Frithiof and his colleagues, sat to the left, opposite the bench where the injured parties' legal counsels had taken their seats. There were more than 70 people in the underground courtroom.

'It's not ideal that the court case has become so large,' Frithiof pointed out in his opening remarks, referring to the number of defendants and injured parties, as well as to the complexity of pinpointing each defendant's role in what the prosecution called The Network.

'But the case needs to be this large to prove intent,' Frithiof continued. From then on, to preserve energy through the days ahead, he and his colleagues took turns addressing the court.

Then the proceedings began. Unlike American court dramas on TV, there was no gavel, there was no 'all rise' when the judge entered the room, and while defendants, injured parties and witnesses did swear an oath to tell the truth, the whole truth and nothing but the truth, they didn't have to stand up nor place their hand on a Bible. Swedish justice is bureaucratic. This courtroom, with its birch-wood furniture, felt a bit Ikea-esque.

With so many charges, going through the evidence was dogged and tedious work. The prosecution went through the drive-by without pause or emphasis, they stated that for Khouri's paralysed cousin, Sherbel Said, the incident had left its indelible legacy.

'A lifetime of suffering,' Frithiof concluded.

At those words, Khouri turned his head left to catch Said's eyes. Khouri wiped away what could have been a mock tear or a real one. Said smiled back. Khouri brought his hands to his chest, holding them just above his heart.

The slop

DURING THE many months that they had represented The Torpedo, his defence lawyers had grown no less sceptical of the evidence. While Jan Karlsson skirted cautiously around uttering outright criticism, he and his junior colleague Elsa Svalsten had their concerns.

'Police investigators have both conscious and subconscious motives,' said Karlsson. 'I dare claim there were conscious decisions to not investigate leads that took them away from their hypothesis.

'And I'm sure there are subconscious motivations too. I'd rather not be commenting, but what you can see …' he hesitated, weighing his words. 'If you look at all the investigation material, both the part that was made public and what we can access as defence lawyers, you can see that they've looked a *bit* at other leads. But they haven't quite managed to make them catch, so they stop looking.'

Svalsten took it upon herself to explain in more detail. The police case file made public, the evidence and statements that form the basis of the prosecution, was a redacted version. Odds and ends, for example 'other leads that didn't catch', end up in what's known as 'slasken' – literally, the slop, and, while journalists can apply to see 'slasken', the police and prosecutors may classify it to conceal witnesses' identities for safety reasons, or redact parts of it.

For defence lawyers, going through 'slasken' is part of the normal order of the day. Any contradictory evidence they find will form the backbone of their arguments in court.

'There's often a lot of that [contradictory] stuff, and that's obviously what you're looking for,' Svalsten said.

In run of the mill cases, the younger lawyer pointed out, it doesn't take long to find conflicting evidence. But in this case, she and Karlsson claimed, the slop painted a picture of investigators abandoning leads that did not fit their working theory. In this particular case, there wasn't a lot of contradictory material at all, she underlined.

Karlsson interrupted, wanting to emphasise a point: in some cases not even the prosecutor will go through the entire case file, including the slop.

'It's always the case, when it comes to these expansive investigations, that the prosecutor hasn't read everything,' he said. 'That's not the way it works. The [prosecutors] trust the police.'

Add to that the particularity in this case that the defendants were being tried en masse, so to speak. Karlsson pointed out that The Torpedo's guilt was tied into Khouri's guilt and to the prosecutor proving the existence of The Network, where Khouri gave orders to The Torpedo, who in turn gave orders to an underling, and so forth down the chain of command ... including defendants such as Travolta.

wh#re

WHEN HE was younger, Travolta had starred in a dark but comic short film called *The Elixir*, which tells the story of Swedish society breaking down when a group of kids find a secret potion that makes dark-skinned immigrants look white. The teens start bootlegging the elixir, and soon everyone has pale skin and blue eyes. The chaos doesn't take long to unfold. In a memorable scene, a harried police officer tells the kids that there are no immigrants left to work in eldercare and where, he asks, are the middle class going to buy pizza on their way home from a boozy evening at a bar if the pizzeria owner has gone off and found a white-collar job?

Turning 'white' has other effects on the boys, who abandon their suburban sociolect and develop a taste for old-school vernacular, and complex sentence structures, that wouldn't sound out of place in an August Strindberg play. One of the boys' badass-loving girlfriend loses interest in him once he stops being a violent little punk (she takes him back after he stops drinking the elixir and beats up a much younger kid in the schoolyard to impress her).

In addition to *The Elixir*, filmed long before his arrest, Travolta had penned poetry while in custody ahead of the trial; he'd added me on Facebook, where he posted a poem addressed to the girlfriend who appeared to have ended the relationship when he was locked up. I wrote down parts of the poem, which was both heartfelt and coarse:

> *the picture of you was the most valuable decoration in my cell*
> *i looked at you from morning till evening*

287

i made a promise that for you my love I'll fight to come home
news of your betrayal hit me hard
but in a way, your silence had me suspecting

you've tattooed my name Joni on your body and claim I'll always
be your number 1

you grew tired of my lifestyle, wearing a protective vest every
day and
looking over my shoulder
wh#re you're fucking someone else
fuck your excuses you were quick to take off your panties

Travolta's sad poem reminded me of something the beat cops said: that their time in custody affected many of the younger boys profoundly, not least Travolta.

He'd always acted out, he would come up too close for comfort and try to pick a fight with the police, but as long as they didn't take the bait and kept calm, Travolta would always back away with a mischievous grin. He could be talkative back then too, but that changed when he was let out. Now, there was little left of his juvenile candour and showmanship, there was just a dense wall of distrust and suspicion. 'I think the restrictions imposed on him in custody really scarred him,' a cop said. Although one time his new suspicious attitude slipped when he and a cop, who'd known him when he was younger, bumped into each other on the street and both leaned in for a hug, until they realised they were on opposite sides of the cops 'n' robbers divide. 'So we just said hello instead,' the beat cop said.

And while Travolta agreed to talk to me about being in custody, and about his poetry – 'I won't talk about my friends,' he informed me – the meeting never materialised. He rescheduled, apologised for doing so. After a while, he posted an update on his Facebook page saying that someone had explained to him that the 'true definition of friendship is loyalty'. He never got in touch again after that and soon removed me as a friend on the social media platform.

At some point in the trial, Khouri had made a point of never ever having had Facebook, and, in fact, that he barely knew what it was, and he communicated with his entire demeanour that such things were for children. There were several instances such as this when Khouri had distanced himself from the younger suspects, whom the police called 'errand boys': the ones who were said to have stolen mopeds for him, acted as scouts for him, and who had been charged with their parts in facilitating the double murder.

In fact, when Khouri talked to me, he denied even knowing who Travolta was. When I described the boy's *Saturday Night Fever* quiff, Khouri said, 'Yes, I recognise him from the trial.' I noted that he said 'from the trial', as though their paths had never crossed before, even though Travolta was with him when they kidnapped Georges from Heron City.

That Travolta apologised to me for cancelling our first meeting made me think that he must have been raised to be polite in all circumstances. Of course, they are all polite at first contact: Assyrians and Arameans respect their elders.

Travolta's apparent and desperate need to be a likeable guy had me thinking. I couldn't help but feel what an easy target for older gangsters he must have been. 'You're right,' a relative of his told me later. 'He really does want to please everyone and I think that made him vulnerable.'

The promise of cash coupled with promises of brotherhood, as long as you prove your worth – and proving your worth could be emotionally devastating for such young boys. As one of them told the police during questioning, 'I've been forced to do things that no teenage boy should have ever had to do.'

As they were no longer stuck in custody, the errand boys filed in and out of the appeals court every day. In the smoking area, they chatted to me a little bit, telling me the police saw 'The Network' everywhere, figments of over-active cop imagination. Like when a few of them were driving quad bikes in the forest recently: 'THE NETWORK are driving quad bikes!' one of the young men exclaimed, mocking the police.

Some of the defendants brought friends with them, who sat with me in the viewing gallery but tired after a while – understandably: I almost fell asleep myself when the prosecution went through the mobile-mast triangulation. They headed outside to buy ice cream. I bumped into them on my way out, perched on top of a bannister inside the lobby, dangling their feet and licking their Daim ice cream cones as if they were enjoying a day on the beach rather than attending a murder trial.

Naknemo

THE VIOLENCE was not over. As the appeals trial began in the winter of 2013, a man was attacked in front of his son in central Södertälje. The kid ran for help.

As an ambulance helicopter flew the man to hospital, the police didn't issue his name. Yet Södertälje didn't need them to issue his name, it didn't matter, the phones were going wild. Within an hour, anyone in the Aramean and Assyrian community who wanted to know knew his name: turned out he was a friend of Khouri's who at one point had been a suspect in the investigation. A tax-agency source told me he had been subject to their investigations, but they'd failed to find dirt on him.

The tax agency, once its staff were drafted to help heal the town's woes, were trying to uncover money laundering within big families. Having a lot of sisters and brothers can prove useful if you need to clean a large chunk of cash. Relatives work too. A niece receives some money, a brother more, a few thousand to your uncle, and as the recipients wire the money onwards, or make purchases at key businesses or in other ways transfer the money, the sums are in turn broken into smaller sums. The criss-cross of transfers make it difficult for the agency to trace the origin of the cash, but they try their best to follow the money. But the man who'd just been attacked, if he was hiding something, was too smart for the taxmen.

Then he died in hospital.

The police kept the details of the murder close to their chest, but that did little to put a stop to the gossip. At the appeals court, one of the younger defendants told me, 'knife to the head', then shook his head and walked into court.

Others say it wasn't a knife, but a screwdriver to the temple. He was first shot, then stabbed in the parking garage of the Luna Mall in central Södertälje. As the investigation delved deeper, the cops found that his death had nothing to do with the skirmishes between rival gangs in Södertälje. It was retribution for another incident, an insult perceived as a violation of honour, paid back in the bloodiest way possible.

When incidents such as these took place in Södertälje, the town was put on display at its ugliest in the media. As crime after crime made the national newspapers, the town seemed like a different universe to downtown Stockholm. And far removed from orderly settings such as the courtroom where The Network were being tried once again. And the differences were also clear to me from a quick glance at the way the defendants were dressed versus the lawyers' expensive attire, which also differed from the journalists' standard smart-casual style.

When I spotted a woman in the viewing gallery with a light-grey suit and a chic necklace, I wondered what paper she could possibly be from. No journalists look that smart. Perhaps the business daily, *Dagens Industri*? But why would they be covering crime all of a sudden? Perhaps some kind of legal trade paper? Nope, turns out she was Claes Borgström's intern. Of course, she was a lawyer too.

But the contrast was most stark in front of me in the courtroom, where the difference between the defendants' and the lawyers' worlds was sewn into the literal fabrics before me. Suits and pencil skirts for the lawyers, hoodies and t-shirts with tracksuit bottoms for the defendants.

There were other differences, audible in the way they spoke. While Khouri himself was well spoken, he spoke with a slight accent. Or rather, it was not an accent, but a cadence, a sociolect.

In contrast, quite a few of the lawyers and prosecutors spoke with the nasal vowels that let slip that they'd grown up in Stockholm's wealthier suburbs. Some even had aristocratic last names.

Their posh way of speaking rendered transcripts from the wiretaps bizarre, almost comical, as they read out loud the frequent profanities caught on tape. 'We were all quick to learn "Fuck your mother" in Aramean,' one of the lawyers had pointed out during a fika break, after smuggling out a cup of coffee from the lawyers' lounge to me, because the coffee in the waiting area was not fit for consumption.

The lawyer had leaned down from her considerable height to whisper 'naknemo', while at the same time glancing over her right shoulder to make sure no one else was listening.

While the lawyers who'd been involved in the case from the start – the first District Court trial began three years before – had learned some Aramean along the way, not everyone involved in the trial was as experienced with a language that might be ancient, but still new to Sweden. Some struggled with the names. The appeals court judge, who was new to the case, had started his first day off by mispronouncing the name of Milad's brother, Bahnan Bahnan. By stressing the second syllable instead of the first, BAH-nann BAH-nann had turned into bann-AAN bann-AAN, Swedish for 'banana banana'.

The error had provoked a quiet, but nonetheless perfectly audible, and rather disdainful huff from a man sitting in the viewing gallery. It was crime reporter Torbjörn Granström from the local newspaper in Södertälje who had travelled up to central Stockholm. A man who knew all the names by heart, having covered what the paper called 'the gang war' for years.

When a lawyer had pointed out the mistake, the judge had corrected himself.

The prosecutors started off the proceedings. Tora Holst took the lead; she was about to do what her team had done in both renditions of the District Court trial: address the history and culture and lay bare the insularity of the Aramean community in Södertälje.

'There is a tradition of scepticism towards the authorities; people prefer to solve conflict within the community, and there is an historic system of mediation. With big sums of cash from illegal gambling in circulation, we believe this created a hotbed for criminality.'

In court, the prosecutor's tone was neutral, the syntax borderline academic; it was correct and stripped of emotion. There was a more powerful way to sum her argument up, I thought to myself, by simply revisiting what the lead detective once told me. 'Bernard Khouri is a little brat who terrorised a neighbourhood,' Appelgren had said. 'The question is what or whom allowed him to do it?'

Best friend

'I'VE LOST my best friend.' That was the only comment Khouri had about the man who had just been murdered down in Södertälje.

A lot can happen in three weeks: when I had spoken to Khouri again after our visiting-room chat, he had ditched me. There wouldn't be a follow-up interview. It was clear to me that, as a reporter for a small online newspaper he must consider to be irrelevant, and as an author who didn't yet have a publishing deal, he considered me worthless. He had decided to speak only with the *Expressen* tabloid, which had just run a long interview with his friend and former best-man-to-be Bülent 'The Godfather' Aslanoglu.

In that *Expressen* article, Aslanoglu had accused Khouri of fucking things up. He claimed that the spat between Eddie's brother Dany and Khouri had messed up a smooth operation – I thought to myself, 'You mean back in the day when loan sharking was civilised?'

That interview stuck in my mind; it seemed to corroborate what Appelgren had said about Khouri losing perspective. That he lost track of what was feasible, pushed people too far.

I understood Khouri's need to respond to Aslanoglu's interview – it had not painted him in a good light while the appeals trial was underway. I also understood Khouri's choice of newspaper. A staff writer for a national newspaper could guarantee reach. I could not.

And while *Expressen* was not so long ago on the edge of financial ruin, it had picked itself up by the bootstraps. It was respectable again, as respectable as a tabloid could be. The reporter's name was Diamant Salihu. 'Diamant' means diamond in Swedish.

'Seriously?' I told Khouri on the phone. 'You're gonna talk to a reporter whose first name is Diamant?'

Diamant Salihu was no spring chicken, but an experienced reporter, and my attitude was not cool, but I was annoyed with Khouri for dumping me. Khouri remained on point.

'Yes, but I won't be flashy like Bülent.'

'Can I write something for another newspaper?' I asked.

'NO NO NO.'

A few weeks later, the *Expressen* article was published. Indeed it wasn't that flashy, Khouri came across as measured, although for those of us who knew more about him – and the evidence against him – one could also say that he came across as deluded.

Khouri said that he knew who killed the Moussa brothers, but would never snitch. It raised an eyebrow and I thought to myself, 'how convenient'. Upon being freed of all charges, a trial outcome which he remained convinced of, he'd like to meet with the Moussa brothers' mother and explain what happened to her sons. He would tell her, but not the police.

Widow

'WE WILL now watch the video from the crime scene,' the judge told the court.

As the appeals trial had inched forward in its subterranean den, month after month had passed. The trial started in autumn and now it was spring again; another winter behind us. Mohaned, Eddie and Yaacoub had been gone for four years, yet still there was no final verdict. Dragged-out torment, but necessary to preserve the rule of law and make sure there was not another mis-trial.

During much of the proceedings, Khouri had been leaning forward with his elbows on the bench in front of him, but with Yaacoub's widow present he sat upright; perhaps in some way to honour the severity of the crimes and acknowledge her loss.

The judge, who was about to instruct the court clerk to press play on the gruesome crime-scene video, turned to Yaacoub's widow. 'You may step outside if you want.'

She stayed.

There was something about her, as she nodded to acknowledge that she understood the content of the film yet wasn't going to step outside, that made me think she was determined not to let the violence scare her off. That she was there to face her husband's killers, no matter what.

The clerk pressed play on the video that one of the responding officers filmed at The Oasis. Eddie had been lying on his back, one leg bent behind him. Yaacoub's body was by the radiator ... as the camera moved in closer to Yaacoub's body, the widow swallowed hard, placing her hand on her chest to quell her sobs. She started to shake but didn't cry. By the time the video ended, she was biting her thumbnail.

When the court went on to show photographs from the morgue, the widow buried her face in her hands at the sight of Yaacoub, his eyes slightly open, staring vacantly in the harsh light above the autopsy table.

Later, during fika breaks, the younger defendants gave her a wide berth. After a recess, several of the youngsters came back into the court lobby and saw her standing there in the narrow corridor. They backed off. At one point, she joined them in the crowded smoking area – where I was busy trying to get the boys to talk. The room went silent. The youngsters stared at their feet.

I admired the widow's pluck. Or perhaps it was more simple than that, perhaps she didn't blame the young ones.

Cross

MILAD'S LAUGHTER came out as a coarse chuckle. He couldn't help it, I'd just told him that Khouri had worn a large cross around his neck during the first day in court. 'Khouri could bring Jesus himself to court and it wouldn't help, no one can help him,' Milad said, pausing. I could hear over the phone that he was lighting yet another cigarette. 'You have to be a kind person to get God's or Jesus's or [the] cross's help,' he said. I heard him take another drag. 'God has to be in your heart,' he added.

He asked if I'd corresponded more with Khouri. 'He sent me a very angry and illogical letter,' I replied, but didn't delve into my conviction that I'd failed my audition, so to speak. 'Well, that's Khouri. Angry and illogical,' said the sanguine Milad. 'He's always like that. I think that if Khouri finds no one to fight with, he fights with himself. That is Khouri.'

Milad couldn't talk long because he had to pick up a birthday cake for his daughter. She would soon be turning 14. 'I found an old Arab woman who makes cakes. They have less cream than Swedish cakes do,' he explained. 'Usually I'd just pick one up from the bakery, but I'm trying to make [my daughter's] birthday party as nice as possible.'

That he couldn't spoil his daughter as he used to, because he was unemployed and broke, pained him the most.

'She remembers Södertälje, that I'd pick her up from school in a nice car. She asks me sometimes why we don't have a nice car anymore, why I don't give her nice things,' he said, adding that he had had high hopes for his business, and his enthusiasm rubbed off on his daughter. Had things turned out differently, he would have been a wealthy man by now, not reduced to this.

There was no way to tell if that was a reasonable assertion, or if Milad had romanticised his old life in Södertälje. Yet it didn't really matter. Whether his wholesale business had been going just well enough to pay the bills or been about to set them up for a well-to-do life was irrelevant, because either would have been better than where he had ended up – out of work, living on benefits.

'It's shameful,' he said.

He had moved into a modest one-bedroom apartment with his wife and daughter, he told me. It was crowded, he didn't hesitate to admit it, but what made him most sad every day was the loss of family. The birthday party was a good example, as Milad thought the guest list was too short.

'How many?' I asked.

'About 40. We've made some new friends at church,' Milad said.

'Forty is quite a lot.'

'Yes, but in Södertälje if I just invited my brothers and their families, and all my cousins, we'd be closer to 200 people,' Milad explained. 'And if you want to have a big party, it's easy to reach 400.'

His teenage daughter had made new friends. At church, some of the older women made sure to spend time with his wife. And there was no shortage of newly arrived immigrants in their new town so there were people from the Middle East to get to know. In 2014, Sweden had welcomed asylum seekers at a rate of 8.43 per 1,000 inhabitants, according to Eurostat. Milad was happy about the new arrivals: they've never even heard of Khouri nor did they know about this network that had taken power over an entire town just south of Stockholm.

'They are new in Sweden, they don't know nobody in Stockholm,' he said.

He and his family had been given new identities and weren't allowed to talk about what happened, or even mention where they came from.

And soon, if the Appeals Court would at long last put Milad's enemies in jail, The Network would be old news. So Milad and his wife and daughter were safe. He hadn't spoken to his brother Bahnan, who also had to leave Södertälje, for a long time, but he had spoken with his parents on the phone a few times. They still supported his decision to leave.

'They understand that I didn't have a choice,' said Milad.

I'd noticed a difference between Milad and Oritha. She was acting not just out of fear but fury; Milad was acting only out of fear, which he didn't hesitate to admit. Milad had no interest in painting an altruistic picture of himself. Quite the opposite, he was fine with admitting that if Khouri had eased up on the pressure, given him and his brother more time to pay and perhaps a bit less to pay, he would have muddled through. He had mourned Södertälje since the day he'd moved. He left because he had to leave, it hadn't been any less or more complicated than that.

'I only care about myself and my family,' he said.

But when I told Appelgren about what Milad had said, the detective interrupted: 'Milad is still a hero.'

Khouri had gone too far, he'd pushed too hard – people will do everything to protect their family, even testify against one of Sweden's most notoriously brutal gangs. And thus Khouri had been the architect of his own undoing. If he was found guilty, that is. The trial was about to reach its conclusion.

Radio silence

A FEW weeks later, as the prosecutors ploughed through endless mobile phone data to plot a sequence of events that pointed to the double murder, The Torpedo turned around to look at Khouri. The younger man put both his hands in the air, smiled at Khouri and shrugged, part amused, part 'What the **** do they think they're proving?'

The mast data kept coming. The prosecutors then turned to the burner phones. As the evidence mounted, the day grew long, and tedious. In a corner, one of the wardens nodded off. The air started to feel thin. Seventy-plus people competed for oxygen in the underground bunker. When the warden jolted awake again, he popped a Fisherman's Friend lozenge into his mouth. One of Khouri's lawyers sneezed. Khouri poured him a glass of water.

After a recess, as people traipsed back into court, a warden asked one of the older defendants if he was a reporter. The man, whom I'd never seen show emotion, shook his head. Said, a much more animated figure, wheeled past. He asked me how the book was going.

'Fine,' I said. (I'd never told him about the book yet it seemed to have become a talking point.) 'You'll all soon be international celebrities.'

He struggled to hide a smirk. I asked him how he was. He looked up at me from his wheelchair.

'You know,' he said laconically. 'I keep on rolling.'

Then he wheeled himself into the courtroom.

Travolta was there. He gave me a *snus* (Swedish snuff), which I tucked under my top lip. I noted the huge tattoo of Jesus on his forearm. At that moment a fat guard bumped into his arm. To me it was clearly an accident, but fury flashed on to Travolta's face. But the rage disappeared as quick as it came and he was all boyish charm again, all smiles. Then he joined the others on the courtroom floor.

At one point during the proceedings, the judge lost his temper. He was talking when he spotted a defendant gleefully reading a newspaper left on the bench by a lawyer.

'Put down the newspaper and pay attention to proceedings!' the judge barked.

The case was all new, complex, and perhaps even gripping to the judge, but the defendant had had to listen to all this three times. It was not that surprising that he'd rather read the paper. 'Being remanded is sooo boring,' he told me later.

It was time for Ungerfält to speak. I wondered how it felt to represent a man, an alleged psychopath nonetheless, who had tried to have you replaced.

Much had been said about a barbecue that parts of The Network attended on the night the Moussa brothers died. A final meeting before the deed, the prosecutors argued. Nonsense, retorted the defence. Ungerfält ran through a list of dates on which such barbecues had previously taken place. The Swedish verb to barbecue is 'grilla'.

'Grilla … grilla … grilla …' he intoned. 'Grilla … grilla … grilla …'

The point being that Khouri and his friends had barbecues a lot; the date in question meant nothing.

At times, Ungerfält opted to mock the prosecution's conclusions, and its choice of language. When all the phones went dead at the same time, for example, 'The Network enacted communication silence'. Those were the prosecution's words. Ungerfält underlined the time in question, then breezily commented, 'People usually do "enact communication silence"…' he paused for dramatic effect, '… when they are sleeping.'

The letter

'I'VE ENTERED the mind of a madman,' I thought to myself as I scanned the letter.

Khouri must have known that things weren't going his way in the appeals trial. So as the hearings drew to a close, the displeased Khouri took matters into his own hands. He wrote the court a letter. It was long, more than 80 pages, and it was thorough. It was also meandering and accusatory. The letter left me ill at ease for days. None of it was new to me. He said the first judge was corrupt, the cops set him and his fiancée up. The prison staff had lost his notes and his computer when they moved him to a new detention centre. Those were his accusations, interwoven with paragraphs ripped straight out of the European Court of Human Rights, including examples of other cases which, he said, had set precedent for his case. Legally binding precedent the Swedish court was ignoring.

Yet any valid points he might have been making were drowned out by the rest of the letter, both because of its length and tone. He swung from stilted legalese to less informal sections that were part pleading, part scolding; desperate for the court to hear his plight. Eighty pages … I only read half at first, because it left me feeling ill – the fury and the fear like heat waves off the page.

For three days, I couldn't shake that feeling. I was used to Khouri creeping into my dreamscape, where he'd provoked both terror and sympathy. This time around it was not so much that he was there, like a character in a film, instead his feelings had infected me. They had pulled me in to his world, and it was unsettling.

I understood the rage now. For the first time, I truly understood why Oritha's family were so terrified of him. I understood what Milad had meant when he spoke of Khouri's eyes, the smouldering fury that set him apart from the more reasonable Aslanoglu.

The question was, would the letter have any effect on the judges? Would it affect the verdict?

Celebration

MILAD, IT turned out, was right. Neither the Cross nor Jesus, and certainly not God, could save Khouri. On 1 September 2014 – more than four years after Mohaned, Yaacoub, and Eddie died – the appeals court issued its verdict.

Bernard Khouri, 33. Life in jail.

They convicted him, among other charges, of conspiracy to commit three murders. Extortion, illegal coercion ... the list was long.

The court stated that Khouri had motive: avenging the drive-by shooting when his friends were injured. They pointed out that Khouri returned to Sweden just 12 days before the double murder. And that the phones, which the police claimed were used in the planning, were acquired just a few days after his return; that those phones had been activated with sim cards that had been handed out for free in Södertälje.

The court sentenced The Torpedo, now 23, to 12 years in jail for the murder of Mohaned and for aiding and abetting the murders of Yaacoub and Eddie. The rest of the defendants fell one by one. Down they went, from top to bottom of the alleged mafia hierarchy, as they were found guilty of various crimes.

The Appeals Court made several amendments to the District Court's verdict; it was less forgiving when it came to the double murder. The court decided to also convict two of the errand boys for their roles in the murder. They'd stolen the get-away mopeds and had visited The Oasis earlier in the day of the murders on a 'reconnaissance mission'.

As a murder had taken place at The Oasis six months before, and given whom they worked for, the court argued that the boys must have known what was coming – the court employed the legal term *likgiltighetsuppsåt* – motive of indifference, which is similar to the American 'second-degree murder'. They were found guilty of aiding and abetting murder.

There was another amendment too, a vital point about the reliability of testimony. The lower court had judged Milad's character and founds his credibility to be 'partially limited'. The appeals court verdict disagreed. In clear terms it called Milad's testimony consistent and sound, and the court underlined there was no reason to question his integrity. And what was more, other parts of the investigation backed up Milad's testimony.

When Milad received a call from his lawyer delivering news of the verdict, he got to work immediately. There was only one thing left to do. He pulled out a large knife. Then he turned to the fridge, where he had a stash, and he fished out the proper amount. Once he found the chopping board, he started to chop the parsley – a rhythmic accompaniment to his elation. The chickpeas, sesame paste, and olive oil went into the blender. It was time for taboulleh and hummus, a proper Middle Eastern mezze spread. It was time to celebrate. And he thought of that list, the one he had started before he fled, the list of names of people who had hurt him and stolen Södertälje from him.

'I know you think I'm awful,' he'd later tell me, 'but they broke me. I have a list here, in my head. I'm counting, I will feel good when they die.'

PART SIX

THE AFTERMATH

2014 to 2016

Metaphysics

KHOURI APPEALED again, this time to Sweden's supreme court. The supreme court said no. It was game over.

But there was still something I needed answering. My thoughts returned to the little boy whose mother was called bad names by his classmates, the boy whose father was said to be dead, the boy who wouldn't listen to his uncle's admonishments. Were you allowed, despite it all, to feel sorry for a man such as Khouri?

'I think so,' said the Moussas' lawyer Claes Borgström, who nonetheless called Khouri calculating and manipulative. He still saw room for pity.

'Who wants to swap lives with a person like Khouri?' Borgström said, as his calm gaze held steady. 'Versé, the French lawyer who defended the butcher of Lyon, said that deep inside, in the deepest recess of every human heart, there's a flowering garden. Of course, that's a bit poetic when you're talking about the worst bad guys, but I think it's well put. Of course that's the way it is, nobody is born evil.'

'I don't believe in evil,' he continued. 'Believing in evil is a way to make things easier for yourself, because if evil exists you can't do much about it. If it exists as a metaphysical force in the universe in and of itself, then you can't change the circumstances that contribute to people perpetrating evil acts. Evil does not exist as a metaphysical force. That is very clear to me.'

Slap in the face

'IN LEBANON, every single person who could be tied to the murders would have got life, they'd never be let out. That would have been justice,' said Alexandra Moussa, Yaacoub and Eddie's sister.

She had, from the start, taken on the role of the angry Moussa, the one who, on her family's behalf, spoke to the media. Her sister Atie couldn't take it – the one time I'd contacted her she started to cry – and their mother Nayla only sometimes granted an interview. The family weren't satisfied with the verdict. The sentences were too short. And because the suspects spent so long detained in the run up to the trial, many had already served their time. So after all this time ... it was an anti-climax of sorts, and Alexandra spoke of her fear of the day Abraham 'The Torpedo' Aho would be released. While Khouri had been sentenced to life, which can mean until death but rarely does in Sweden, Aho had been sentenced to 12 years. Four years had already passed since he was detained, and he could also, now that he'd been jailed, end up getting early parole for good behaviour. Alexandra had done the maths.

'Abraham Aho could be out in four years' time. He'll be free soon, while I've lost two brothers. And I hope Khouri doesn't get out in 18 years' time. The sentences are ridiculous, it makes no sense, the justice system is so sick in Sweden.'

Things got worse for the family a year later. In June 2015, the state agency tasked with regulating payments to the victims of crime decided the family wouldn't receive any damages. The decision cited the court's description of the turf war: 'Eddie and

Dany collected debts with violence and threats of violence. Yaacoub ran The Oasis, where it is considered highly likely that illegal gambling took place.'

Somewhat simplified, the law limits payments to victims of crime who knowingly put themselves at risk.

'The Crime Victim Compensation and Support Authority considered it highly likely that the crimes had their origin in criminal activity. By entering into that type of activity, they subjected themselves to a higher risk of being hurt.'

Alexandra was furious.

'Not even mum gets money,' she said. 'And it's not about the money, it's about principle. We lost the ones we love the most. This decision is a slap in the face.'

Stomach pains

WHEN I met up with Alice Ekengren a couple of years after the verdict, she had long since left the Södertälje police. She had taken a job up in Stockholm, then fallen pregnant. Soon after returning from parental leave, she'd told her boss that baby number two was on its way. 'Well, you're a fine recruitment, aren't you?' her boss had joked, facing the task of finding a substitute to cover for her.

Ekengren was five months pregnant, her belly big but not huge, when she let me into City South police headquarters for our interview. The police station is situated in an odd slice of town. The southern island of Stockholm used to be called 'Knivsöder', 'Knife South', because of its high crime rates, but had morphed into a quiet, bourgeois mecca. Overpriced noodle shops, a ladies-only gym with pink equipment, photo-book stores. Yet remnants of Knivsöder remained. The local pharmacy was still doing a brisk trade in methadone, the drug abuse centre was just around the corner. Which all meant that Ekengren, now an investigator, had more than enough on her plate.

It had nothing on Södertälje, however. And Södertälje was still never far away because she could recount with ease details of her many experiences down there, such as the night she tried to use Cosy Friday as a bargaining tool to get the young boys to go home. So long ago now, yet so much of it stood out in detail, like reels of an old movie.

'Most of those boys were on their way into organised crime,' she said. 'And as far as I've been told, most of them are rather heavy-duty criminals now.'

'When you're that kind of cop, a beat cop, it's a relationship, and you become more than a cop. You're their buddy, their enemy, their social worker, their teacher, their guidance counsellor. I mean, you become everything to them. And it's a complex relationship, it's a love-hate thing.'

Ekengren had slipped from past to present tense. Her memories seemed vivid, even those before that fateful double-murder summer, when she was 'only' pouring her entire soul into saving the boys she saw slipping into crime.

'And you know they can't say, "I like you, you're OK" because they hate the cops, you know. Cops are assholes,' she said. 'Sometimes you feel like you got through to them, then you meet them the day after and it's "Whore! Cunt, I'm gonna kill you." When you work here in the city, nobody knows your name. Down there, I was Alice everywhere. I couldn't go anywhere without hearing "Alice, Alice! What's up?". And when I wasn't on duty they'd ask my colleagues, "Where's Alice?"'

Her tone changed from amused to sad as Ekengren started to explain how much she had cared for many of the young boys. She knew now that she had been naïve. She had wanted to save them, but could barely even save herself. Her sleep had suffered; the stress caused stomach pains and heart palpitations.

'There's nothing left of you in the end. You can't stay in these neighbourhoods for more than a few years. You can't take it, it becomes too personal.'

Ekengren filled up her cup of coffee in the sunlight-flooded police canteen. To one side of the room, an entire wall was covered in film posters with her colleagues' faces photoshopped on to the faces of the actors in *Ghost* and *Star Wars*.

'Oh, this,' she said with a wry smile. 'Office party.'

She paused for a moment.

'I don't want to speak ill about anyone, but I'm not sure that all my colleagues here in the city would have the strength to do the job we did in Södertälje.'

Responsibility

THE LAST time I met Özcan Kaldoyo, the local journalist, he was even more critical of his own community than he had been during previous meetings. As I tried to find out why, it turned out he had been diagnosed with cancer. 'God, he's saying his piece as he stares death in the face,' I thought to myself.

Although the prognosis looked good, Kaldoyo was more combative than usual and spared no criticism of the churches in particular, but not just of them.

'How did you turn out this way? So honest, and so critical?' I asked.

'My father was like this, he never took anything at face value, he always asked questions.'

A few months later, I sent Kaldoyo his quotes, to make sure the translation to English was okay with him. He made few amendments, adding only that he understood why his community had this tradition of silence, that it was not easy to stand up for yourself after decades, even centuries, minding your own business.

'You could say that in the Middle East, we worked like donkeys, were treated like pigs, and saved up money like a bee, because we thought we could use the money to save our skin,' he had told me, adding that persecution damages the soul, and deprives men of their pride.

A few days later, I got another email from Kaldoyo. It was short.

'I would just be curious to know, and I wonder if you could ask the people you've interviewed, what responsibility they think they have for what happened in Södertälje?'

Eddie

FIVE YEARS almost to the day after the murders, Eddie's old fan Conny Chamas met me at a railway station. It was a nondescript Stockholm suburb; two tracks for the commuter trains, two for the national railways. The latter rarely stop. People rarely stop here unless they are going to the nearby hospital or to Stockholm's southern District Court. Chamas wasn't really stopping either. He was off to England to see if he could find work as an assistant coach. He still kept an eye on Assyriska – how could he not?

The club had run into financial troubles. All those player purchases that Chamas once grumbled about were ill-financed, the accounting was in deep disarray, and Assyriska was deep in debt. Already the previous year, the municipality had stepped in and said it would help, on two conditions: Get drive-in football sessions going, and spend more effort on the girls' teams. Assyriska's fans rallied to help. The furniture store owner Jakob Rohyo had been one of them, donating cash to keep the club afloat. The club survived again. When Assyriska met Syrianska in a September 2015 derby, the mood had been high and I'd noticed Eddie's mum sitting in the stands, watching Assyriska take home a 2-0 win. Five years had passed since her sons had died.

All Assyriska fans remember that day; most people in Södertälje do. At The Oasis, the gamblers Philip and Issa running for their lives as a gunman with a Kalashnikov ended Eddie's life, moments before the second gunman shot Yaacoub three times in the throat. The text message on detective Appelgren's phone. The friend who called Nayla, warning her about a shooting at her son's place. Yaacoub's wife showing up at the crime scene, fearing she had been widowed. And Dany showing up too. A beat cop writing a memo that one of the errand boys stood in the crowd outside The Oasis, his face crumpled in shock. The officer who couldn't plug the radiator leak, and instead picked up his phone to film the bodies, as water, blood and dust mixed into pinkish grey sludge on the floor. The 6am phone call to Eddie's team-mate Andreas Haddad, the bosses at Assyriska having to tell their players that the brothers hadn't survived.

'I just remember how sad everyone was,' Chamas said. 'People really believed that [Eddie] would go far. You were basically waiting for a foreign club to buy him. You pinned a lot of hope on him as a player, especially as a lover of Assyriska.'

The brutality of the murder had not come as a shock to Chamas.

'You always knew that things happened in Södertälje. You'd heard a lot, you'd seen a lot. [Some people] are like Neanderthals who resolve conflict with violence. And there's this prestige, there's no forgiveness. "If you wrong me, I'll kill you." And sometimes that's not enough: "I will kill you and your entire family."'

'I'm sure similar things have happened to many Assyrian families in Södertälje,' he said. 'It would have never become such a big thing if it hadn't been Eddie Moussa.'

PART SEVEN

THE PRICE

2016 to 2018

Press freedom

A YEAR and a half had passed since I met Conny Chamas to talk football and murder. The trial against The Network was long since done and dusted, and by this time many of them had already served their prison sentences. I saw them sometimes, when I was out and about in Södertälje during the summer of 2016, where I had taken a job full-time for public service radio.

I was curious to know if they knew who I was. At a local restaurant – the owner once told me that 'Khouri was really well-liked' – two of them sat a few tables away from me at lunch. I was on the phone and needed to write down a phone number, so seeing an opportunity I walked over to them and asked if I could borrow a pen. 'No problem, you're welcome,' they said without a flicker of recognition on their faces.

And, in truth, why should there be? Journalists had been scampering after them for years, and in the courtroom the reporters sat behind them. There was no reason for them to have memorised my face. Yet at times I did wonder how they would react to the book, which had been set to be published three months after I saw them at the restaurant.

It was time for me to let this story go. For the past four years, my research had been the equivalent of a part-time job on the side of my full-time job.

As publication neared, I let the closest family members of the victims know, I told Yaacoub and Eddie's sister to prepare their mother, I emailed the contact I had for Yaacoub's widow to let that side of the family know.

Then I wrote a letter to Khouri's immediate family, explaining that they were welcome to give me an interview, there was still time to include their views in the book, but they were not obligated to do so. I said that I'd like to speak about Khouri's childhood, adding some details about what in particular I'd like them to explain to me. To make sure I was understood, an Arabic-speaking colleague translated the letter and I sent off both that and the Swedish version in the same envelope.

No response. I hadn't expected one, but I had done my duty as a reporter and gave them the chance to reply.

In early December of 2016 my phone rang. It was Khouri's aunt, who was polite to me but confused. 'What book?' she asked.

That's when I realised that Khouri had not mentioned our interview to his family, and I wondered if he'd even himself understood that his refusal to give me a follow-up interview did not spell the end of my book. That I was neither seeking nor in need of his approval to continue.

His aunt asked me to write to Khouri in prison, which I agreed to do.

Shortly after, one of his friends called me; he was not unfriendly either but even more confused than the aunt, having tried to google me. He told me that Khouri was 'angry' at me, then fired off questions about the book.

'Did you speak to any of us or is the book just based on the police case file?' he asked. 'I've spoken to Khouri,' I said, 'and given several of you the chance to speak with me.'

The man who was calling was not one of them, so I added 'You're welcome to give me an interview.' He said no.

'Are you using our real names?' he asked.

'The verdict's public record,' I replied. 'So yes, I'm using your names.'

During the phone conversation, I got the impression that Khouri's friend was less annoyed at me than he was at Khouri for making him run his errands.

'Is it okay if his dad calls you?' he asked.

'Sure,' I said and, as I knew Khouri's father had a home in Paris, I added 'and I speak French'.

When call *numero trois* made my phone light up, it was a Swedish, not a French, telephone number. Being at this point rather rattled, I taped the ensuing conversation and later looked the number up – it was a burner phone.

Yet again, the conversation was friendly but Khouri's father passed on a message from Khouri that I couldn't use the material – I was unclear which parts of the material, or all of it, but regardless Khouri was giving a journalist orders; in a country that has the world's oldest press-freedom laws.

'C'est moi qui decide, pas lui,' I told his father – I'm the one who decides, not him.

'My son's very annoyed,' his father said with what sounded like a barely suppressed sigh of resignation.

I came dangerously close to answering with 'your son was born annoyed' but thankfully I managed to hold my tongue. It wouldn't have been just unprofessional but also potentially dangerous: I was not about to pick a fight with Khouri, or make worse the one I seemed to have started by accident.

His father then told me Khouri didn't want me to use his name … a prohibition that was ridiculous given that Khouri had been front-page fodder for years. 'Your son's a public person, and, *monsieur*, we have press freedom in Sweden,' I said.

Just like Khouri's aunt before him, the old man asked me to write to his son in prison.

With each one of those phone calls, my concern had grown bigger. After speaking to Khouri's father, I fired off a rambling, fear-laced email to my publisher. Yet, I was also hoping that this meant perhaps he'd give me that second interview? If so, we'd have to stall publication by six months.

My publisher, however, said that the 'changes in the security situation' meant they would not be publishing the book at all. I tried to reason with them, but to no avail; they were unflinching.

Fine, I thought, I'll find another publisher. Or publish the damn thing myself.

While I thought my now ex-publisher was over-reacting, I felt a nagging worry growing stronger in my chest ... perhaps I was under-reacting?

Phone call

I WROTE to Khouri in prison, who responded with a letter accusing me of contacting his mother 'who doesn't speak Swedish' to get his attention, which I now had – 'Bravo,' he wrote.

That was when I remembered what the cop had said to me many years before when I met Khouri when he was in custody – he'd told me, 'Be straight with him' – and now I understood that Khouri really could see hidden agendas everywhere. As if I'd go through his mother just to get him to talk. I wrote back to him and said that giving his mother a chance to speak with me was a matter of showing respect to her and to him. To get him to understand that there was an actual book now, I sent him the names of the chapters, including one about his childhood. When I got a long letter back, where Khouri talked 'family honour' – 'One does not write about mothers and girlfriends' – I suspected that one chapter's name in particular had triggered him.

After that communiqué from the maximum-security wing of Kumla prison, I decided there was a clear solution to the problem – to apply for permission to visit him, talk it out, everything would be fine. Maybe I'd have to tweak the chapter.

So I returned to my day job in Södertälje and went about my tasks as usual. I might have become an expert of sorts on the town's dark underbelly, but since taking the radio job I was covering everything from town hall politics to housing issues. Asking questions like, why did they close that youth club, why don't the football clubs encourage the girls to play too? Or, which daycare centres are the most popular?

One lunchtime, after an interview at a sought-after daycare, I walked along the main street, thinking about lunch. Maybe sushi at the Angry Lady? – the affectionate nickname for the town's best but dour sushi chef who'd set up a hole-in-the-wall restaurant on a side street.

My phone started to vibrate in the back pocket of my jeans. The number had a regional dialling code that I didn't recognise. Hm, I thought, who's this? Then answered: it was Kumla prison.

'I'm calling to inform you that we have reported Bernard Khouri to the police for making illegal threats against you,' the prison employee told me. 'He instructed a visitor to send a number of people, whom he named, to speak with you about the book. Then, he held his hand up in a way that could be interpreted as a gun.'

'Seriously, is he stupid?' I responded, because I was confused: having always considered Khouri to be a creature driven by profit, I wondered what was in it for him to threaten a journalist when he was still hoping that his conviction would, through some new evidence or yet-to-be discovered legal technicality, be overturned? And it'd lessen the chance of parole. Is he stupid?

'I can't comment on that,' the prison officer said. 'He has also sent you a letter – we read everything that he writes – where he refers to himself as a "big Man", with a capital M.'

'Well, Khouri has always had an anarchistic relationship with capital letters,' I said.

I hurried off the main street to stand with my back to the wall in an alley – just days ago I had spotted one of Khouri's best friends and fellow convicts walking through the centre of town.

So no sushi. I spent the rest of the afternoon on the phone. I called the journalists' union first, then my boss, then our security department's 24-hour phone line. The head of security called me back within minutes, the head of my radio channel soon after. They told me to go back to the office and wait.

Death penalty

AT MY office, I gathered my things. I closed down my computer, gathered all the batteries I had bought at a discount store to never let my radio recorder run out of juice. I sorted papers, threw some out, kept others. There were a few Christmas presents for a friend that I'd forgotten to post in time; I gathered them up, then I waited.

A friend showed up to keep me company. I gave him more details, telling him that I'd sent Khouri the chapter names. 'NO NO NO don't send him the chapter names,' he said, shaking his head.

'But Khouri has a right to respond to the contents of the book,' I replied. My friend shook his head again, 'No! No! No!'

My friend, an Aramean, then gave me a speech about how Sweden needed to reinstate the death penalty because people like Bernard Khouri didn't deserve to live. 'Seriously, what's he contributing to society?' – and then told me twice that 'you Swedes' need to realise that 'us Arameans' need tougher rules.

There was just no way I could have a philosophical debate about capital punishment at that time, so I didn't say anything, instead focussing on trying to shove the Christmas presents into a far too small, padded envelope. It was not going very well.

'Ann, stop! I'll fix a bigger envelope and send them this afternoon,' my friend said. 'Leave them to me, you have enough to think about.'

We spotted movement out in the dark stairwell: it was a private security contractor – whom we'll call Laurent – who was checking that the stairs were empty before he guided me out to a van with tinted windows and we drove off.

The van carried me across the canal. I gazed down at Astra Zeneca, one of the many industries that had defined the town for decades. But nowadays, the town was associated more with the mafia than anything else, which I had been so brutally reminded of with one single phone call.

And I was reminded of what all those crime victims told me about being forced into witness protection, about leaving their homes. This was what they had all meant, what the witnesses had meant about seeing things for the last, and thus almost for the first, time. How everything looked new. St Ragnhild's church spire glowed in the light from the sinking sun. It was winter, two days until the New Year, and soon night would fall, at 3pm.

I wondered if it would be the last time I would see this town.

We drove past the flat I rented one summer, past the cemetery. Not even I would cross it at night. I had always been more afraid of ghosts than of people, because you could reason with people. At least that's what I had thought until now, until the warning.

As we joined the traffic on the motorway, the sky was ablaze in pink, the setting sun hazy between strips of cloud. Then we just drove and drove. North north north towards Stockholm, towards safety.

One way to kill me, I realised, would be to drive straight into our van, but they wouldn't risk their own lives, I reckoned. I knew any attempt on my life was unlikely, but fear trumps reason and my mind raced, sorting through scenarios. And, for some reason, I thought about what I was wearing on this day that could be my last.

A long-sleeved, mottled grey T-shirt, skinny jeans, curling boots. Standard reporter uniform in winter. And large grey underwear with polka dots in black.

'I will die with polka dot pants on,' I thought. 'And they're big too, big like the ones in *Bridget Jones's Diary*.' And I remembered my beloved grandmother, who I had so often visited in Liverpool, saying that one should always wear nice underwear just in case one was hit by a bus. I would have been better served by recalling her last words to me when she'd said goodbye: 'Ann, I've never worried about you for a second, you're hard as nails, just like I am.'

Laurent asked me to point out my house on Google Maps. They were taking me home to pack a bag.

'Where will we take you after that?' he asked.

'I haven't booked a hotel room yet, all my boss said was not to check into a suite at The Grand,' I replied.

Then I hesitated.

'Laurent, should I give them my real name? It's just, I can't stop thinking of one quote in the book, from one of the witnesses, that Arameans own half of Stockholm.'

Laurent's colleague caught my gaze in the rear-view mirror, and nodded.

'I was thinking the same thing,' he said.

Grozny

BUT FIRST we went home. Laurent jumped out of the van to check the communal garden, the stairs to my flat. I joined him shortly after. The flat looked the same. Of course, I had been there not that many hours before. I wondered when I would see it again. My striped sofa, the Persian carpet. I started packing, threw all my expensive face creams in the overnight bag – being threatened by a mob boss was no excuse for poor skin care – then five different outfits, all black, my running shoes in case I needed to sweat out the anxiety.

I watered my plants, started the dishwasher, emptied the bin, looked through the books by my bed. *The Shots in Copenhagen*, about the Islamist death threats against Swedish artist Lars Vilks, felt too poignant.

At home, I was done packing. We left. Climbed into the van. I started to think about Vilks, who had lived with bodyguards for many years now thanks to a cartoon of the Prophet Mohammed. I thought of Salman Rushdie. And I realised that the worst might not be the fear, but the endless hours of day when your movement was curtailed. How would you fill them? Could other people my age, as they rushed from dropping the kids off at daycare to work, then squeezing in the gym while thinking of dinner, could they understand what having too much time would feel like? Had I destroyed my own life?

As we drove into town, all the roadworks confused the GPS. Central Stockholm was a mess. We passed under a bridge, turned right to avoid the cement road blocks at a building site.

'It looks like Grozny,' said Laurent who, I'd just learned, was half-French and a war veteran.

'But surely you didn't fight there?' I said.

'Of course not, but I've fought against many Chechens.'

'Ah, the mujahideen, of course. You said you were in Afghanistan, with the French, where were you? Helmand?'

'Yes.'

'What was your first impression when you flew into Afghanistan the first time?'

'That it was beautiful but hostile territory,' he answered.

'That's what I thought too, when I flew into Kabul in 2009,' I said. 'I thought no one but native fighters could ever survive in those valleys and crags, you'd need to know every boulder, every dip of the land to hide. And how could we ever win there?'

Laurent nodded. I felt forced to add that I had been shocked by my instinctive use of 'we', the 'How can WE win there' that had popped into my head, because I'd never supported the war, never felt the Swedish soldiers, who'd also been deployed alongside their allies, were fighting in my name.

'We follow orders,' Laurent said as we pulled up to the hotel. 'But none of us thought we'd be able to stay long enough to make any difference. I don't know how many schools we built that were torn down within days by the Taliban.'

It made me think of the parallels to Södertälje. That the second-largest police investigation in Swedish history had locked up more than a dozen gang members, but that the cash economy and loan sharking lived on, that old habits die hard.

And I thought about Bernard Khouri. About how the tone between us had turned so ugly. It wasn't like this two years ago when I'd called him the first time to set up an interview.

'Our first meeting can be off the record, if you want,' I had offered one of Sweden's most infamous gangland bosses.

When, over that tinny line, the then still young manhad said there was no such things as off the record.

And I had thought just one thing.

'So be it.'

And so it was. I had kept writing. Juggling research with a full-time job, it took years. And then I found myself checking into a hotel two days before New Year's Eve. Laurent helped me with the bag. The receptionist greeted us with a warm smile.

'Are you celebrating New Year's with us?' she asked and looked at us like we were a couple.

'Not exactly,' I said, in a way that was confused, slightly amused, and I could see the look on Laurent's face – his gaze was telling me to play it cool, not make any jokes or allude to the real situation.

'Work trip,' he told her.

Voodoo doll

WE WERE having coffee in Oritha's living room when she asked me about Khouri threatening me. She was attentive and calm as I gave her the details. 'Believe me, Khouri has no money left to pay people to go after you,' Oritha said.

She had been hardened by the last few years and while she thought that I, and my employer, over-reacted to the death threat, she understood how I felt. And in knowing recognition, she started to finish my sentences for me.

'I just felt like a …'

'A toy, a voodoo doll,' Oritha interrupted.

'Swedish Radio sent bodyguards …' I continued.

'Surely it wasn't that serious?' she said.

'No, I agree, but when that kind of thing happens, you become …'

'Shaky,' Oritha filled in.

'Even the small possibility of something happening …'

'I get it,' she said.

'And that's when I understood how effective threats are,' I concluded.

Once my fear had started to subside, I'd been thinking about the difference between intellectual versus emotional understanding of what it was like to be a victim of crime.

'Well, you know,' Oritha said, 'our situation's nothing compared to those who died.'

Seven years had gone by since The Network threatened her family. Oritha hadn't moved back to Södertälje. She'd moved several times. After a period of time in the police safe house, she'd moved to an affluent Stockholm suburb. Not just to provide her children with a permanent home, but because she disliked living off taxpayers' money.

The family had moved a third time after Oritha bought her own house; she had put the blue and yellow Swedish flag outside the front door. 'I call myself a citizen,' she said. 'You take responsibility.' Her comments made me think of the TV series *The Wire*, in which the police officers use the term 'citizen' for witnesses who cared about doing the right thing.

'What's a "citizen" in your eyes?' I asked Oritha.

'It means that you don't let people like Khouri walk all over your rights – walk over the rights of my children,' she answered. 'Who the hell is he? Who the hell are The Network?' she added angrily.

She felt safe in her new town. 'There's a police station around the corner,' she said, pointing towards the centre of her new little town. 'The personal-protection unit don't get in touch often anymore, but the station's just around the corner,' she said.

The modernly decorated house – a far cry from the old-fashioned Middle East-inspired furniture in her parents' home – had a lived-in, cosy feel, with pictures of the kids hung on the walls. Oritha made some coffee, and placed a plate of cinnamon buns on the table. 'I live like a total "Svensson",' she said, sinking down into a low and deep, light-grey sofa.

Even though she wouldn't be moving back to Södertälje, she now felt safe enough to visit her family. Usually, she didn't run into any problems, but she told me that she, not long ago, had run into one of Khouri's friends in one of the malls. He had shouted names at her, calling her a 'whore' and a 'snitch', for good measure adding 'you snitching whore'.

As they'd been on the mall's upper floor, Oritha had to contain herself not to push his wheelchair down the escalator. Instead she'd shouted back at him. She admitted that her tirade matched his in vulgarity.

Then there'd been another incident, when a younger member of The Network had somehow got hold of her new telephone number. 'He called me and was just screaming "snitch, whore, snitching whore" and telling me he was going to fuck my mother,' she recalled. 'So I just told him to come over so I could teach him how to fuck his own mother.'

After that, she changed her number yet again.

Broadcasting House

EVERY MORNING, I went to work to keep up appearances. Or at least, that's what I thought I was doing. Later on my colleagues told me that during the first weeks after the death threat, I'd been pale, shaky, losing weight and staring into walls.

I didn't cry until one morning when I got a panicked email from one of my interviewees, a relative not just of Eddie Moussa, but also second cousin to a key witness.

She'd always been adamant that people had to stand up against people like Khouri, but now she too was scared, and she had sent this email at four in the morning – seemed there were two of us who couldn't sleep. She told me that Khouri's friends were badmouthing her relatives in Södertälje, because word was out that her family had spoken to me.

Her email caused me to crack. Out on the parking lot at work, I kicked at the snow and cursed Khouri and all his friends. I found myself slipping into the borderline racist 'us and them' rhetoric that I despise.

'Seriously,' I snarled as one of our armed guards looked on as I cried. 'We spent hundreds of millions of kronor locking them up, why do they still have so much power?'

My boss sent me to a crisis therapist.

'That they come after me is one thing, but trying to intimidate my interviewees is unacceptable,' I hissed in our first session.

In the ensuing weeks, I heard myself, as if possessed by a demon, use the word 'fitta' – Swedish for 'cunt' – more times than in the previous 20 years put together; usually reserved for Khouri or my ex-publisher, but also for the police investigator who'd never even called me to take a statement about Khouri threatening me. She'd never worked in Södertälje, but a quick look on Google would have informed her of who he was and what he was capable of.

At Broadcasting House, my bosses ruled out a return to my job in Södertälje. I locked myself in a recording studio to cry. My employer found me a new job in-house. I calmed down. Life went on. But not like before.

Eventually, I moved back home. The police made sure my address didn't show up in public records, so Khouri's friends couldn't find me even if they tried – and, in all likelihood, they were not even trying.

'You know, it costs money to kill someone, and why would anyone put themselves on the line for Khouri?' one cop told me. 'The worst that can happen is that they shoot you in the leg.'

'Good thing I don't play competitive volleyball any longer,' I told him.

RIP

MILAD SOUNDED resigned when I phoned him up and told him about the death threat, but didn't ask me for more details. He sounded stressed. In contrast, Oritha wanted to know more, asking me about my first publisher's decision to pull the plug on the book. 'I just felt,' I told her, 'that they didn't quite understand that this was a book about real people.' They'd proposed a book cover with a close-up of a bullet drenched in blood, I told her, which I'd vetoed because it was insensitive to the Moussa family.

'This isn't a game,' Oritha had said. 'And it's not a game for me either, even though I'm not afraid of death. When they threatened me the last time, I told them "Death lives inside my doors, so come on over."'

Her son Leon had been close to death several times over the past few years. Specialists had operated on his heart recently. As the operation had taken place in Lund, a town in the very south of Sweden, Oritha hadn't been home when a letter had arrived from the Tax Agency, who were tasked with keeping witnesses' identities out of public records. The letter informed her that they would no longer do so – the need for protection is re-assessed after a few years, but the Tax Agency does give the person in question time to appeal their decision. 'I was in Lund for Leon's heart operation, so I'd not been home to read my post, and I didn't see the Tax Agency's letter, and they removed the protection,' Oritha explained.

'It's been put in place again,' she said. 'I'm not scared for my own sake, I'm scared that someone close to me will be hurt.'

I told Oritha about the letter I'd got from the police informing me that they had closed down the investigation about Khouri threatening me. 'Typical,' Oritha said. 'You got one of those standardised letters, right?'

'Yep,' I said, explaining that I'd written a furious email to the police officer who was in charge, telling her that she may not have understood how dangerous Khouri was. She'd replied that she had to prioritise threats that were made in person.

Oritha and I went through incidents where we'd been in touch with the police, the competent and the less competent, and in the end I asked her about the investigation into The Network. 'What's your opinion on the lead investigator, Gunnar Appelgren?' I asked.

'He was given a job to do and he did it, but the police have focussed far too much on Khouri,' she said, echoing what I'd heard a thousands times from other people. 'There are others out there.'

Her youngest son, clad in a football shirt, appeared from his bedroom, where he'd been playing with one of Leon's assistants so he wouldn't overhear our conversation. He was bored. He crept towards the plate with cinnamon buns. 'One bun,' Oritha said. 'No more. And then return to your room.'

The boys had a room each in the new house. Her two younger sons had rooms overlooking the garden, while Leon's room faced the street. Against all odds, he was about to turn 12.

Just a few months later, towards the end of 2017, Leon's assistant sent me an email.

Hi! How are you! I'm sorry I've not been in touch! I don't know how it's been going with you and the book! Hoping for the best.

Difficult for me to write this but as you've in a way stayed with us over all these years. Got bad news that I can barely write. Our angel Leon has left us!

I read and re-read the letter … it was just so horrible. The assistant hadn't included any more detail about why, when or how Leon had died. Picking up my phone, I sent her a text message – I was heartbroken for the family. She responded quickly.

He turned 12 on 10 October and he was doing super well but then on 23 October the shock came from nowhere! My fighter my angel n the one who loved life more than anything!

She was so polite, as always, and in the midst of her own grief was still showing concern for me. She asked me how I was doing. I replied that I was fine now and that if Khouri's intention was to silence me it had had the opposite effect because once the fear had subsided I was left only with anger. Not against him per se, but because organised crime had become so entrenched in Sweden that it threatened the free press.

Yet again, the assistant answered me almost straight away.

Good, stand up for yourself. [The Network] are used to people giving them everything and people being deprived because they consider themselves to be God ruling over humanity! You have power over your own life n nobody else decides how you should live. That's how I feel!!

For 12 years I've worked with Leon my angel who showed me life and the meaning of everything in life. The strength he gave me that people took for granted shall not be wasted. What he gave me will live within me for ever.

Then she added a final flourish about The Network.

And let's hope that people learn some manners!

Old School

MY THOUGHTS were still, at times, frenzied, they'd loop and loop until I knew I was borderline manic. My dark humour was keeping me afloat. But underneath I was hurting. I was not the first person Khouri had hurt, of course not, and he'd hurt other so so badly, ordering the murders of men who were sons, brothers, cousins, husbands, fathers, whose deaths left aching voids in the hearts of their loved ones.

I couldn't and wouldn't compare the gravity of loss, yet my losses did start to stack up. In just a few weeks, I'd lost my book contract, my beat reporter job, and I'd lost my home, in a sense, when I'd been forced to live elsewhere for a month.

I was also close to losing faith in the police for not having taken my case seriously. The police did, to their credit, assign me a contact person with the personal-protection unit. He was an ex-Södertälje cop and knew Khouri well. I checked out his credentials by phoning another officer – whom I trusted because he was a grumpy truth sayer. He said my contact person was good, 'old school', and not 'an idiot like 90 per cent of the police force'.

Old School and I spoke several times, and whenever he called to check up on me, he barked his last name instead of a hello. I barked back – Törnkvist! – and it became a standing joke between us.

When I went to meet Old School for the first time in person, he offered me black coffee – 'How on earth does he know I take my coffee black?' I thought to myself, wondering if experienced cops just know these things – and he apologised for not having any doughnuts.

I quickly liked and trusted him.

At one point, Old School re-read the report that Kumla prison made to the police. One detail had escaped me. I already knew that Khouri held up his hand 'in a way that could be interpreted as a gun' but I assumed he'd done so at chest height to conceal it from the wardens. But no, Khouri had held his hand up under his chin. 'God I'm naive,' I thought, 'why didn't I realise this before, he wanted to be seen.' He was making sure the message reached me. He was talking to me in the only language he was truly fluent: the threat of violence.

Imagining him with his hand under his chin, I felt a stab of panic and blurted out 'What a loser!'

'I know!' Old School shrieked with laughter. 'Even for a psychopath he's so POMPOUS!' While I didn't find the situation particularly amusing, I couldn't help but laugh.

Khouri, meanwhile, sent me a letter and denied he ever threatened me. I'd said, he reminded me, that I wanted to interview the people he was 'sending to me'. That's true, I had said I wanted to interview the rest of The Network. But the newborn cynic in me just thought that he was trying to cover his tracks, and that's why he named them, when giving orders, in the first place. Bravo. Bravo, Khouri.

Altar

I WENT to see Oritha shortly after Leon's death. A candle was burning in a small candleholder – a little altar to Leon – with a quote in English on the wall above it: 'It doesn't matter where you go in life it's who you have beside you.'

Oritha went through photos and videos on her phone, stopping at one film and holding the phone up to show me. She hadn't pressed play, so I saw just the opening image, in which Oritha was lying next to her son. She had dark rings under her eyes and it was clear she had been crying.

At first glance, it looked like Leon was sleeping. He was a bit swollen around the jaw and cheeks, and had a smattering of pre-teen acne. But when you looked closer at his shirt, it was drenched in blood. Oritha could tell that I didn't want her to press play, it was just too heartbreaking, so she lowered her phone.

'When the ambulance arrived, it was too late,' she said. 'Every time we had to move it drained his energy. Khouri and his gang killed my son.'

The family buried Leon in the Södertälje cemetery in late 2017.

Oritha lit a cigarette under the kitchen fan. She had a new tattoo with Leon's date of birth and the date of his death on her right arm, which she massaged cream into. She hadn't opened Leon's room since he'd died. In the bathroom, they hadn't removed the gurney with the hose that she and the assistants used when they gave him showers.

'Was testifying worth it?' – that was my final question to Oritha. She didn't answer. She was quiet for such a long time – a contrast to her usual rapid-fire answers – that her dog, lying close to Leon's altar, looked up with concern.

'When it comes down to it,' she finally said, 'we make our own choices, because we live in a free country. In the end, I choose, I decide what to do, even if it means that I'm killed.

'And Leon provided me with motivation,' she said, before pausing … 'I don't know what to say,' she continued. 'Was it worth it? Yes and no, no and yes.'

Her voice was gathering strength and volume, and I noticed that my shoulders were tense, as though I was watching a scary film, because it was scary, it was a scary question to ask whether testifying was worth it, because if it wasn't, why should others testify?

'Yes, it was worth it,' she finally said. 'The Network devoured my children's rights, but it was a difficult decision. Having a child with special needs, changing all his routines, missing doctors' appointments, missing physiotherapy, and everything else. I knew that I could lose my son any day, but we could all die any day, you could walk over the street tomorrow and [be hit by a car] and die.'

The first part of our interview – going over the timeline and checking facts – had meant Oritha's answers were short and concise, but now, as I remained silent, she couldn't stop speaking. She was furious as she spoke about The Network. 'I hope that the people who threatened us rot in hell, I hope they die. If they lay dying in front of me I wouldn't help them because they didn't care about my children. Excuse my language, but I piss on them, they can go to hell.'

To encourage others to testify, she said, the government needed to change the law and introduce longer prison sentences in order to get criminals off the streets. 'Threats, extortion, what do they get?' she said. 'Four years perhaps?'

Then she started to ask me questions:

'Why are you writing this book? You've worked on it for so long.'

'I want our country to become a better place,' I said.

'You actually think that's going to happen?' said Oritha, lifting a sceptical eyebrow.

'Onc can hope,' I said. 'I wrote this book because I'm obsessed with justice. But I'm not going to sit here and pretend to be all noble and pretend that I didn't write it for my own sake: I was bored at work, journalism is superficial.'

'Yes, it is,' said Oritha, who had declined all interview requests during the trial.

'Was it worth it for you?' she asked me.

'It has to be worth it,' I replied. 'It has to be worth it to not let yourself be silenced.'

But the truth is I had let myself be silenced, at least in part. After Khouri's letter telling me that 'the code of honour must NOT be broken', I had removed part of the chapter that had angered him.

And one thought thus played on repeat in my mind: *Even I follow fucking orders.*

Epilogue

IN THE summer of 2019, about a year after the Swedish edition of this book was published, a friend of mine in Södertälje sent me a screen grab of the local newspaper website. The article informed me that an important 'key witness in the Södertälje case' had died suddenly.

I scanned the article – the key witness was a woman and 37 years old. Because I didn't want to believe it, I refused to believe it, trying to find ways to make the headline not be about Oritha. 'There were other key witnesses,' I told myself. 'There were other women who testified.'

But I knew, even as I refused to face my fear, that there was no one else who was a key witness, 37 years old and female in the trial against The Network. There was only Oritha.

As I stared at the article that evening, I became frantic, calling my family, calling my friends, speaking fast and incoherently as reality sank in.

When I reached out to Oritha's family, they confirmed that the article referred to her. They had found her slumped on the sofa, not breathing, and even though her brother started CPR straight away as they waited for the ambulance, Oritha never regained consciousness. And the world's poorer for it. I told her family that 'Sweden owes her a debt of gratitude that can never be repaid' and I meant every word.

Oritha was a rare creature, which I think is quite clear in the pages of this book. After its publication here in Sweden, readers got in touch asking me to thank her for standing up to the mafia.

A friend asked me if The Network were behind her death, but the police said there was no suspicion of foul play. I don't know why she died and thought it too insensitive to ask the family for any medical details, but she had told me the year before that her psychologist thought she had post-traumatic stress disorder. Which in my eyes means that we can point a finger of blame at The Network.

While they did not break her spirit or her resolve, the death of her son, which she pinned on them, broke her heart. And there are limits to what a person can take, even a person like Oritha. 'The way I see it,' I told a friend, 'The Network murdered her too, it just took them nine years to do it.'

At work, shortly after Oritha's death, we held a brainstorming session in the newsroom about how to cover the increasing number of gang-related murders in Sweden – unfortunately, the unusual brutality of The Oasis murders had turned out to be a harbinger of much worse things to come. At the meeting I said we should look at the long-term mental health consequences of testifying despite death threats and having to upend your life when you go into witness protection.

Then I started to tell my colleagues about Oritha, but my voice failed me. I had to stop talking because I was seconds away from bursting into tears. My boss, used to me stalking the corridors in high heels looking angry at the state of the world, looked a bit shocked at seeing me so emotional.

While I only met Oritha in person twice, I felt that I knew her quite well. We kept in touch over iMessage for months, her giving me feedback after watching my TV interviews about The Network. She thought I was unusually outspoken 'for a Swede' and praised my courage. I've been called brave before, but being called brave by her, the most courageous of women I've ever met, meant more to me than anything.

Oritha was a role model not just as a witness but also as a mother. She was, as a colleague of mine put it, 'the ultimate tiger mummy' who'd fought to keep her son alive for so many years.

Even though he had been ill since birth, the trauma of losing Leon was obvious to anyone who knew her. Just reading about what happened was enough for my father, who choked up when he reached the chapter about his death.

Oritha's family are now taking care of her two younger sons. Ahead of her funeral, the family opened Leon's grave so they could place her coffin with his. Upon hearing this, my only thought was: *She's taking care of him even in death.*